Joseph Epstein is the editor of *The American Scholar,* the quarterly magazine published by Phi Beta Kappa. He teaches literature at Northwestern University and is also the author of *Divorced in America* and five collections of essays, *Partial Payments, Once More Around the Block, Plausible Prejudices, The Middle of My Tether,* and *Familiar Territory.*

AMBITION
THE SECRET PASSION

JOSEPH EPSTEIN

ELEPHANT PAPERBACKS
Ivan R. Dee, Inc., Publisher, Chicago

To the Memory of Martin F. Maher
(1908–1975)

AMBITION. Copyright © 1980 by Joseph Epstein. This book was originally published in 1980 by E. P. Dutton and is here reprinted by
arrangement with the author.

First ELEPHANT PAPERBACK edition published 1989 by Ivan R.
Dee, Inc., 1332 North Halsted Street, Chicago 60622. Manufactured in
the United States of America.

Library of Congress Cataloging-in-Publication Data
Epstein, Joseph, 1937–
Ambition, the secret passion.
Reprint. Originally published: New York: E. P. Dutton, 1980.
Bibliography, p.
Includes index.
1. Success in business—United States. 2. Ambition. 3. United
States—Social conditions. I. Title.
[HF5386.E57   1989]   89-11775
ISBN 0-929587-18-9

PREFACE TO THE 1989 EDITION

This book, I have sometimes thought, was, in its original publication, ill-timed. It was written about an idea whose time had almost but not quite arrived. In 1977, in the wake of what seemed to me the spread of the fraudulent communitarian notions of the counterculture, I sat down to write a book in defense of the idea of ambition. But only a few years after the book appeared, ambition, it seemed, no longer required any defense. *Ambition* was first published in 1980, and in 1981 Ronald Reagan swept into the office of the Presidency for the first of his two terms—a time, as all liberal critics seem to agree, of unexampled selfishness and greed. I myself happen to think that better examples can be found, but it is true that over the past decade we have seen great publicity for such phenomena as insider stock traders, junk-bond dealers, a youthful class of earnest money-makers known to journalism as "Yuppies," and other assorted wheelers and dealers. Nowadays it is refreshing to meet someone who isn't currently only three courses away from completing his or her MBA, with which he or she hopes to acquire such goods and services as will make left-wing journalists and others with a taste for public moralizing positively quiver with delight.

I don't believe that my book contributed heavily to making the world safe for ambition. I certainly did not write it in the hope of clearing the way for the MBA army. What I did have in mind in writing this book was that ambition was too much a part of human nature to be denied, that it is in itself an object of wondrous complication, and that its complicatedness repays serious study. Too great ambition, as all the great writers, historians, and philosophers knew, can be deadly; what is perhaps less well known is that too little ambition can also kill, through an atrophying and eventual wizening of those qualities that, whether we wish to acknowledge them or not, are among those that make us most human. Ambition remains a great historical and literary subject.

A common feeling upon having finished writing a book is the wish that you could begin again, for only now, having written the book, do you feel that you know how it really ought to have been written. To have your book reprinted does not eliminate this feeling, but it does give you a chance to point out a thing or two you might have handled differently upon rewriting. I shall restrict myself to one item: I wish I had delineated more thoroughly than I do in these pages the notion of empty ambition, by which I mean ambition tied to no greater desire, concern, or vision than sheer self-promotion and getting ahead. It is empty ambition that has given ambition itself a bad name. Still, as one oughtn't to allow the phenomenon of drunkenness down the hall to destroy one's pleasure in a good bottle of wine, so oughtn't one to allow the emptily ambitious to deter the attempt to understand ambition itself, without which life truly would be empty of all the achievements that make it so endlessly interesting.

J.E.

June 1989

... the most secret of all passions, ambition ...
—HERMAN MELVILLE

One would need to be a God to decide which are the failures and which are the successes in this life.
—ANTON CHEKHOV

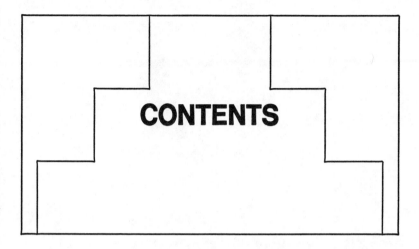

CONTENTS

AMBITION

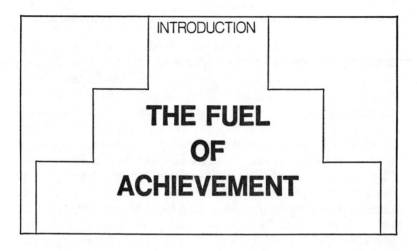

THE FUEL
OF
ACHIEVEMENT

Ambition is one of those Rorschach words: define it and you instantly reveal a great deal about yourself. I do not mind revealing a great deal about myself—and in the pages that follow, doubtless do—but I hesitate to lock myself into a definition that, though precise, is also needlessly confining. Even that most neutral of works, *Webster's*, in its Seventh New Collegiate Edition, gives itself away, defining ambition first and foremost as "an ardent desire for rank, fame, or power." *Ardent* immediately assumes a heat incommensurate with good sense and stability, and *rank, fame,* and *power* have come under fairly heavy attack for at least a century. One can, after all, be ambitious for the public good, for the alleviation of suffering, for the enlightenment of mankind, though there are some who say that these are precisely the ambitious people most to be distrusted. Yet, if a brief definition is needed, I should define ambition as the fuel of achievement.

If ambition be the fuel of achievement, then what order of achievement does it propel? Surely ambition is behind dreams of glory, of wealth, of love, of distinction, of accomplishment, of pleasure, of goodness. What life does with our dreams and expectations cannot, of course, be predicted. Some dreams, begun in selflessness, end in rancor; other dreams, begun in selfishness, end in large-heartedness. The unpredictability of the outcome of dreams is no reason to cease dreaming.

To be sure, this fuel of achievement, as I have defined ambition, can throw off some highly noxious fumes. Ambition, the sheer thing unalloyed by some larger purpose than merely clambering up, is never a pretty prospect to ponder. The single-mindedly ambitious is an old human type—"Cromwell, I charge thee, fling away Ambition," wrote Shakespeare in *Henry VIII.* "By that sinne fell the Angels"—and scarcely a type that has gone out of style, or soon figures to. As drunks have done to alcohol, the single-minded have done to ambition—given it a bad name. Like a taste for alcohol, too, ambition does not always allow for easy satiation. Some people cannot handle it; it has brought grief to others, and not merely the ambitious alone. Still, none of this seems sufficient cause for driving ambition under the counter, in an undeclared Volstead Act.

By this I do not mean to say that ambition, like white shoes for men or virginity for women, has gone or been driven out of style. It hasn't. Or at least not completely. In our day many people, goaded by ambition, go in for self-improvement programs of one kind or another: speed reading, assertiveness training, the study of books calling for looking out for number one and other forms of aggressiveness. But such activities have always seemed déclassé, and the sort of person who goes to est today thirty or forty years ago was enrolled in a Dale Carnegie course. In most respects, though, it appears that the more educated a person is, the more hopeless life seems to him. This being so, ambition, to the educated class, has come to seem pointless at best, vicious at worst. Ambition connotes a certain Rotarian optimism, a thing unseemly, in very poor taste, rather like a raging sexual appetite in someone quite elderly. None of this, of course, has stopped the educated classes from attempting to get their own out of the world—lots of the best of everything, as a famous epicure once put it—which they continue to do very effectively. To renunciation is thus added more than a piquant touch of hypocrisy.

If the above assertions seem overstated, consider what seems to me the unarguableness of the following assertions. If one feels the stirrings of ambition, it is on the whole best to keep them hidden. To say of a young man or woman that he or she is ambitious is no longer, as it once was, a clear compliment. Rather the reverse. A person called ambitious is likely to arouse anxiety, for in our day anyone so called is thought to be threatening, possibly a trifle neurotic. Energy is still valued, so too is competence, but ambition is in bad repute. And perhaps nowhere more than in America.

The degradation of ambition is not an exclusively American phenomenon. But a case can be made that it has hit America particularly hard. For many years America has represented Europe's idea of the coarseness of which ambition, cut loose of the moorings of tradition, is capable. All that American energy, placed exclusively in the service of getting on, getting in, getting ahead—of sheer getting—was viewed as crass in the extreme in the nineteenth century and scarcely less so in the twentieth. Americans themselves soon enough picked up on this view, and our own writers have provided ever-fresh mintings of the American upstart: Daisy Millers, Silas Laphams, Carrie Meebers, George Babbitts, Jay Gatsbys, Flem Snopeses, Sammy Glicks. The pusher, the hustler, the self-starter, these became if not the essential then the dominant American type in the eyes of the world—and in all the type's true ignominy. How widespread the type has really been, and continues to be now, is difficult to know. Referring to his own character Sammy Glick, the novelist Budd Schulberg has written: "But the Sammy-drive is still to be found everywhere in America, in every field of endeavor and among every racial group. It will survive as long as money and prestige and power are ends in themselves, running wild, unharnessed from usefulness."

Well, money and prestige and power have always and everywhere been viewed as ends in themselves as well as means to quite useful ends—and, it ought but does not quite go without saying, not in America alone. Consider Dickens's Uriah Heep, Balzac's Monsieur Grandet, the first the rankest opportunist, the second the most tireless miser, one pure English, the other pure French, yet neither is made to stand in as a representative Englishman or Frenchman—the correct assumption being that any complex society throws up such types. But the American hust-ler/pusher/self-starter is taken not to be universal but repre-sentative of a national type: a fish indigenous to American wa-ters, a distinctly American species.

Not a very great deal is known about the origins of ambition in the individual. Instead we have a bundle of clichés, some of a higher kind (such as Freud's remark that a man sure of his mother's love is born to be a conqueror), some of a lower kind (such as the notion of the Napoleonic complex, which holds that all short men seethe with ambition). Alfred Adler, in an essay entitled "On the Origin of the Striving for Superiority and of Social Interest," argued that the striving for superiority and perfection "is given to *every* person and must be understood as *innate,* as a *necessary and general* foundation of *the develop-ment of every person.*" Ambition is thus, according to Dr. Adler, in us all. Yet Adler did not approve all ambition. The striving *"to master one's fellow man,"* he deplored. As a social-ist, Adler preferred ambition channeled into a *"cooperating community."* Ambition, for Alfred Adler, will come to fruition in "an *ideal* society yet to be developed, which comprises *all* men, all filled by the common striving for perfection."

Alfred Adler here sounds, if somewhat indirectly, a common theme in discussions of ambition: that ambition is a perverse quality to possess in an unjust society. Who, after all, wishes to rise to the top of a burning building? To succeed in a society that is itself shoddy is no great mark of distinction. On the contrary, it implies that one might oneself be shoddy. Forgetting for the moment that all societies are unjust, with perhaps the most unjust being those that claim to have been founded upon justice, is there anything to this idea that society is not worthy of peo-ple's ambitions—that society is not good enough, essentially, for the individual to wish to succeed in?

Certainly there is something rather new in this notion. Not Balzac nor Stendhal nor Dickens, three great writers in whose novels ambition often has a place very near the center, needed to pretend for a moment that the societies of their day were clean and well-lighted places. But this did not disqualify their heroes' ambitions, at least not necessarily; in some ways it even ennobled them. For these writers life was life, and ambition, toward good and bad ends, was part of it. As André Maurois, one of Balzac's biographers, put it: "Balzac does not judge but merely notes. To change the form of society is only to change the people in power; the species are changeless; there will still be workers, bureaucrats and rascals in carriages—another lot, that is all."

One must be wary of ambition, one's own and the next fellow's, especially where it contends against things of the spirit, yet today most people have gone well beyond wariness into a crippling ambivalence. This has immeasurably complicated the place of ambition in contemporary America. Ought ambition, for example, to be something one encourages in one's children, or for that matter in oneself? Ought one to look terrifiedly or admiringly upon the ambitious man or woman? Is he or she intrinsically the enemy or instead a savior of sorts, supplying the motor power that keeps the furnace humming? Because such fundamental questions continue to receive confused and contradictory answers, because the worth of something so fundamental as ambition has been cast in foggiest doubt, people live with confusion and contradictions running up the center of their lives, in a state of perturbation, distraction, and fretfulness.

While Americans as a nation are in fact rich, we feel ourselves to be, somehow, poor. While we have in recent years shown ourselves capable of surmounting bulky problems—pollution for one, extravagant population growth for another—yet we continue to feel ourselves impotent and hopeless. All this suggests a people that has lost its way, its energy, its dreams —in a word, its ambition. Ambition represents the spirit of futurity. The fuel of achievement drives one's thoughts into the future. To be ambitious is to be future-minded. But we do not seem to live in a very future-minded epoch. "Not even the future," said Paul Valéry, "is what it used to be"—a remark that applies aptly to us. Whether the loss of belief in ambition has caused this loss of confidence in the future, or the loss of confidence in the future has caused the loss of belief in ambition, is difficult to say. But that the two are connected is not arguable.

It seems unarguable, too, that ambition in the United States today is losing—if it has not already lost—its justification in the common culture. History has known periods of greater and lesser human energy; and those periods of greater energy have been periods when ambition was a passion in good standing. In *The Century of Louis XIV*, Voltaire remarks on the four most admired historical epochs: Periclean Athens, Augustan Rome, Italy under the Medici, and France under Louis XIV. Since Voltaire's day one might wish to add to the list the United States of presidents Washington through Jefferson and England under Queen Victoria. But what all these periods have in common is their lack of equivocal feeling about ambition. Not that ambition in any of these periods failed to produce its usual perversities, from the Athenian Alcibiades to the American Aaron Burr. But whatever its excesses, ambition has at all times been the passion that best releases the energies that make civilization possible.

Writing of ancient Greece, E. R. Dodds observed, "The Greeks were not so unrealistic as to hide from themselves the plain fact that the wicked flourished like a green bay tree." But the Greeks did not go the additional step to find the wealthy or powerful inherently corrupt. In Homer, Dodds remarks, "the rich are apt to be specially virtuous." Wealth and contentment tend to be the attributes of the virtuous in the Old Testament as well. In the Christian view, the pendulum has swung back and forth, from the doctrine that the meek shall inherit the earth to Max Weber's perception (set forth in *The Protestant Ethic and the Spirit of Capitalism*) that, among the Calvinists of the sixteenth and seventeenth centuries, a sign of being among God's elect is success on earth. As a general statement it seems unexceptional to say that Christianity has not necessarily despised ambition, although it has tended to view excessive preoccupation with ambition for worldly things as misguided.

Yet there can be no blinking the fact that ambition is increasingly associated in the public mind chiefly with human characteristics held to be despicable. Ambition is most often confounded with aggression; and aggression, make no mistake, is scarcely thought an admirable quality. The ambitious person is generally thought to be single-minded, narrowly concentrated in purpose, bereft of such distracting qualities as charm, sympathy, imagination, or introspection of the kind that leads to self-doubt. Success is said to beget success, but ambition begets distrust. Even in quite serious contemporary American novels, a character drawn as ambitious is not a character to think well of; more likely, he is someone meant to be ridiculed, or taught hard lessons, or brought down with a thump. Such a character, if a man, is likely to be without depth or dimension; if a woman, she is likely to be a shrew, a cunning bitch, an advertisement for all that a woman ought not to be. Man or woman, the ambitious figure is meant to demonstrate that the possession of—or, more accurately, the being possessed by—ambition puts an end to natural feeling.

Perhaps the one novel that no serious writer in America would care to write today is one about a man who sets out to succeed in life and does so through work, decisive action, and discretion, without stepping on anyone's neck, without causing his family suffering, without himself becoming stupid or inhumane. Now it might be argued that there is no basis for a novel here because there is no conflict. But anyone who knows the world at all knows that to set out with legitimate ambition and to achieve what one had set out to achieve without diminishing oneself is to have led a life filled with conflict. Yet it is a novel unlikely to get written so long as that other, more familiar novel —which has the ambitious man or woman confront society and either go under or win out only at the cost of his or her decency —provides, as it evidently does, so much comfort.

In the middle of the third century A.D., Cyprian, Bishop of Carthage, wrote to one Demetrianus, Roman proconsul of Africa and himself a pagan:

> Now since you are ignorant of divine knowledge and a stranger to truth, you must in the first place realize this, that the world has now grown old, and does not abide in that strength in which it formerly stood. This we would know, even if the sacred Scriptures had not told us of it, because the world itself announces its approaching end by its failing powers. In the winter there is not so much rain for nourishing the seeds, and in the summer the sun gives not so much

heat for ripening the harvest. In the springtime the young corn is not so joyful, and the autumn fruit is sparser. Less and less marble is quarried out of the mountains, which are exhausted by their disbowelments, and the veins of gold and silver are dwindling day by day. The husbandman is failing in the fields, the sailor at sea, the soldier in the camp. Honesty is no longer to be found in the marketplace, nor justice in the law courts, nor good craftsmanship in art, nor discipline in morals. . . . So no one should wonder nowadays that everything begins to fail, since the whole world is failing, and is about to die.

Unlike Bishop Cyprian—now Saint Cyprian—most of us do not believe that the world is coming to an end. But there is nonetheless a fairly strong feeling that the world is pretty well used up. The implications of this feeling are many, but not least among them is that those who hold it, who feel that the world and they themselves are exhausted, are left without a dream. In a used-up world, of course, a dream is quite pointless, as is ambition, the fuel of future achievements. Yet without dreams of achievement, and ambition to fuel them, life itself might as well be over. It is one of the arguments of this book you are about to begin that ambition in America has been unrelievedly, almost systematically, discouraged by men and by conditions. In the process a natural appetite has nearly lost its justification, although that does not mean that the appetite itself has disappeared. Ambition cannot be altogether suppressed, although it can be twisted and perverted. But always at a high cost. "True vice," wrote George Santayana, "is human nature strangled by the suicide of attempting the impossible."

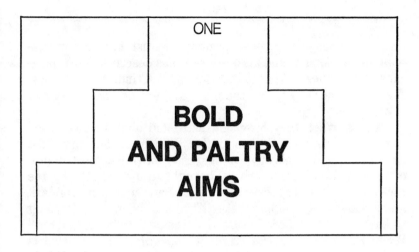

ONE

BOLD
AND PALTRY
AIMS

Dr. Franklin

Begin with Benjamin—Ben in the good diminutive of American style—our first well-publicized success and premier go-getter. Ben Franklin is a representative and an exemplary American. He is also an acid test: what one loves about America, one is sure to love about Ben; what one loathes about America, one is sure to loathe about Ben too. He is representative in being a bit like all of us. He is exemplary in being more than a bit better. Of common clay, he polished himself until he ended up marble.

The great democratic virtues—energy, industry, prudence, practicality—Ben had them all. Their obverse side—opportunism, a knack for turning everything to personal advantage, an eye for the main chance—all these Ben had as well. His measure for all things was the flat dead measure of the useful. Of Deism, the reigning religion of his circle when he was a young man, he wrote: "I began to suspect that this doctrine, though it might be true, was not very useful." Of poetry, he wrote: "I approved for my part the amusing one's self with poetry now and then, so far as to improve one's language, but no farther." He was himself the poet of common sense.

As a young man, Ben Franklin thought to become a different sort of poet, but his father quickly put him off that. Sound advice. He was, in talent and temperament, almost everything

else but a poet—shopkeeper, printer, scientist, inventor, statesman, revolutionary, and (as one writer has described him) "part-
time philosopher." What it was Ben did full-time is a nice question. Full-time, he kept on the move and got on and, of course,
ahead.

Poets, when they have not distrusted him, have despised
Benjamin Franklin. William Carlos Williams called him "the
greatest winner of his day," adding that "he presents a voluptu-
ousness of omnivorous energy brought to a dead stop by the
rock of New World opportunity." D. H. Lawrence, a poet of dark
and bloody thoughts, hated Ben. "The soul of man," according
to Lawrence, "is a dark forest," and he saw Ben "fencing it off."
When Ben came to write his *Autobiography*—a work that is
perhaps the first in a by-now long list of how-to and self-help
books on achieving success—he charted a list of thirteen virtues,
running from Temperance to Humility, and graded himself on
each. He scored, one need scarcely add, very well. Under the
twelfth of his virtues, that of Chastity, Ben noted: "Rarely use
venery but for health and offspring, never to dullness, weakness,
or the injury of your own or another's peace or reputation."
D. H. Lawrence had a field day with that list. "Middle-sized,
sturdy, snuff-colored Doctor Franklin," he wrote, "one of the
soundest citizens that ever trod or 'used venery.' " Very amusing, except that one can bet that Ben enjoyed his venery much
more than D. H. Lawrence ever did.

For all his moralizing, for all his immense practicality, for
all his business-mindedness, Benjamin Franklin seemed to have
had a damned fine time on earth. If there is a rub, this is it: for
Franklin, success was a pleasure. He hopped from achievement
to achievement. His list of accomplishments—as writer, as inventor, as public servant, as scientist, as businessman—is of a
length sufficient to induce drowsiness. Yet no three or four items
—his experiments with lightning, his invention of the Franklin
stove, his initiation of the first public library in America—quite
captures him either. He specialized in variety.

Un-French though Benjamin Franklin seems, the French,
when as our ambassador he lived among them, adored him. He
showed up before them in a coonskin cap. He knew how to play

any role yet always remain himself. He is the chief American Enlightenment figure—our Voltaire, allowing for a substantial discount in style and a proportionate increase in utility. The critic Sainte-Beuve remarked of Benjamin Franklin that "he was wily for the public good." Which he most certainly was—though while at it, he didn't do badly for himself either.

"An impassioned man is seldom witty," said Stendhal, and more than one commentator has remarked on Ben's lack of passion. There is something to it. He did not drink, he went for long stretches without meat, he slept only four hours a night. This left time for the larger indulgences: for getting on. He had a taste for the ladies. "I attempted familiarities (another erratum)," he notes in his *Autobiography.* He had an even greater taste for giving advice, much of it of an astonishingly high quality: "He that is secure is not safe." "He is not well bred that cannot bear ill breeding in others." "Cunning proceeds from want of capacity." "Fish and visitors stink in three days." Excellent shots, and there were a great many others, such as the one that advises that the best way to get into a person's good graces is not to do a favor for him but ask a favor of him. For a plain man he was supremely subtle.

Benjamin Franklin was the promise and the dream, the special American vision made flesh. "How little origin is to happiness, virtue, or greatness," he not only wrote but by his own life demonstrated. A pilgrim who made progress, a nonfiction Robinson Crusoe, he begins humbly walking down Chestnut and Walnut streets in Philadelphia eating a great puffy roll and carrying two others and then before one knows it he is at the French court dandling a *comtesse* upon his knee. "As constant good fortune has accompanied me even to an advanced period of my life," he recounts in his *Autobiography,* "my posterity will perhaps be desirous of learning the means which I employed, and which, thanks to Providence, so well succeeded with me." The "means" are to remember that appearances count as much as reality, to keep one's shoulder to the wheel, to secularize the teaching of Christianity, to practice frugality, industry, and temperance, and (although he does not say this outright, it comes through) to have a near genius for life. Life, Franklin instructs, is of

plastic, a substance within the power of each of us to mold—
preferably, to mold by proper ambition into success. As for happiness, he wrote: "Human felicity is produced not so much by
great pieces of good fortune that seldom happen as by little
advantages that occur every day."

In ways simple and complex, ambition is tied to success, as
means to ends. Etymologically, the definition of the word *success* begins with a neutral ring. Its earliest definitions refer to
sequence, to following upon, to coming after. When it first
becomes involved with the notion of fortune, it still retains something of this neutrality. Hence the second definition offered by
the *Oxford English Dictionary:* "2. The fortune (good or bad)
befalling anyone in a particular situation or affair. Usually with
a qualifying adj." The *OED*'s third definition formulates the
word as we understand it today, without need of qualification:
"3. The prosperous achievement of something attempted; the
attainment of an object according to one's desire: now often with
particular reference to the attainment of wealth or position."
The American *Webster's* falls in line with this last definition:
"2b: a favorable termination of a venture; *specif:* the attainment
of wealth, favor, or eminence."

What none of these definitions encompasses is the context
for success. As an idea, a notion really, success is a detached and
quite lonely phenomenon. It is an idea without an ideal. The
Greeks had the ideal of citizenship to live up to; success and
citizenship, or fealty to the *polis,* were one and the same. The
Romans had the ideal of excellence; fame and power and large
holdings had their place, to be sure, but always in the context
of the Republic and then, later, the Empire. Under the Church,
the official ideal of success entailed serving God: hagiography
took secure precedence over biography. With the Renaissance
and its accompanying gradual secularization of life, wealth and
fame and the power conferred by politics come into their own as
things worth pursuing in themselves. But even here, as we learn
from Machiavelli, Fortuna reigns—Fortuna, an amalgam of fortune and fate, is understood to be a tricky matter. It is some-

thing to be appeased, this Fortuna, to be played to—thus Machiavelli's instructions to his Prince to do all that can humanly be done to have it on his side. Yet it is understood, too, that one can make all the correct moves and still go under. Failure, the absence of success, was terrible, a disaster—one could pay for it with one's head—but not yet what it would come to be in later centuries. What failure would come to be was disgrace: one could retain one's head, but only to hang it in shame.

In the modern world, and especially in America, a new distinction, a cruel twist, has been added: not to succeed means to fail. Leaving aside for a moment what it is that constitutes succeeding—something that depends upon where one starts out from, what aspirations one sets for oneself, what league one chooses to play in—the crux of this distinction is that it enters everyone in the race for success. The need to succeed, in other words, can also be viewed as the need to avoid failure. And as to which is greater, the hope of success or the fear of failure, this, in individual cases, does not always allow a clear answer.

Whether people are born with a desire—more than a desire, a need—to succeed is a question bound up with one's views of human nature. But as soon as one makes assertions about human nature, the waters grow murky. Mention that mankind is inherently aggressive and counterevidence can be brought to the bar of tribes who have lived pacifically—and happily within their pacificity. Mention that mankind is inherently acquisitive and counterevidence can be brought of sects that have lived without any conception of private property. Mention that mankind inherently gravitates naturally (and selfishly) to wanting the best for itself and evidence can be brought of people who have lived in near-perfect communality. To make any broad assertion about human nature—that men and women are, say, essentially aggressive, acquisitive, selfish, in sum, oriented toward success—is to call to mind exceptions, to invite skepticism, to enter the flux of controversy.

Less arguable is the assertion that some conditions bring to the fore certain human qualities more than others. In this regard, much in American history can be seen to conduce to the development of precisely those qualities that aim its citizens toward seeking success. Aggressiveness, acquisitiveness, a strong desire to get on—a puerile Marxism might view these as habits historically ingrained by ruthless capitalism. Yet it is more reasonable to assume they have been intrinsically nurtured by life in America. Until recently, in Italy or France a man might be a waiter and be perfectly content to do his job well; his son might just as contentedly follow suit. Not, however, in America. In America a man works hard at being a waiter precisely because he does not want his son to be a waiter; and if his son does turn out to be a waiter, any pride or pleasure he might take in the job is likely to be irrevocably soured by his sense of having failed by not having advanced over the situation of his father.

To offer a one-sentence gloss on American history, ours has been a country of vast opportunity, enormous wealth, tremendous social fluidity, and a powerful belief in progress. Allowing for some exceptions, Benjamin Franklin was correct in noting that in America "How little origin is to happiness, virtue, or greatness." The American Revolution, in its social and economic aspects, was a revolution not of rising but of continual expectation—a revolution that is perhaps only now beginning to wind down. Onward and upward had for a long while been the prevailing American spirit. And why not in a country one of whose chief myths, that of Abraham Lincoln, posits the possibility open to all of going from log cabin to White House? If the Lincoln myth was one day to be replaced, in the person of John F. Kennedy, by the reality of a modestly talented and intelligent young man traveling the shorter distance from Boston to the White House backed by his father's money—well, it still suggested that America was a land of possibilities.

Now there have always been arguments that possibility in America has been a very selective matter. In the most recent argument of this kind, *Who Gets Ahead? The Determinants of Economic Success in America* by Christopher Jencks and others, the authors have concluded that they "could not isolate any single personality characteristic that was critical to success." In an earlier volume, *Inequality*, Professor Jencks had asserted that success was tied above all to family and, to a lesser extent, schooling. Now, in *Who Gets Ahead?*, the emphasis has shifted to "the structural features of the economy." Yet little room is allotted for the ideas that are in the air, and that get into some people's heads but not into the heads of others. One might argue, say, that blacks as a group have not progressed as smoothly as have whites—a proposition that is no longer quite so true as it once was—but this does not answer the question of why some blacks do progress very smoothly indeed. Or why among members of the same family one brother succeeds and the others do not. Ideas are of course more difficult to measure than economic indicators or IQs, but all other things being equal —and all other things are becoming more and more equal—it is one's point of view about effort, success, ambition, that can be decisive. A systematic devaluation of possibility and of the prospects for progress have in them a self-fulfilling prophecy.

"Progress is our most important product" runs the advertising tag of the General Electric Corporation, but the tag could as aptly be applied to America as well. If the United States could be said to have not so much an ideology as an underlying assumption governing its general behavior, both as a nation and as a people, then that assumption has been progress—progress unrelenting and unremitting. Lewis Mumford has written about the philosophical naïveté inherent in the assumption of progress along with the social and ecological wreckage that has often been its natural consequence. The "simplistic formula for Progress," Mumford writes, "created the overriding imperative that the very victims of the power complex meekly accepted: one must go with the tide, ride the wave of the future—or, more vulgarly, keep moving. The meaning of life was reduced to accelerating movement and change, and nothing else remained. . . . Bigger and bigger, more and more, farther and farther, faster and faster, became ends in themselves, as expressions of godlike power; and empires, nations, trusts, corporations, institutions, and power-hungry individuals were all directed to the same blank destination. The going was the goal—a defensible doctrine for colliding atoms or falling bodies but not for men."

Yet when that is said, when the ironies of progress and the contradictions implicit in believing in it unstintingly are noted, it still remains to be remarked that in America it has been exceptionally difficult not to believe in progress. In the short run, in the span of one's own lifetime, who has not seen astonishing progress? The vast improvements in material well-being are too many and too obvious to require example. In the long run, much of this may not have constituted true progress at all—the increased use of the automobile, the development of the high-rise building, the invention of atomic weapons—but then in the long run, as John Maynard Keynes once rudely remarked, everyone dies. Because of our particular situation, living on a wealthy and largely undeveloped continent, Americans have been permitted a belief in limitless horizons as perhaps no other people. "An American may do with impunity," Charles W. Eliot wrote, "what a European could only do in the spirit of the most reckless gambler or in the confidence of inspired genius. Freedom, and the newness and breadth of the land, explain this favored condition of the American." Archibald MacLeish, coming at the same point from a different angle, once put it: "The American journey has not ended. America is never accomplished. America is always still to build. . . . West is a country in the mind, and so eternal." America is a country always becoming rather than being; nothing if not a land of perpetual new beginnings. If much of this was a myth, considering the attitudes it embodied and engendered and the actions it motivated, it was by and large a good and useful myth, putting hope in people's hearts and ambition for betterment in their heads.

If Americans have been in one sense favored by being allowed the fullest belief in progress, in another sense they have been the people most tyrannized by this same belief. As with deficit financing, so with the belief in progress: what may make sense for a nation is often ruinous for an individual. And a belief in progress—in one's own progress, unabated and ever upward —can be ruinous. The imperative of the belief in progress is that, Coué-like, every day and in every way one *must* get better and better. Next year, next month, next week, tomorrow, must be better than last year, last month, last week, today. When it is not, people feel lost, abandoned, cheated. Corporate vice-presidents have nervous breakdowns because they realize they can advance no further in their careers. Corporate presidents leap from thirtieth-floor windows because they have nothing more to conquer. One's children drop out, or otherwise let one down by not turning out better than oneself. Merely to hold one's place, to stay still, is viewed as a form of stagnation—of death. What is the point? What is the meaning of it all? Why go on churning? Questions, these, prompted by disappointed believers in progress—by victims of an *unexamined* belief.

Little of this is news. "The rat race" it was once called, but called, it is necessary to add, by those who most strenuously participated in it. Having affixed the label, they did not drop out of the race; instead they ran—and continue to run—all the swifter. A prize, despite all the awareness of the exhausting pace, was presumed to await the winners—money, fame, the ease of eminence, the good life itself—and the prize was one still deemed worth striving for. Exhortations to slow down, attacks on the shallowness of success as an empty ideal, were—and continue to be—unavailing. People, men and women, see life as a smorgasbord of choices: a Mercedes or a Plymouth, a daughter at Harvard or at secretarial school, first cabin to Le Havre or Greyhound to Yellowstone, to be the boss or the bossed. Who, given a choice, wouldn't know which to pick? In America, moreover, the Mercedes, Harvard, first cabin, being the boss, along with being preferable are also altogether possible. Justifications, if any are needed, exist for preferring them. To put the matter in what seems its least selfish light, they are often to be preferred for the sake of one's children, if not for oneself. Jules Michelet, the great nineteenth-century historian of the French Revolution and the chronicler of the role of "the people" in history, when it came to his own grandson's education, remarked to his son, "Let us not engage in false democratic attitudes." The boy, Michelet made clear, must have the best.

Can wanting what one construes to be the best—for one's family but for oneself as well—be rooted out of people? Can the desire for primacy be quenched? In the modern age the record is clear, and not good. No society has eliminated such desire without squelching liberty along with it. In times of national emergency—the English during World War II are a notable example—people have been known to pull together, sacrificing individual desire for the common good, but for the most part it is every man for himself, within known limits of what is allowable. Totalitarianism and disaster are the only known stopgaps for the free competitive spirit, and America, for better or worse, has thus far escaped having to undergo either.

Instead, Americans undergo much introspection about ambition and success—most of it of a self-lacerating kind. The national catechism in recent decades has had to do with unrelenting lectures on organization men, affluent societies, lonely crowds. "Offhand," the novelist Walker Percy writes, "I cannot think of a single first-class novelist who has any use for the most 'successful' American society, namely life in the prosperous upper-middle-class exurbs, in the same way that Jane Austen celebrated a comparable society." The very people who are excoriated in such books are, of course, those who buy them. But to little purpose, except to make many of their authors themselves successful.

Purpose is the great question behind the struggle for success. "To what purpose is all the toil and bustle of this world?" wrote Adam Smith in *The Theory of Moral Sentiments.* "What is the end of avarice and ambition, of the pursuit of wealth, of power, and pre-eminence?" Some people answer, There is no purpose to the toil and bustle, no end to the pursuit, and, so answering, drop away to tend their own gardens, to read their books and think their thoughts, to savor perhaps the feeling that they are above the mass. But the great majority hang in, struggle and strive, their efforts to get on and up made with greater or lesser self-assurance.

Curiosity Shop □ They were in their forties and had known each other for more than thirty years. At lunch in a Chinese restaurant, one asked:

"What would you do if you had eight million dollars?"

"Not much differently than I do now. Oh, maybe I'd buy a house somewhere in Greece. We went there two years ago on a cruise. It is as beautiful as everyone says. But I wouldn't quit working. It has taken me too long to learn to do what I do, and it's only now that I am beginning to feel I do it well. How about you?"

"I think I'd take more short vacations, maybe read more. I would go to Yankee spring training every year, though I've done that the past two years anyhow."

"Would you quit working?"

"I don't love my work as much as you do, but retirement is death, of that I'm convinced. Maybe I'd work a little less than I do now. Hard to say."

"We grow old, friend. Imagine what this conversation might have been like twenty or even ten years ago."

"Yes, I suppose we would have found sexier things to do with eight million than put it into Greek real estate or use it to buy a little more time for reading."

"If we're still alive, what will this conversation be like in, say, twenty-five years from now?"

"You may be ready to settle for a condominium in Florida, I to want to buy less time for reading."

"And eight million dollars may not be enough to pay for these two orders of eggroll and shrimp with lobster sauce, the check for which I hereby stick you with."

Failure has about it none of the ambiguity of success. It is not a problem; it is a pitfall. Failure implies waste, loss, incompletion; it means being cut off, left out, beaten. It is bad, sad, and to be avoided. One of the nicest things about success is that it isn't failure. Failure is especially a danger in America, a land where success has always been such a distinct possibility. Gertrude Stein found it a puzzle why success was everything to American men "when they know that eighty percent of them are not going to succeed." Disraeli wrote that "our business in this world is not to succeed, but to continue to fail, in good spirits," but the philosophical calm behind that remark could come from only one source—years of success.

Failures seem to fall into one of three general kinds: not reaching high enough, overreaching, wanting courage. Translated, these mean too little ambition, too much ambition, coward-ice. Many gradients of failure fall somewhere in between, and it is noteworthy that not only are there more reasons for failure than for success but the former is usually easier to account for than the latter. You can't argue with success, an old maxim has it, but a better maxim might be that there is no explaining success. (In fact, what is there better to argue with than success? What is the point of arguing with failure?) Failure is more easily explained, even pinpointed. He lost his nerve. She didn't follow through. He moved too soon. She waited too long. He needed more capital. She appeared too hungry. He hadn't the right connections. She was too pushy. He didn't have enough drive. The list of reasons for failure can be extended ad infinitum.

Some people have been said to have failed at success, but fewer are noted for having succeeded at failure. Success brings with it a host of problems, but failure is grinding, flat, and grey. The desire for success, as Emile Durkheim remarked, "is at the very basis of our social life." Perhaps that is why failure carries with it such a heavy penalty in personal chagrin: to fail, in Durkheim's sense, is not only to go under oneself but to be an affront to the society in which one lives.

Failure does, however, carry with it two luxurious emotional states: that of placing the blame for one's failure outside oneself and that of self-pity. One can blame one's failure on one's social origins, one's parents, one's bad luck, one's competitors, one's family, or, on a grander scale of accusation, on what some are pleased to call " the system." One can also blame it on one's fine character and general excellence. William Hazlitt, in an essay entitled "On the Qualifications Necessary to Success in Life," makes essentially this case in the best prose in which it has ever been made. "Fortune," Hazlitt writes, "does not always smile on merit," and when he has gotten through listing, by way of negation, those whom fortune does smile upon he has constructed a near-perfect rationale for failure. (The essay, it should be mentioned, was written at a particularly bleak time in Hazlitt's own career, when he had suffered professional humiliation, financial difficulty, and the sting of feeling his enormous talents going unappreciated.) Fortune (or success), for Hazlitt, smiles upon those who are thought wise rather than upon those who are truly wise, "for it is for the most part only necessary to seem" wise. It smiles upon those who are "qualified for certain things, for no other reason than because they are qualified for nothing else." Again: "The way to secure success is to be more anxious about obtaining than about deserving it." To have too high a standard of refinement, to have too great a respect for the public, to have a simplicity of manner, to have no pretensions, to have taste and wide interests, to have delicacy, to have sincerity and straightforwardness, to have a higher regard for realities than for appearances—to have any of these qualities is to be assured of being held back from success. Apart from possessing the reverse of all these admirable qualities, the only positive quality helpful to success that Hazlitt mentions is *constitutional* talent, by which Hazlitt means no more than a good constitution such as will bring about physical stamina. A weak mind in a sound body, he says, is more clearly destined for success than the reverse, and he further comments that it "is more desirable to be the handsomest than the wisest man in his Majesty's dominions, for there are more people who have eyes than understandings."

Enough truth is contained in what Hazlitt says—despite his own autobiographical reasons for saying it—to make his argument cogent. Single-mindedness, vulgarity, hot-blooded desire, deviousness, animal energy, attention to appearances, and the rest do often make for, or at least aid, success. With modern variations, Hazlitt's arguments continue to be made in our own day. Successes have even been made attacking the qualities that go to make success. Among writers and painters, though not among scientists and businessmen, a cult of failure has arisen, which finds its icons in men of talent or even genius who have gone to their graves with their abilities unrecognized, their careers unkissed by success. The allure of such figures—James Agee and Sylvia Plath are recent examples—is fairly evident: see how genius goes unappreciated, is hounded, and finally cut down in our country (or system or time). With such models for failure, to succeed is to become a bit vulgar, the very fact of

one's success attesting to one's own shoddiness, for the gist of
the argument on behalf of failure is that true quality falls by the
wayside and only the shoddy really succeeds.

But a problem arises. True, the good and the gifted often do
not meet with success in this world, yet just as often, perhaps
more often, they do. Where exceptions on both sides are so
plentiful, there can be no rule. And where there is no rule, where
virtue and talent are at least as often rewarded as not, failure
carries with it, and always will, a nagging doubt in the heart of
the failed.

Curiosity Shop □ He was near seventy; the results for all
intents and purposes were in. A most complex matter, the as-
sessment of a long life, a summing up and final grading of a
man's worth. From his early twenties he was marked out as a
man of the highest promise, a brilliant young scholar, possibly
one day a philosopher in the old-fashioned, grand sense of the
word, certainly a person to watch. Now, almost fifty years later,
it was clear he had not quite delivered on this early promise. He
was everywhere well thought of, generally granted distinction,
had met the great men of his time. But what would he leave
behind? Measures for determining such matters do exist, after
all. A businessman can tell the score at any moment by totting
up his assets; a man such as he, by what he had written. What
he had written was brilliant but cumulatively slight. The problem, insofar as it could be gauged, was that he had too great an
appetite for the social life; he too much enjoyed his stay on earth.
This propensity was abetted by a marriage to a wealthy woman.
With the carrot thus placed perpetually in his mouth, the stick
over his head was removed. He frittered away his ideas in talk.
He, who could have been a great man, ended up an interesting
and a pleasant one. How, then, assess him? In the charitable
view one could say that he gave pleasure to his friends and took
pleasure from his days. Of how many others could as much be
said? And was that not sufficient? But what view did he himself
take? I came, I saw, I felt it was not really worth conquering?
Or: I enter oblivion leaving nothing behind. Was it all a wretched

mistake? Impossible to know yet endlessly fascinating to speculate upon.

Ambition is unequally parceled out, and one of the great divisions of mankind is between those who have it and those who
don't. This appears to have been so always and everywhere. The
religious thinkers of India, for example, long ago distinguished
between the Way of Renunciation, Meditation, and Contempla-
tion and the Way of Action. Ambition is one of the great trans-
formers of personality—a shaping force par excellence of
human character. To have ambition or to be without it affects a
person's conduct in every regard: one's sense of time, place,
relations to other people, feelings about one's self, and views
about the rationality or irrationality of the world. Gibbon speaks
of "the jealous and unsociable nature of ambition," a characteri-
zation that does not forestall his admiration for men whose
ambition directs them toward ideals he believes in. The value of
ambition is one of the great issues in life and in literature, which
might be formulated thus: Can a person learn more by testing
himself, through ambition, against the world, and only by reaching for his highest limits acquire knowledge of his depths? Or
is it only by renouncing ambition, by living within oneself, that
true self-knowledge is available? Ranged on one side of the issue
are Balzac, Stendhal, and Dreiser; on the other are Dostoevski,
Kierkegaard, and Kafka.

Of course, the issue is not quite so clear-cut as all that.
Behind the determination to be ambitious or to renounce ambition, a perennial argument is carried on within most people,
whichever their choice. Emile Durkheim, whose point this is,
writes: "The active, ambitious type upbraids the more passive
one for losing his life, neglecting his duty to the 'here and now,'
and shaking off responsibility for the actual by taking refuge
with a Higher Reality which commits him to nothing. The passive type retorts, by maintaining that his opponent is sacrificing
his inner 'self' to the 'world,' and that instead of minding his own
soul, he concentrates upon purely mundane objectives.

"In both cases," Durkheim continues, "there can be genuine

and spurious solutions; whichever alternative is finally decided on, it is always possible that the result in practice will prove to be a mere caricature of the real potentialities of the choice." Durkheim does not say so flat out, but he gives ample reason to believe that he feels that the person with ambition has much the better of it—that the way of ambition holds out to those who take it a surer sense of direction, a better purchase on reality, and a firmer feeling of control over their lives than the way of renouncing ambition. "The attitude of 'not caring for tomorrow,'" he writes, "which is equally characteristic of tramps, Bohemians, and mendicant friars, and distinguishes them from the man striving for success, conceals a life in which there is little clarity and much darkness and impenetrable gloom."

What Durkheim tends to overlook, and what becomes a problem in our time, is the end result of ambition. What happens when the goal is reached? What if, having lived a life caring for tomorrow, tomorrow turns out to be an empty promise? Quite apart from the prospect of one's ambitions being short-circuited along the way—life, after all, is filled with the most complicated wiring—what if one realizes them completely, and after doing so achieves a clarity too glaring to live with?

Nor is all that much known about the origins of ambition. Why do some people burn with it, while others, apparently wrapped in metaphysical asbestos, never feel its heat? The answers that commonsense psychology provide are not very satisfactory. One gets ambition from one's parents. But where do one's parents get it from? Why does it take in one child, and not in his two brothers and sister? "Though it has not been written about much," the novelist Nathan Asch began an essay about his relationship with his famous father, the novelist Sholem Asch, "the children of famous artists do not have an easy time, nor do they usually end up well. There is more apostasy, suicide, homosexuality, fraud, and lying, as well as plain ne'er-do-wellism among them than among children of other kinds of people." Nathan Asch's remark can be extended to the children of the greatly successful generally, not merely to those of successful artists alone.

Is it better for the succoring of ambition to be born to

parents whose own lives have been immensely successful, or to parents whose lives have been only mildly so? Or is it better yet to be born to parents whose lives are marked by failure—and thus to have passed on to one the impetus of a negative example? Yet again, is it better not to have both parents? Orvis F. Collins's book *The Enterprising Man*, a study of the founders of 110 companies, noted that an inordinately large number of these men lost a parent either to death or to divorce early in their lives. "The picture that comes through from the interviews is one of the lonely child, grubby fists in tear-filled eyes, accepting the loss and facing a dangerous future." Is the key to success, as Hemingway once claimed it was the key to being a good writer, having an unhappy childhood? Is ambition really as simple as a wish to make the most of one's abilities and thus to get the best the world has to offer? Does it arise from a consciousness of superior worth? Or is it instead really a more or less secret desire for revenge for humiliations received? A cover for fear of being discounted as a negligible person? A disguised cry for love and attention? Or the acting out of some other psychic scenario? Not known, nor soon likely to be.

What is known is that some societies do encourage ambition by offering up certain fairly clear ideals of success. Although by now it has become a great baggy-pants cliché into which many discrepant types have been made to fit—Catholics, Jews, middle-class blacks, any ardent workers—Max Weber's idea of the Protestant Ethic, applied, as Weber applied it, to the Protestant countries of seventeenth-century Europe, is still compelling in its broader lineaments. Weber found the components of the Protestant Ethic—hard work, ascetic living, thrift—in the teachings of John Calvin, which placed religion in support of the methodical pursuit of one's "calling," and created in the process the ideological reinforcement for the moral discipline, the spirit, that made possible the development of industrial capitalism. As Weber viewed it, men who lived by the Protestant Ethic were not principally animated by the love of money; money was instead a by-product of the pursuit of their calling. Yet the accumulation of wealth, a sure sign that one had successfully worked at one's calling, was also a sign that one was among God's Elect.

Ambition and success, in other words, had religious support.

The main point is that different societies hold up different ideals for success and, by implication, determinants for failure, and thus view ambition differently. In seventeenth-century Protestant Europe, ascetic capitalism was the ideal. In early nineteenth-century France and Spain, the aristocratic was the ideal. In late nineteenth-century England, wealth formed part of the ideal of success but it was not decisive; to have money, as Henry James noted, was an advantage, but to lack it was not a disgrace. At the same period in America, our Gilded Age, extravagant wealth yoked to piety of utterance and manner seems in many quarters to have been dominant. Sometimes the ideal, though still given official lip service, is eclipsed by the real. Thus in Soviet society, the tough-minded yet mediocre seems, if not the official ideal, then in reality the type that flourishes best. And in the America of our day—well, that is a complicated question.

Tocqueville, as usual, is instructive. He entitled a chapter of *Democracy in America* "Why There Are So Many Men of Ambition in the United States But So Few Lofty Ambitions." Tocqueville was viewing America only a half century or so after the consolidation of its successful revolution, and he observed: "Every American is eaten up with longing to rise, but hardly any of them seem to entertain very great hopes or to aim very high. All are constantly bent on gaining property, reputation, and power, but few conceive such things on a grand scale." The equality prevalent in democracies, Tocqueville believed, had much to do with the nature of ambition in America. Although a few men do achieve great opulence in democracies, most realize that their desires must be "confined within fairly narrow limits. Hence in democracies ambition is both eager and constant, but in general it does not look very high. For the most part life is spent in eagerly coveting small prizes within reach."

Ambition also, in Tocqueville's view, had certain imposed limits in America, where people, as he saw it, cared less for the interest and judgment of posterity and were more completely absorbed by the moment. "They are much more in love with success than with glory," Tocqueville wrote. "What they especially ask from men is obedience. What they most desire is power. Their manners almost always lag behind the rise in their social position. As a result, very vulgar tastes often go with their enjoyment of extraordinary prosperity, and it would seem that their only object in rising to supreme power was to gratify trivial and coarse appetites more easily."

Tocqueville ended his chapter on a plaintive note, complaining that Americans have an insufficiency of pride and too low a view of themselves and of humanity. "I think," he wrote, "that nowadays it is necessary to purge ambition, to control it and keep it in proportion, but that it would be very dangerous if we tried to starve it or confine it beyond reason. . . . But we should be very careful not to hamper its free energy within the permitted limits. I confess that I believe democratic society to have much less to fear from boldness than from paltriness of aim. What frightens me most is the danger that, amid all the constant trivial preoccupations of private life, ambition may lose both its force and its greatness, that human passions may grow gentler and at the same time baser, with the result that the progress of the body social may become daily quieter and less aspiring."

Curiosity Shop □ There is a fantasy commonly held by many who have been given a liberal arts education but who lack either the talent or the opportunity to practice any of these arts. It runs something like this: Very well. I will spend the first fifteen or twenty years of my life striving in the canyons of Wall or La Salle streets, or in the law courts, or in the long halls of corporations, and during this time, through concentrated exertions, I will pile up enough money to free myself forever from such grubby pursuits, and devote the remainder of my days to the Higher Things: literature, philosophy, music, beautiful pictures. Alas, it is a fantasy seldom achieved. But it makes all the more interesting the career of an American writer who seems to have spent the first fifteen or twenty years of his adult life living for the Higher Things, establishing himself as an important, indeed an extraordinarily influential, art critic. Once having done so, he has been free to spend the remainder of his days in the buying and selling of paintings—in short, in business. A perfect reversal of the common fantasy. What a wonderful world!

Henry Adams

"How little origin is to happiness," Benjamin Franklin asserted. "How much origin can be to unhappiness," Henry Adams might have replied. Henry Adams had a taste for paradox, but, more important in this instance, he could have submitted his own life in evidence. No child, certainly, as he himself put it, "held better cards than he." Of the principal founders of the Republic, Washington, Franklin, Jefferson, and John Adams, only the last left legitimate male descendants. John Adams was Henry's great-grandfather; Samuel Adams was a kinsman; John Quincy Adams was his grandfather; and Charles Francis Adams, congressman, statesman, and minister plenipotentiary to England during the diplomatically delicate years of the American Civil War, was his father. Henry Adams was the scion of the greatest, perhaps the only authentically patrician, family America has ever known. For one born into such a family—America's first family—no expectation could be too grand, no vision of one's potential achievement too ambitious. Yet Henry Adams considered himself a failure, a pitiful bust-out. He had lost all hope long before he died, and he died grasping at theories to explain the universe, and his own lost place in it, that he himself was not altogether convinced of. Was Henry Adams a failure? When a man who is not obviously a failure so frequently insists that he is—as Adams does time and again in his autobiography—it is in order to ask what it would have taken for him to have regarded himself a success.

But first let us tot up Henry Adams's accomplishments, which were not few, however little he himself made of them. He lived well, met and was highly regarded by many of the great men of his time, some of whom he knew on intimate terms and many of whom—among them John Hay, secretary of state for both McKinley and Theodore Roosevelt—actively sought out his advice. After Harvard, Henry Adams served as secretary to the American legation in England during his father's brilliant ambassadorship, which gave him a box seat for witnessing history in the making. Seven years later he returned to Washington, where he set up as a journalist of reforming spirit, and caused an immediate stir. E. L. Godkin, editor of the *Nation,* remarked of his journalism that it "justifies his title to the family name," and that he had "peculiar powers as an assailant . . . an instinct for the jugular and carotid artery as unerring as that of any carnivorous animal." Adams contends that he found himself in a state of "continual intoxication" over politics, but was uncertain what he really wanted. "Certainly not office," he wrote, "for except for very high office I would take none." He next turned to academic life. His performance during a seven-year stint as editor of the *North American Review* and as an assistant professor of history at Harvard—he held both jobs simultaneously, with no evident sign of strain—was roundly adjudged brilliant. Of his historical writing that came out of these years, particularly his nine-volume *History of the United States During the Administrations of Jefferson and Madison,* Carl Becker wrote that he had produced "a history which for clarity, tight construction, and sheer intelligence applied to the exposition of a great theme, had not then, and has not since, been equalled by any American historian." *Democracy,* one of the two novels he tossed off when he returned to Washington to live, was a great succès de scandale, which, being a portrait of the vulgarities of Washington political life as it was lived under the administrations of Grant and Hayes, was what he fully intended it to be. *Mont-Saint-Michel & Chartres,* his book on the Middle Ages, was both a critical and a commercial success. *The Education of Henry Adams,* though privately printed and distributed only to friends during his life, has since become an American classic, one of a small shelf—perhaps containing fifteen or twenty volumes—of truly indispensable books in American literature. Although late in her life his wife committed suicide, under circumstances that even now remain clouded, Henry Adams's marriage appears to have been a beautiful one, lived out before a background of independent wealth, quiet elegance, and extreme refinement. After his wife's death, he lived out his last years alternating his home quarters between Paris and Washington, doing much traveling, and always carefully tended by nieces till his death at the age of eighty.

His wife's death aside, the road Henry Adams traveled

through life is notable for its lack of bumps, potholes, or other obstacles. "Most men would have been satisfied with the life he lived apart from the books he wrote," the historian Carl Becker rightly remarked, "or with the books he wrote apart from the life he lived." What, then, was wrong? What was Adams's complaint about? "What was the matter with Henry Adams?" the novelist Owen Wister once asked Oliver Wendell Holmes, Jr. "He wanted it," Holmes replied, "handed to him on a silver platter." Comfortable to believe, especially coming from so keen an intelligence as Justice Holmes, but more appears to have been involved.

True, in defense of Holmes's reply, there was much of the snob in Henry Adams. In the notes for a story, Henry James has a character named Bonnycastle, who is modeled on Adams, say when discussing a forthcoming dinner party, "Hang it. There's only a month left; let us be vulgar and have some fun—let us invite the President." Shortly after graduating from Harvard, Adams noted two traits at work in himself: "One is a continual tendency toward politics; the other is family pride." The two, alas, did not mix well in the time in which it was given him to live—the Gilded Age, the Era of the Robber Barons. Yet Holmes and Henry James, given similar conditions, found space enough to exercise their ambitions and to win through to distinguished and successful careers in which they were rightly able to take pride. Why not Henry Adams?

However strong his attraction to politics—the U.S. government, it might be said, was the Adams family business— Adams's family pride, commingled perhaps with his overly refined temperament, did not allow him to join in "the dance of democracy," as he disdainfully referred to the patronage politics of his day. An aunt noted of her nephew Henry: "He wished to be a force, and yet takes no part in life's high destiny. . . . Advanced in thought, knowing and strong, he sees clearly and acts mildly. . . . He cannot act—he sets himself as the universe."

"Autobiography," George Orwell wrote, "is only to be trusted when it reveals something disgraceful. A man who gives a good account of himself is probably lying, since any life when viewed from inside is simply a series of defeats." So did Henry

Adams view his life from the inside—a series of defeats, or miseducations. But for all the evasions, the paradoxes, the ambiguities of Adams's autobiography, for all that he kept insisting that he was not only a failure but a man whose failure remained a riddle to himself, he points out quite clearly what it would have taken for him to regard himself a success. A man who was well educated, who succeeded, for Henry Adams, was one who was able to "react, not by haphazard, but by choice, on the lines of force that predominated in the world, someone able to throw his life into the main 'stream of tendency' of the period into which he was born"—someone, in other words, who left his mark on the world. To leave the world changed as a result of one's having lived in it—this for Henry Adams was what success meant and what a proper education fitted a man out to do. And this, precisely, is what Henry Adams felt he did not (could not, would not) do.

Justice Holmes used sometimes to stop in at Adams's house on his way back from the Supreme Court, and find his friend Henry "playing the old Cardinal; he would spend his energy in pointing out that everything was dust and ashes." Poor Adams. Holmes noted: "He was kind, sad, and defeated, although another man would have thought the same life a success." What he had accomplished, Adams seems truly to have felt, did not matter. To have the admiration of professors and intellectuals was not enough—not for an Adams it wasn't. Carl Becker persuasively argues that the problem with Henry Adams was that "his genius was at war with his ambition." Adams's genius was for reflection, criticism, scholarship, but his ambition was to leave his mark upon a world wider than that peopled by men and women with sufficient mental equipment to make his books accessible to them—a piddling minority, then as now. He was an Adams, and an Adams does not get off so easily. High birth can carry burdens that may sink a man.

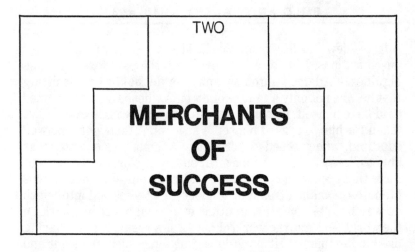

TWO

MERCHANTS OF SUCCESS

John D. Rockefeller

Such was the gravity of his bearing that, not yet twenty years old, John D. Rockefeller was everywhere known as "Mr. Rockefeller." Before he was thirty he ran the largest oil manufactory in the world. Less than ten years later some men with whom he had done business speculated upon his age. One man said: "I guess he is one hundred and forty years old—for he must have been one hundred years old when he was born." His agelessness derived chiefly from his imperturbability, a certain aloof and distanced quality. It was a quality he had had from early boyhood. When in later years his fame had spread, people who had known him as a boy were interviewed to attest to his early abilities. They could think of none, except that he used to walk along in a somewhat dazed way and seemed always to be thinking. We can now guess what he was probably thinking about. He had a one-track mind, he was a single-track genius. Business was his life.

His origins were scarcely humble but neither were they very grand. The Rockefellers settled in this country sometime in the 1720s, and lived here more than a century without a trace of a hint of distinction. John D. Rockefeller's own father was an itinerant trader, mostly in medicines; he was what was then known as an "herbal physician," and in Richford, New York, where John was born, his father was sometimes called Doc. He was a man with dash—handsome, large, with a taste for fine horses. His son later acquired this taste and also something of his father's acumen in business, this last learned the hard way. "I cheat my boys every time I get a chance," the older Rockefeller said. "I want to make 'em sharp. I trade with the boys and skin 'em. I just beat 'em every chance I get." If anyone apart from his father ever beat John D. Rockefeller, there is no known record of it.

Knowledge of horses and a rudimentary business savvy are chiefly what Rockefeller learned from his father. His mother's contribution to his character was greater. While his father was flashy, his mother was solid. While his father was erratic, off on long business trips, then returning in the night, his mother was steady, always there, holding things together. While his father was of this world, once accused of horse-thieving and once actually indicted for rape, his mother was spiritual, a teetotaler, plain-spoken, devoted to her church. John, when he grew up, tended to be more the man his mother was. An anecdote illustrates the kind of person she was. Once John and his brother William had disobeyed her and gone out late at night skating. As they were doing so, another boy who was with them had fallen through the ice, and the Rockefeller boys were able to pull him out, saving his life in the act. When they reported the incident to their mother, she embraced them for their bravery, then punished them for disobeying her. "Wilful waste makes woeful want," his mother used to say, in a maxim fully as boring as it is true. Her son wasted not and neither did he want. He had no interest in clothes, food, vice plain or fancy. "I never had a craving for anything," he said, and there is not, on this score, much reason to doubt his word.

He did have dreams, though, dreams of business: of deals and opportunities. It was an age when business was the elite profession, and one in which men began young. Carnegie, Gould, Jay Cooke, Morgan, Frick, all began in their adolescence. John D. Rockefeller began at sixteen, as an assistant bookkeeper for a firm of commission merchants and produce shippers in Cleveland, and in later years celebrated his first day on the job as a

festal occasion. He early determined never to work in a shop or
store. His father had decided against sending him to college. "I
hadn't the advantages of a college education," he once remarked. How much more might he have accomplished if he had
gone to college—or how much less?

He was dogged, determined, and good at arithmetic. Quick
to seize opportunities: "When it's raining porridge," his sister
Lucy once said, "you'll find John's dish right side up." No brutality or aggressiveness to him; nothing of the swashbuckler businessman, the wheeler-dealer, the showman. He made up for this
with persistence, love of order, curiosity about facts, and an
unwavering attention to detail. Attention to detail was part of
the secret of his early success. He was a saver; tithed to the
Baptist church on limited income; carried his lunch to work. "I
lived within my means," he said. Once in business with partners,
then for himself, shoring up modest victory after modest victory, he spoke to himself in bed at night: "But be careful. Pride
goeth before the fall. Nothing in haste, nothing ill done. Your
future hangs on every day that passes. . . . Look out or you will
lose your head—go steady."

He was cautious but courageous—a careful plunger. He
took on loans of such size as to make his early partners tremble.
He learned that other men's money had its uses. "We should
borrow whenever we can safely extend the business by doing
so." He had no known distractions. He found adventure in business, spiritual nourishment in his church, social life among his
family. His life was organized for success. He tended to give off
a somewhat chilling effect on people who met him. He com-
manded complete calm in crisis. He planned everything eight or
nine moves ahead. He had the mind of a first-rate chess player:
analytical, concentrated, monomaniacal. Of his inner life very
little is known. Possibly he had none.

If luck played a part in his rise, it was that he came of age
around the time of the first great oil strikes in Pennsylvania. Oil
provided the second American gold rush. It was the time of the
Great Barbecue, as the Gilded Age was sometimes referred to,
and oil was to be a major ingredient in the sauce. It was a wild
and brutal business—men catching themselves aflame, horses

dying under their extravagant loads, millionaires created every afternoon, scenes of squalid wealth sloshing about in liquid gold. Sizing up the scene, the young John D. Rockefeller found the potentialities of refining oil far outweighed the risks of producing it.

The history of Standard Oil is the history of American business over the past century, and by no means writ small. It is the story of an unexampled rise with perhaps a stumble or two along the way but no real fall. It is, eminently and ultimately, the story of John D. Rockefeller. "We were all boys together," he later noted of his associates, "having a lot of fun as we worked hard every day." That no doubt depends upon one's interpretation of a good time. As for the boys, among them Henry M. Flagler, John Archbold, William Rockefeller, and H. H. Rogers, they were an odd crew of differing temperaments who taken together made up one of the most astute collections of business executives in the history of the nation. H. H. Rogers (men who had done business with him claimed that the H. H. stood for "Hell Hound"), for example, was merciless in his business dealings, yet it was he who paid for Helen Keller's education and later bailed Mark Twain out of his nearly impossible financial difficulties. Flagler, one of his earliest partners, described his relationship with Rockefeller as a friendship founded on business, adding that this was to be preferred to a business founded on friendship. Although Rockefeller kept in the background—taciturnity, indeed a penchant for secrecy, was part of his nature—it was he who led these men and orchestrated the fortunes of Standard Oil. Uniting audacity with precision, imagination with caution, he put together an empire. "Mere money-making has never been my goal," he said, having acquired more money than any man, including himself, could ever have dreamed of. "I had an ambition to build."

Like most businessmen who were successful on the grand scale, he did not put much stock in pure capitalism. "Men like spoiled children," is the way he described those petroleum producers who insisted on overproducing and hence depressing the market for their product. He preferred efficiency to individualism. Expansion, as he saw it, meant economy—so he expanded

and expanded and expanded, until by the 1880s the Standard was
the richest industrial company in the United States, the richest,
in fact, in the world. From his earliest days he cut out middlemen
in the name of efficiency. Later he would cut out—usually buy
out, sometimes snuff out—competitors in the name of efficiency.
He was not against competition except when it was inefficient.
It frequently was inefficient, so he swallowed it. Heady individualism, wildcatting, the let-'er-rip spirit offended his sense of
order and love of system. He advocated industrial discipline, and
practiced it. He was for "progressive" measures. He used the
word *progressive* a good deal, and when he did it was usually
synonymous with the word *profitable*.

In some ways better than its counterparts among the levia-
thans of nineteenth-century American business, the Standard
never cheated its investors by manipulating stock (à la Jay
Gould) or watering it (à la J. P. Morgan); it paid somewhat higher
wages than other industries, and hence was seldom struck; it set
up a liberal pension plan. In other ways it was no better than the
times in which it throve. Dependent upon transportation, it engaged in every possible bit of finagling with the railroads: re-
bates, drawbacks, anything that would knock out what Rockefeller felt to be "ruinous" competition. No business of his would
be entirely at the mercy of the vagaries of supply and demand
or of cutthroat competition if he could help it. And he could help
it. The solution, as he saw it, was combination and expansion. "I
believe the only way to succeed is to keep getting ahead all the
time." Early in what was to be a great growth industry—the
inventions of the automobile and the airplane were to make its
growth inevitable—he expanded into all phases of the oil business (refining, exploration, production, shipping, marketing)
until he controlled something like 95 percent of the oil business
in the United States along with an ample trade in Europe, Asia,
Africa, and South America.

"General propositions in regard to either competition or
monopoly are full of snares," the economist Alfred Marshall
noted, and whether Rockefeller's innovations in forming combi-
nations, trusts, and what the Supreme Court in 1911 finally
found to be a monopoly were really the wave of the future is less

to the point than the fact that his actions were against the grain of American sentiment about open and free competition in business. As the Standard grew in size and efficiency, Rockefeller grew as a figure of public contumely. Women in the Allegheny Valley used to frighten their children by telling them, if they behaved badly, "Rockefeller will get you if you don't mind." Exposés began to appear, chief among them Ida M. Tarbell's *The History of Standard Oil* and Henry Demarest Lloyd's "The Study of a Great Monopoly," both charging gain ill-gotten and corruption all around, with Lloyd remarking that the Standard "has done everything with the Pennsylvania legislature except refine it." Some of the charges were true, others false, all fitted out to make excellent newspaper copy. Rockefeller answered none of them. "I will not engage in controversy," he had said early in his career, a point he held to. The Standard was sued by competitors, charged with sabotage, with price-slashing to drive out competitors. In all this litigation high principles were invoked, but at bottom profits were involved. Amid the various rumors flying about, the *New York World* wrote: "Certain ribald and envious persons have asserted that the Standard Oil Company is aiming at the control of the solar system. . . . It is but an act of justice to state that this is not the case. The Standard Oil Company is entirely satisfied at present with controlling the earth."

Rockefeller maintained his imperturbability throughout, keeping his own counsel. His capping comment about his role in one of his earlier controversies seems to apply to his later ones: "It is between me and my God." The morning that Judge Kenesaw Mountain Landis fined the Standard Oil Company of Indiana $29,240,000 (in a decision later reversed), Rockefeller learned of it on the golf course; he commented briefly that this appeared to be the maximum fine, and then finished his round. Some said he was the most hated man in America. Cartoonists had a field day with him. Articles carrying such titles as "Rockefeller: Man or Monster?" appeared regularly in the press. Every calumny was spread about him, not least the story that his father had bigamously remarried. In the face of all this, he retained his equanimity. John Singer Sargent, who painted his portrait, afterward commented: "Here is a man at peace with God."

"The money God gave to me" is the way Rockefeller referred to his ever-increasing fortune. In France he told the mayor of the town of Compiègne: "It is foolish to believe that any man in the United States is worth a billion dollars. I am not worth one third of that amount." Later his net worth was estimated at $900 million. He was able to shore up such a sum because most of it was earned before there was an income tax. He was also clever in his investments, and seemed to have a piece of the action everywhere. In the 1890s he made large investments in the Pacific Northwest, including steel mills, railroads, lumber, ore deposits, and real estate. In the Middle West, he gained control of the Mesabi iron range, which he later sold off to J. P. Morgan for $55 million. Peter Finley Dunne's Mr. Dooley said of the Rockefellers that they were "a kind iv society f'r th' previntion iv croolty to money." Such was the extent of the fortune he had piled up that, in later years, after his effective retirement from Standard Oil, he let his office know that he need not be contacted for any investment under $2 million.

Although no official notice of it was given, Rockefeller left Standard Oil in 1897. He had been going into the office less and less, and now he went in not at all. The next phase of his career was the philanthropic one. Here he applied the same principles that had worked so well for him in business, those of combination and cooperation. He had developed a feeling, bordering on the mystical, that God had given him so much money so that he might benefit the welfare of mankind. Over the years he gave away $550 million, being the chief donor to the University of Chicago, the Rockefeller Institute for Medical Research, the Rockefeller Foundation, and many hundreds of other institutions. He tended to give his money quietly, no big splash connected with his benefactions. Once, when one of his large donations was made public, he received in the mail 15,000 applications for money the first week and a total of 50,000 before the month was out. Unlike other great givers, he had no ulterior motives, not even tax breaks, which had not yet come into existence. Unlike Andrew Carnegie, the other great giver of the age, he had no wish to know the famous and the powerful. Unlike J. P.

Morgan, he required no adulation. He gave with surprisingly few strings attached: no building named after him while he lived, no ceremonies connected with benefactions, the minimum accompanying publicity.

Although there was nothing of either the public relations gesture or the tax write-off gambit behind Rockefeller's charitable donations, in some quarters his money was held suspect. "Tainted money" was the charge made by Reverend Washington Gladden when Rockefeller donated a (for him) mere $100,000 to the Congregational Board of Foreign Missions, even though the Board was later discovered to have actually solicited the money. Around this time Senator Robert M. La Follette pronounced John D. Rockefeller "the greatest criminal in the world." In the presidential campaign of 1908, Rockefeller, a lifelong Republican though not a man keenly interested in politics, announced he would vote for Taft, which delighted the Democrats and caused Taft, such was the unpopularity of Rockefeller, to eschew his support. If Rockefeller, now an old man, was wounded by any of this, he never publicly registered his hurt. Ivy L. Lee, the public relations specialist, was hired on toward the end of Rockefeller's life not at Rockefeller's but at his son's request.

Nothing, it seems, daunted the old man. He had no whims, he bore no malice. A streak of bad health plagued him in 1890, when he underwent a digestive ailment and generalized alopecia, a nervous disorder that caused the loss of all his hair, eyebrows included. But for the rest of his life his health was good. He golfed, he planned the landscaping of his homes, he kept a hand in the stock market. Everyone around him testifies that he never knew a moment of boredom. His son and he shared a relationship of mutual respect and unequivocal love. Jo Davidson, the sculptor and a tough judge of human character, after doing a sculpture of Rockefeller, remarked: "Maybe you have strolled along the left bank of the Seine and picked up an ancient volume bound in dusty leather. You handle it. It belongs to another world. You open it. The print at first is difficult to read. The *s*'s look like *f*'s; the spelling is strange. But you read on and you come to a phrase familiar, human, appealing, and it acts like an open sesame. That to me is John D. Rockefeller."

He died in his sleep at 4:30 Sunday morning, May 23, 1937, at the age of ninety-eight.

Three large elements are entailed in determining the destiny of any individual: first, the conditions of his birth, his parents, and the talent and intelligence he is born with; second, the circumstances actual and intellectual surrounding his time on earth; and third, and closely connected with the second element, the ideas and beliefs he holds. (A fourth element, some might argue, is luck or the role of accident; although in discrete instances luck can loom large, it is not usually so dominant or decisive as these other three elements.) But, given the cards one is dealt at birth and those one draws fairly early in life, the question is, What makes a life significant? A number of different standards can be invoked. There is the standard of the cash box. There is the standard of good works. There is the standard of public opinion. There is the standard of harmlessness, or doing little to make life poorer for one's fellows. There is the standard of altering history, or changing the life of one's time. There is the standard of being, in some ineffable way, a force. "You may not like him," Henry Luce, the founder and principal owner of Time-Life, Inc., once said of General Douglas MacArthur, "but he meets the test of greatness. He *fills* the living space around him. He cannot be trespassed upon, or toyed with, or subtracted from. Whatever ground he stands on, it is *his.*"

Henry Luce's test of greatness does not allow much room for most of mankind. Under it, Julius Caesar and Muhammad Ali would qualify, but Alexander Pope and Mother Teresa would not. But then greatness, as Henry Luce envisioned it, is different from significance, as William James, who wrote an essay entitled "What Makes a Life Significant?" envisioned it. Greatness, for Luce, is a measurable matter, power and colossal wealth being the counters employed, and as such it is quick to exclude. Josef Stalin's alleged question, How many divisions has the Pope?, provides a stellar sample of such reasoning carried to its logical conclusion. To have shored up a few millions of dollars, to have become an accomplished artist, neither of these can be sufficient; nor, it nearly goes without saying, is merely leading a good life, or coming to some keen perceptions about the world around one. Sacrifice, no matter what the cause, does not enter it; not even an honorable death scores points. Greatness, as Henry Luce perceived it, was evinced in power and control. Heady stuff, and for a certain kind of man immensely attractive.

Greatness scarcely figures in William James's notion of significance, although interestingly the great world does. James thought that one's place in the world mattered a good deal, yet it was not everything. Among other things, how one acquires one's place counts importantly. With the balance that was habitual to him, James wrote: "But, instinctively, we make a combination of two things in judging the total significance of a human being. We feel it to be some sort of product (if such a product only could be calculated) of his inner virtue *and* his outer place —neither singly taken, but both conjoined. If the outer differences had no meaning for life, why indeed should all this immense variety of them exist? They must be significant elements of the world as well." Inner virtue, for James, is only valid "when the inner joy, courage, and endurance are joined with an ideal." Yet an ideal itself is not sufficient to significance; it must have the added "dimension of active will, if we are to have *depth*, if we are to have anything cubical and solid in the way of character."

For William James, then, a fusion is required to bestow significance: the fusion of ideal aspirations and "pluck and will." Moreover, James held that "the thing of deepest—or, at any rate, of comparatively deepest—significance in life does seem to be its character of *progress.*" What makes morally exceptional, or significant, persons different from the rest, in James's view, is that "their souls worked and endured in obedience to some inner *ideal*, while their comrades were not activated by anything worthy of that name." James does not spell out what the exact nature of these ideals are—although we know from other of his writings, with his castigation of the "bitch goddess of success" and lusting solely after money—that they are not simple. In fact, he remarks that "these ideals of other lives are among those secrets that we can almost never penetrate, although something about the man may often tell us when they are there."

James's idea of what makes a life significant is admirably flexible; that it also comports with the reality of human character and conditions is another of its advantages. The marriage of an inner ideal with courage, fidelity, and endurance in seeking to realize that ideal is splendidly nonexclusionary: it leaves open the possibility of human significance for poets and businessmen, statesmen and mothers, lovers and tycoons. The tyranny of conformity is absent from it. The mystery of human personality is respected by it. It is well worth remembering.

Curiosity Shop ▫ He was in his middle fifties, and on his desk sat a thick manuscript. His writing had brought him fame and the love of many beautiful women. The manuscript on the desk would, as he had more than an inkling, soon bring him much money as well. From the outside his life seemed smooth and enviable. He had a lucrative professorship and an admirable reputation as a writer of great and serious production. His personal life was a bit messy—his second marriage had only recently collapsed—but then so were the lives of many people in his circle. A writer younger than he was seated across the desk from him, and he was in a talkative mood.

"I think I may have written a very good book here," he said, laying his hand on the manuscript, "but I have to tell you that such sense of accomplishment as I have felt about it has been brief. Already I am looking around for another book to write, already the itch is upon me. Resting content is a thing I seem unable to do. Where does all this energy, this urge to keep firing away, come from? You know S. L. [here he named a well-known woman writer]? Twenty-five years ago, when I was only beginning to establish myself, she described me as 'another Jew-boy in a hurry.' She didn't say it to me, of course, but it got back to me. I hated her for it then, and, though the sting has over the years become less, a part of me hates her for it still. I can't ever forget it. Another Jew-boy in a hurry. It's a devastating remark. I have had all these years to contemplate its accuracy, and I am still not sure that she was altogether wrong. That's what galls."

On the matter of achieving success, America has never for very long lacked an ample literature on, as Henry James once put it in an entirely different context, "the dear little deadly question of how to do it." This literature, the how-to literature on success, is not exclusive to America. In England, for example, Daniel Defoe wrote manuals on how to succeed in business, even though he had himself endured bankruptcy and debtors' prison. Samuel Smiles, author of such works as *The Lives of Engineers, Character, Duty,* and *Self-Help,* flourished by teaching the adjustment of the human spirit to technical progress and the lesson that anyone could succeed in Victorian England. But where a Samuel Smiles has been a fairly lone marcher in the cause of success, America has generally had a parade of such men. For a how-to literature to succeed there has to be a want-to spirit abroad in the land—and this America has never lacked.

The first notable American work in this line—and to become notable a work instructing people about how to succeed must itself succeed in acquiring a fairly large audience—was Benjamin Franklin's *Poor Richard's Almanack,* and particularly its most frequently quoted segment, "The Way to Wealth." Perhaps more than anything else this work has contributed to the popular notion of Franklin as the epitome of American practicality, if not narrow-minded shrewdness. Certainly Franklin, as a dispenser of information on how to succeed, was part wily, part platitudinous. But if he was wily, it was because wile was required to survive in the American colonies; if he was platitudinous, it should be remembered in his defense that he himself initiated many of what have since become platitudes. Time is Money, God helps Those who help Themselves, Creditors have better Memories than Debtors—these are all Franklin's formulations, not, as he was quick to admit, absolutely original with him but rather the product of "the Gleanings I had made of the sense of all Ages and Nations."

" 'Tis hard for an empty bag to stand upright," Franklin wrote in his guise as Poor Richard, and no other single sentence of his composing better connects his teaching on success to the meaning of his own extraordinary life. Whenever one is tempted to write off Franklin as a grumbling and grasping American hustler, it is well to recall that at forty-two he effectively retired from his various businesses to devote the remainder of his life—he lived to the age of eighty-four—to learning and public service. In his *Autobiography*, the first American success story, he recorded his rise "from the poverty and obscurity in which I was born, to a state of affluence and some degree of reputation in the world." The point of his life, however, was not affluence, but the freedom that affluence made possible to do good works and think clear thoughts without the distractions of business and financial worry. Franklin spent a goodly amount of energy in his *Autobiography* extolling the merit of individual prosperity; it was, as his life handsomely showed, not individual prosperity that was of primary interest to him but what such prosperity made possible.

Apart from his exemplary personal accomplishments, Benjamin Franklin represented a new, and peculiarly American, historical type: the self-made man. Europe had known the type of the self-made man, but there he had never gotten a very good press, and was in fact slapped with such contemptuous labels as *parvenu, nouveau riche,* and *arriviste.* But contempt of this kind was only possible where an aristocracy existed from which it could issue. Colonial America having no such securely established aristocracy, no one was better fit to fill the role of an elite than the self-made man. In his useful and thorough book, *Apostles of the Self-Made Man,** John G. Cawelti remarks that "Franklin's conception of self-improvement was closely related to his belief in the necessity of a self-selecting and self-disciplining elite, men of virtue voluntarily assuming the leadership of society." Cawelti goes on to connect Franklin's ideas on this

---

*Professor Cawelti's book has proved a most helpful guide to the enormous literature on success and self-improvement, and anyone who touches on the subject cannot but be very grateful to him.

score to Thomas Jefferson's notion of a "natural aristocracy," one that would not become an entrenched party of interests, as had other aristocracies, but would instead formulate the new values for the new society that was America and in the process be replenished by those who were capable of living up to these new values.

Although neither Franklin nor Jefferson was a notably religious man, their ideas about success had behind them considerable religious support. In the seventeenth and early eighteenth centuries in America, orthodox Puritanism, whose leading figure was Cotton Mather (1663–1728), stressed business as a worthy calling, and hence a vital part of religion. Individual prosperity, in this view, was a clear reflection, if not a direct result, of individual piety. A Christian, according to Mather, should follow his calling with "industry," "discretion," "honesty," "contentment," and "piety," looking out always, it nearly goes without saying, for one's religious or general calling to serve God, which is primary. "Let not the *Business* of your *Personal Calling,*" Mather wrote, "swallow up the *Business* of your *General Calling.*"

The secular and the religious strains of the success gospel handsomely reinforced each other in the United States during the first half of the nineteenth century, much to the profit of the figure of the self-made man. Self-made status was claimed, not altogether truthfully, by the likes of Daniel Webster, General William Henry Harrison, and Henry Clay. The career of Abraham Lincoln was of course to be the ultimate expression of the self-made-man legend. Ministers and secular writers alike, while preaching the virtues of success in a general way, offered little practical advice, but instead emphasized the development of moral character—with its attendant virtues of industry, frugality, enterprise—from which success would inevitably follow. The way to become self-made was to make oneself over through the cultivation of moral character: a task that was deemed doable and eminently worth doing. Ralph Waldo Emerson, in such essays as "Self-Reliance," "Wealth," and "Success," had few qualms about it. Emerson, whose writing straddled the religious and the secular, was perhaps the last first-class American mind to tout success in general terms. "Poverty demoralizes," he wrote. "Wealth brings its own checks and balances," and "The counting-room maxims liberally expounded are laws of the universe." Up through Emerson, virtue and success were in no wise seen as incompatible; on the contrary, virtue was the cause that brought about the effect that was success. And, by extension, ambition was a quality to be encouraged.

But other forces were at work that tended to wrench the notion of success from the philosophical and religious frame that Mather, Franklin, Jefferson, and Emerson had placed it in. Tocqueville, on his visit to the United States in 1838, had already remarked upon the restlessness of Americans, the national hunger for mobility in one or another of its forms. "Death at length overtakes him [the American], but it is before he is weary of his bootless chase of that complete felicity which forever escapes him." In this setting, one of ever-expanding opportunity and the great hunt for personal happiness, individual success, as opposed to success of a kind that would strengthen society, became primary. The same moral terms were used—the need for self-discipline, for the rigors of industry, thrift, conscientiousness—but the message commenced to change. Success for the greater good of society was subtly altered to read: every man for himself.

In the process the repute of ambition was altered. Ambition no longer had such interesting and admirable supporters as Franklin, Jefferson, and Emerson. It had become less a communal, more an individual matter. Mark Twain, in a book such as *The Gilded Age*, could make fun of ambition, putting it down as chiefly cheap-jack striving. Henry Adams came to feel that public ambitions were not fit for civilized men in America. The public man and man of letters tended increasingly to be supplanted by the businessman in the American pantheon. And this, at a time when business was in one of its great freebooting phases, did not do the reputation of ambition much good.

While lip service never ceased to be paid to the moral foundations of ambition and success, it soon became overwhelmingly evident that virtue did not necessarily go hand in hand with them. Swashbuckling financiers and entrepreneurs such as the

Vanderbilts, Daniel Drew, and Jim Fisk, men of great commercial energy and savvy, enjoyed immense successes behind which no moral content could be discerned. P. T. Barnum, he of "the sucker born every minute" aphorism, sold almost half a million copies of his autobiography (published in 1854) and went about the country delivering his lecture "The Art of Money Getting," of which Horace Greeley noted that merely hearing it was "worth a hundred dollars in greenbacks to a beginner in life." In the second half of the nineteenth century, the promulgators of self-help, self-culture, and self-improvement were less and less ministers and literary men; the gospel of success was now taken up more and more by businessmen. Andrew Carnegie was a leading spirit here, and in such books as *Triumphant Democracy* (1886), *The Gospel of Wealth* (1900), and *The Empire of Business* (1902), he spoke to the point that only one path to success was possible: that of business. In Carnegie's clear and strong prose, general principles, such as proffered by Franklin and Emerson, gave way to practical advice of a most specific kind. "Aim for the highest," Carnegie wrote in *The Empire of Business*; "never enter a bar-room; do not touch liquor, or if at all only at meals; never speculate; never endorse beyond your surplus cash fund; make the firm's interest yours; break orders always to save owners; concentrate; put all your eggs in one basket, and watch that basket; expenditure always within revenue; lastly, be not impatient, for, as Emerson says, 'no one can cheat you out of ultimate success but yourselves.' "

Ideas frequently trail events, text rolling on heedless of context. Even as Andrew Carnegie wrote, "Look out for the boy who has to plunge into work direct from the common school and who begins by sweeping out the office. He is the probable dark horse that you had better watch," the idea of the self-made man, of the smooth ascent from rags to riches, was being undermined by the more complex economic and social organization of American life as well as by the substantial flow of immigrants into the nation. Men write about one kind of nation while outside their study windows another kind is coming into being. Woodrow Wilson, in *The New Freedom* (1913), remarked on this point when he noted that "the originative part of America, that part into which the ambitious and gifted working man makes his way up, the class that saves, that plans, that organizes, that presently spreads its enterprises until they have a national scope and character—that middle class is being more and more squeezed out by the processes which we have been taught to call processes of prosperity."

A reflection of the phenomenon Wilson described can be found in the novels of Horatio Alger. The Alger legend has by now long since acquired a legend of its own, made possible by the fact that no one any longer reads these novels which once were a staple in the diet of young boys growing up in America. Professor John Cawelti, who appears to have read them all, is excellent on their rather surprising contents. An interesting case, Alger was not himself much of a success. Although his novels sold exceedingly well, he did not make what would have been profitable royalty arrangements with his publishers but instead sold them outright for comparatively small sums. What money came in went directly out again in charity of one sort or another.

If Horatio Alger was not much of a capitalist in the conduct of his personal affairs, neither was he, in his novels, a great partisan of rugged individualism; and only "within narrow limits," as Professor Cawelti puts it, was he "an admirer of pecuniary success." The Alger novels demonstrate very nearly an obsession with luck—his newsboys and other urchinlike characters depend heavily on being discovered by the successful businessman who will launch them on their own way. These heroes turn out to be dominated less by the spirit of buccaneer capitalism than by that of middle-class scrupulosity. Alger stresses their dressing and speaking carefully; their being especially adept at arithmetic, in a bookkeeperly way, is of particular importance. Acquiring the new watch or the good suit is often a momentous event. The young Alger heroes have what Professor Cawelti nicely calls the "employee virtues: fidelity, punctuality, and courteous deference." Very far from being eaten up by ambition, the middle rungs of success—the secure clerkship, the junior partnership—are as high as they figure, or even wish, to climb. "On the whole," the professor writes, "Alger's formula is now accurately stated as middle-class respectability equals spiritual grace," and, given this, Alger himself is most accurately considered "a teacher of traditional manners and morals rather than an exponent of free enterprise."

Others were ready to take up the banner of glorious personal success on the field of free enterprise, however, and beginning late in the nineteenth century and continuing on into our own day a new figure arose to boost the worthiness of the struggle for life's glittering prizes. Neither minister, nor writer, nor even necessarily experienced businessman, the success specialist arrived on the scene. Such a man did not so much lay down principles or practical advice as he taught techniques. Finding some support for their notions in the doctrine of Herbert Spencer and in Social Darwinism, the success boosters assumed fierce competition to be natural to men—survival of the fittest, dog eat dog, red claw of nature, and all that—and highlighted the pleasures of coming out on top. Disciplining oneself, avoiding temptation, cultivating virtue and self-improvement, generally became, in their writing, less important than self-confidence, aggressiveness, and a keen sense for the commercial kill. Character, in their view, counted for a good bit less than personality. The man built for success had a successful personality— he was a go-getter, had magnetism, possessed that mysterious but nonetheless unmistakable "certain something" that caused him to win through.

Orison Swett Marden was among the first of these new specialists, merchants whose product was success, the thing itself. His magazine—called, properly enough, *Success*—spread the new word, and its tone was one of unrelieved boosterism. The title of one of Marden's most popular books, which conveys the spirit behind his writings, is *Pushing to the Front; or Success Under Difficulties.* Success, in his view, was for everyone who had sufficient nerve to seek it out; those who had not the nerve were by definition failures, the nature of their failure being, precisely, a failure of nerve.

To the spirit of boosterism was added a strong strain of anti-intellectualism, which is perhaps nowhere better exemplified than in George Horace Lorimer's *Letters from a Self-*

Made Merchant to His Son, a book that sold more than 300,000 copies in 1902. Lorimer's rostrum was *The Saturday Evening Post,* of which he was editor. Although his own origins were far from humble—he was the son of a successful minister and had gone to Yale—Lorimer's editorial line at *The Saturday Evening Post* stressed unending possibilities in a land of unbounded opportunities: "It is possible for a young man to go as a laborer into the steel business and before he has reached his mature prime become, through his own industry and talent, the president of a vast steel association." Pushing such a line, Lorimer, during his tenure as editor, had raised the circulation of *The Saturday Evening Post* from a few thousand to roughly three million.

The *Letters from a Self-Made Merchant* first ran in Lorimer's magazine, and they proved to be one of the most popular features *The Saturday Evening Post* ever published. The inspiration for Lorimer's self-made merchant is said to have been P. D. Armour, the Chicago meat-packer and a classmate of Lorimer's at Yale, and the form of the *Letters* is a one-sided correspondence from John Graham, also a meat-packer, to his son Pierrepont. When the correspondence begins, Pierrepont is at Harvard, and it continues through the early days of his going to work for his father's firm and ends, twenty letters after it had begun, with the young man about to be married. The style is folksy, the tone confidently commercial. Independence, competence, self-assertion, a tunnel vision to the main chance, are the traits the father wants to imbue his son with. Even though he has sent his son to Harvard, culture of any kind, education, even pleasure, is viewed as so much frippery. "Repartee makes lively reading but business dull," Graham writes to the boy. "What the house needs is more orders." The point of education is neatly polished off in the following manner: "There are two parts of a college education—the part you get in the schoolroom from the professors, and the part that you get outside of it from the boys. That's the really important part. For the first can only make you a scholar, while the second can make you a man." Although he is the boss's son, young Pierrepont is assured that his way will not be made any easier by that fact: "I can't hand out ready-made success to you. It would do you no good, and it would do the house harm." Object lessons abound: "Money talks—but not unless its owner has a loose tongue, and then its remarks are always offensive. Poverty talks, too, but nobody wants to hear what it has to say." And so it goes, a steady rain of hard and homiletic advice on promotion, the uselessness of sentiment, art, theory, the usefulness of saving, seizing opportunity by the throat, and plain damn hard work.

Because Lorimer's *Letters,* despite their being written in what then passed for a peppy style, are intrinsically rather commonplace, even boring, it is worth inquiring into why they met with the enthusiastic reception they did when first published in *The Saturday Evening Post.* (Some 5,000 readers wrote to the magazine about Lorimer's *Self-Made Merchant,* most of them in an approving way.) Perhaps the most persuasive reason is that these *Letters* helped perpetuate a set of beliefs which no longer had as much connection with reality as they once did but to which people wished nonetheless to cling. Chief among them was the belief that conscientiousness, concentrated energy, unrelieved effort, and a sharp eye for the taking advantage of such opportunities as presented themselves are all that are really needed to become a great success.

Congenial though it might be to believe this, a study of the business elite around the turn of the century showed that other factors—factors having less to do with character than with connections—were probably more decisive. In a study entitled "The Recruitment of the American Business Elite" (1950), William Miller found that in 1900, men born to poor immigrant or farm families were for the most part excluded from the business elite. So, too, were blacks, Indians, Mexicans, and Orientals along with southern and eastern Europeans and their descendants. Those Jews who had attained business-elite status did so in exclusively Jewish firms—many of them begun by their fathers or other relatives. Most firms, according to Miller's study, failed "to recruit for their executive hierarchies members of religious or national minorities. . . ." Four out of five members of the business elite were native-born of parents themselves born in America. Among Protestant denominations, Methodists and Baptists were greatly underrepresented, Episcopalians and

Presbyterians greatly overrepresented. (Recall the old single-sentence sociology of American Protestantism, which runs: A Methodist is a Baptist with shoes; a Presbyterian is a Methodist who has gone to college; and an Episcopalian is a Presbyterian who now lives off his investments.) Most of those men who had achieved elite status in business came of fathers who were themselves business or professional men. What was more, contrary to the view that held that there was no better place to start on the way to success than at the bottom, few of the businessmen in Miller's study went off to work at an early age and a disproportionate share attended college.

This is not to say that success in American life was effectively blocked off to all but the well-connected—it was not, and is not now—but only that the old recipes for success had lost some of their meaning. Put another way, the American Dream of success had begun to take on some of the properties of an American Myth of success. This did not at all mean that Americans generally ceased to lend credence to the myth. The peddlers of success in the years to come—the Dale Carnegies, the Napoleon Hills, the Norman Vincent Peales, and their various epigones—continued to command large audiences for their product. But their voices began to sound more hollow even as their advice on how to succeed became more specific.

Curiosity Shop □ In *King Lear*, Shakespeare has the character referred to as Fool say:

> *Fathers that wear rags*
> *Do make their children blind;*
> *But fathers that bear bags*
> *Shall see their children kind.*

Some fool.

In his famous book, Dale Carnegie put forth his own life as evidence that the American Dream was still eminently obtainable. The biographical note accompanying *How to Win Friends and Influence People* tells of a young man who had to overcome rural poverty to attain success. With his family unable to afford the boarding fees at State Teachers College in Warrensburg, Missouri, the young Dale Carnegie had to ride horseback six miles each way to attend classes. "He had only one good suit." He was too light for the football team. It was only by joining the debating team, at his mother's suggestion, and becoming proficient at public speaking, which built his confidence, that Carnegie escaped an inferiority complex and a life of obscurity. Escape, as is now well known, he did. He took to the road with his confidence-building techniques, beginning in 1912 lecturing for two dollars a night at the YMCA, eventually attracting larger and larger audiences for higher and higher fees, and finally (in 1936, in the middle of the Depression) distilling his accumulated wisdom in *How to Win Friends and Influence People*. By 1970 the book had sold more than 9 million copies, and Carnegie had courses teaching the Carnegie method in more than 1,000 cities in the United States, Canada, and forty-five countries abroad.

Himself in the American tradition that the historian Daniel Boorstin has labeled the Go-Getter, Carnegie offered a manual designed to enlarge and improve the breed of Go-Getters. His lessons in *How to Win Friends and Influence People* are part self-hypnosis, part con, part good sense of a fundamental kind. Carnegie sets out to cultivate the salesmanly virtues, which, formulated in a single sentence, would read: Repress the demands of the self on behalf of that higher good—closing the deal. Smile, be a good listener, become genuinely interested in other people, make the other person feel important, avoid argument, and so on, such are Carnegie's rules. "Let me repeat," he writes, "the principles taught in this book will work only when they come from the heart. I am not talking about a bag of tricks. I am talking about a new way of life."

Dale Carnegie was not a fool; sedulously applied, his various rules and principles would no doubt be helpful to any salesman. (It needs be said, however, that Carnegie, like almost all writers on self-improvement, assumed the existence of a great mass of men who were not following his advice, which, in Carnegie's case, with his millions of readers and others who have taken his courses, is not necessarily a safe assumption. A delicious comedy sketch could be done about the meeting of two Carnegie disciples, neither knowing the other had learned from Carnegie, each smiling, avoiding argument, pumping up the other—and getting absolutely nothing accomplished.) Carnegie himself was, obviously, a first-class salesman. In *How to Win Friends and Influence People* he has the interesting habit of quoting William James, John Dewey, Socrates, Woodrow Wilson, Alfred Adler, and Theodore Roosevelt alongside industrialists, bankers, and attorneys as if all were equally engaged in the same enterprise—that of success through salesmanship, or getting other people to do what you want them to do. Carnegie does not waste any time justifying success. His assumption throughout is that of course the game is worth the candle. Thus in another of his books, *Biographical Roundup* (1946), he reveals himself to be impressed with success in its bulkier forms. Among the subjects in *Biographical Roundup* are George Bernard Shaw, Bob Hope, Madame Chiang Kai-shek, and Josef Stalin. "The main thing," Carnegie quotes Stalin as saying, in one of the greatest unconsciously ironic remarks of perhaps all time, "is to have the courage to admit one's errors and to have the strength to correct them in the shortest possible time."

If Dale Carnegie taught *How to Win Friends and Influence People*, Napoleon Hill, author of *The Think and Grow Rich Action Pack!*, teaches how to win over and influence oneself. Hill claimed to have learned "the money-making secret that has made fortunes for hundreds of exceedingly wealthy men" at the feet of Andrew Carnegie, that "canny, lovable old Scotsman." Mind control is what Hill's book is about, and he offers thirteen steps for acquiring "burning desire" and turning that desire into piling up the rewards available here on earth. His is mainly a book of instruction on self-mesmerization; from it one learns to think oneself into a successful frame of mind, blocking out fears, channeling the subconscious, developing a sixth sense for sighting opportunities, even transmuting sexual energy into money-making power. ("This study," Hill notes, "disclosed the fact that the major reason why the majority of men who succeeded do not begin to do so before the age of forty to fifty, is their tendency to dissipate their energies through overindulgence in physical expression of the emotion of sex.") Even the preparation for success, as taught by Hill, is very nearly a full-time task. Hill instructs his readers to memorize this list, reread that chapter, write up and memorize a plan for one's success, repeat one or another bit of homiletic advice upon waking or before falling off to sleep—and in general whipping oneself up into a fine froth of frenzied enthusiasm for succeeding.

As with Dale Carnegie, so with Napoleon Hill, the intrinsic value of success, its point and meaning, went unquestioned. Other writers, Norman Vincent Peale chief among them, attempted to establish a religious basis for the ideal of success. In *The Man Nobody Knows*, Bruce Barton, the advertising man, attempted to show that Jesus Christ was essentially a deft and hugely successful businessman, or at least an exemplary success. After all, Barton's reasoning ran, Jesus started with nothing but an idea and ended up with a worldwide movement. (Lord Beaverbrook once wrote a similar book about Jesus Christ, arguing, in his case, that Jesus was the first great journalist. The genre is not all that uncommon, offering as it does the immensely satisfying notion to its authors that not only are they doing the Lord's work but that indeed the Lord was also doing theirs.) But Peale's and Barton's books were probably preaching to the already converted; President Eisenhower, for example, who was scarcely in need of positive thinking, was nonetheless said to be a great fan of Peale's. Such books, though, were less for intellectual consumption than for what in Mr. Barton's business of advertising is known as reinforcement; most people who read them had already bought the product before coming to them—the product being, of course, shortcuts to success. "The world," Justice Holmes wrote, "longs for some cheap and agreeable substitute for hard work and welcomes every promise. So humbug has the most friends."

In a different realm, the sociologist Charles Horton Cooley, sensing that the ideal of success was coming under fire, stirring resentment, and no longer clearly in harmony with much social reality in the United States, wrote to deplore the "doctrine that selfishness is all we need or can hope to have in this phase of life." Cooley continued: "Economists have too commonly taught that if each man seeks his private interest the good of society will take care of itself, and the somewhat anarchic conditions of the time have discouraged a better theory. In this way we have been confirmed in a pernicious state of belief and practice, for which discontent, inefficiency, and revolt are the natural penalty. A social system based on this doctrine deserves to fail."

Cooley called for a reordering of standards for success. To achieve such a reordering, he believed, would require no change in human nature—Cooley also believed in the existence, in fact in the usefulness, of the competitive spirit—but only in the instigation and direction of its impulses; it would mean "chiefly firmer association and clearer ideals of merit. . . . Freedom, self-expression, and the competitive spirit would be cherished, but [must not be allowed to] degenerate into irresponsible individualism."

Not long afterward, John Dewey took off on a tack similar in some regards to Cooley's. Professor Cawelti ends his book, *Apostles of the Self-Made Man*, with a discussion of Dewey, whose thought about success he, Cawelti, finds most impressive. Cawelti writes: "By emphasizing the inextricable relationship between the individual and the community and by insisting that a failure of community meant a breakdown of individuality, Dewey went far beyond the traditional ideal of rising in society to mark out an important new direction for democratic thought." But just how far beyond the traditional ideal John Dewey went is a bit difficult to make out, as this example from Dewey's thought that Professor Cawelti quotes, will demonstrate:

> To learn to be human is to develop through the *give-and-take* of communication an *effective sense* of being an *individually distinctive* member of a *community;* one who understands and appreciates its beliefs, desires and methods, and who contributes to a further conversion of *organic powers* into human *resources* and *values.* [Italics added.]

Nearly every key phrase in this passage is fogged in by clouds of obscurity and vapors of vagueness. Precisely who gives and who takes, and how much of each? An "effective" as opposed to an "ineffective" sense? An "individually distinctive" as distinguished from an "individually indistinctive" member of a community? What, moreover, constitutes a community? What are the "organic powers" Dewey has in mind, and which the "human resources and values"? John Dewey was never noted as a felicitous prose writer, but here his obscurity has a reason behind it beyond mere crude phrasing. By the time he came to consider them, something had happened to ambition and success in America that had left them in tatters such that not all the patchwork language in the world could put them quite back together again.

Curiosity Shop □ Pascal, in his *Pensées*, remarks that "it has struck me that all men's misfortunes spring from the single cause that they are unable to stay quietly in one room." Corollarily, he adds that "the happiness of men in high position is due to their having a number of people to amuse them, and their power to keep themselves in this state." Pascal would himself have been amused to see a phenomenon taken up by some of the successful in our time—that of installing telephones in their automobiles. Surely this records a true advance. Whereas once men were unable to stay quietly in one room, now they are unable to stay quietly in a car. Sighting an expensively dressed man in the back of a Lincoln limousine talking over the telephone, doing business as usual, Pascal would have understood. "What advantages have a superintendent, a chancellor, or a first president," he wrote, "beyond the fact that, thanks to their position, from dawn onwards a great number of people come from all parts to see them, so that they have not an hour of the day free to think of themselves?"

The Dynasts

Although it is difficult to arrange, one reasonably certain way to attain success is to have a strong-willed and intelligent mother who is disappointed in her husband and thus channels all her emotional energy and ambition into you, her son. A man assured of his mother's love, according to Freud, is a conqueror. Pierre

Samuel du Pont, founding father of the Du Pont dynasty, the long line of lords of Delaware, was never in doubt about his mother's love. As a child, Pierre suffered rickets, which left him with bowed legs and a permanent limp. He was short. A broken nose disfigured his face. A childhood attack of smallpox put on the finishing touches, leaving his cheeks and neck riveted with pockmarks and his eyesight near to ruined. But none of this finally mattered. Nothing, after all, so improves the looks as a high opinion of oneself, and a high opinion of himself is a thing Pierre du Pont never lacked.

Born in 1739 in Paris, Pierre was, like Jean-Jacques Rousseau, the son of a watchmaker. His mother, the central figure in his early life, was Anne Alexandrine de Montchanin, the youngest child of a noble though impoverished family. Like her husband, she was a Protestant; unlike him, she had expectations in life. Samuel du Pont was content to be a good watchmaker and a good Protestant. Anne had higher things in mind. Disappointed in her husband, she took her chips off him and bet them on her son. Samuel du Pont, who could neither read nor write, believed a man should not be educated beyond his station. Anne believed that was exactly the point to which a man—or at least her son—ought to be educated: the point where his possibilities might be limitless. She filled her little son's head with tales of nobility, of romance, of conquest. She found the best teachers for him, campaigned to elude the rude fate her husband had in store for the boy. Pierre, if she had her way, would not be the man his father was.

Madame du Pont's bet looked from the first to pay off handsomely. Pierre had a quick mind and a hunger for learning. The ambition bred into him by his mother was nearly matched by the ambition of his first teacher, a provincial pedagogue who, seeking to gain the patronage of the wealthier families in Paris, put Pierre's precocious learning on display. At the age of twelve at a public exhibition Pierre, drilled in classical learning and literature, came through without flaw. Yet another exhibition of his prowess was planned but was canceled by the rector of the University of Paris, who was not keen to advance the fortunes of a teacher not associated with the university, as Pierre's was not. Notoriety resulted. Samuel du Pont had had enough. Pierre would take up a place at his father's shop. Let there be an end to these pretensions!

Greatly though he disliked it, Pierre remained in his father's watch shop until his sixteenth year, when, in 1756, his mother died from the effects, spiritual and physical, of losing two children in childbirth in the same year. His mother dead, life with his father impossible, Pierre set off on his own. He sought, through the force of his mind, to attract attention to himself from the aristocracy. He was able to arrange a meeting with the Duc de Choiseul, first minister to Louis XV, who held weekly audiences with the public at Versailles. Pierre planned military strategy, he studied economics, he wrote memoranda proposing radical reform for the governance of France. He published, anonymously, a pamphlet. Slowly he became tangential to circles of influence. The aristocratic radical Mirabeau and Quesnay, physician to Madame de Pompadour, became acquaintances and in time sponsors of Pierre's. He began to correspond with the exiled Voltaire. Benjamin Franklin and, later, Thomas Jefferson became his friends during their respective tours in Paris. Antoine Lavoisier, the chemist, was yet another friend. The gimpy little son of the Paris watchmaker was keeping company with the great figures of his age.

Pierre du Pont, the classic young man on the make, had fallen in and out of royal favor, but when the French Revolution came he was a hunted man. Robespierre personally sent men out on a house-to-house search for him. Captured and placed in La Force prison, while awaiting the guillotine Pierre was saved by Robespierre's fall from power. Not long afterward stuffed back in behind La Force's dank walls, this time under Napoleon's radical directors, Pierre du Pont was scheduled to be shipped off to Devil's Island, the penal colony on French Guiana, when Talleyrand, another of Pierre's well-placed friends, managed to spring him at the last moment. Enough was enough. Along with his two grown sons, Victor and Eleuthère Irénée, Pierre, now in his sixtieth year, determined to try the Du Pont luck in America.

Pierre had lost none of his grand vision. With money he hoped to borrow, he planned to buy up millions of acres of land in Virginia, to detach eventually his holdings in the state, and to rule the land as a separate kingdom. The Du Ponts sailed in the autumn of 1799. The ship, a vessel named the *American Eagle*, ran out of stores, and before the voyage was over the Du Ponts ate soup made from boiled rats. More characteristic of the family style, though, was that their baggage included not one but two pianos.

The Du Ponts were not without connections in America. There was Thomas Jefferson, and Alexander Hamilton was the family's first lawyer in America. Among Pierre's first gestures in the New World was to put a bit of space between the syllables of the family name—Dupont became Du Pont. Of his two sons, Victor Marie and Eleuthère Irénée, Pierre held out greater hopes for Victor, the older. Dapper, gay, generally more worldly than his younger brother, Victor looked to be more valuable to Pierre's plan—since his land-buying scheme had to be set aside for lack of funds—of beginning the firm of Du Pont Father, Sons, and Company, which would, as he hoped, make millions handling the American trade of various European governments. When Eleuthère Irénée, his younger son, came to Pierre with the idea of starting a gunpowder factory—the art of making gunpowder in America was then in a primitive state—Pierre showed little interest. But Irénée, who had earlier worked with Lavoisier (initially as a bookkeeper), was not deterred by his father's lack of enthusiasm, and did indeed set up a mill to manufacture gunpowder on the bank of the Brandywine River in Delaware under the name of E. I. du Pont de Nemours & Company.

A stone-hut-to-skyscraper story commenced. Irénée began while England and France were at war, and his gunpowder works, called the Eleutherian Mills, had part of the action; which is to say, the profits. Victor meanwhile flopped in various enterprises. Pierre never took an active hand in the mills, though he was by no means otherwise inactive. He played the role, in a complicated way, of middleman in the sale of Louisiana from France to the United States. Before long, both Victor and Pierre moved to the Brandywine to live in the shadows of Irénée's already successful gunpowder business.

Despite death in the family and disaster in the mills—occasional explosions, however elaborate the precautions, were to mark the history of Irénée's dangerous business—the trend was upward toward greater and greater prosperity. An element of prosperity indeed seemed built into the business: gunpowder was needed around the world for war; and gunpowder, in America, was needed for peace: for mining, for clearing the way for the railroads then everywhere being laid, for much else beside. As Irénée built mill after mill, his buildings winding round the course of the Brandywine and out of sight, Pierre wrote to his wife, then living in Paris, that these mills were so many hens laying so many golden eggs. When Pierre died, at the age of seventy-seven, he was buried in a clearing near the Brandywine called Sand Hole Woods. Henceforth all the Du Ponts would be buried there, the line of Victor to the right of Pierre's grave, the line of Irénée to the left.

E. I. du Pont de Nemours & Company was the family business par excellence. Wearing boots with wooden pegs to prevent explosions, Irénée worked the mills among his employees, all of whom he knew by name. His wife and daughter taught the powdermen's children reading and writing and tended to their various family needs. Irénée's eldest son, Alfred, learned chemistry at Dickinson College in Philadelphia, after which he went into the mills, where he was much respected among the powdermen. Henry, another of Irénée's sons, went to West Point, and later worked the business side of the mills, where he became a potent administrator. The Du Ponts tended to take a paternal view of their employees. Sons of powdermen, most of whom were Irish Catholics, were assured jobs in the mills where their fathers had worked. Men injured in accidents were kept on the payroll until they got well. Widows received pensions. Irénée's own wife, Sophie, was crippled in an explosion at the mills. Blood and bone, the Du Ponts were tied to the Eleutherian Mills.

Business doubled and redoubled. Alfred Du Pont, working in his laboratory on the Brandywine, had improved the process of manufacturing gunpowder, making the Du Pont product all the more marketable. A trend of interesting consequences, not least for the business itself, was the intermarriage of Du Pont cousins, the first of which took place between Victor's son Samuel Francis, a naval officer, and Irénée's daughter Sophie. Other Du Pont cousins would intermarry in future generations; and still later important Du Pont executives who were not themselves of the family would be married to Du Pont daughters, thus at one stroke tying them to the family and to the business, if the two were any longer actually separable. People would often speculate on the effects of the Du Ponts' intermarriages, looking therein for an explanation of some of the family's odd behavior: a strain of nervous breakdown, divorce, sexual adventurism (one Du Pont male was shot in a brothel).

In 1834, the year he had set a production goal of 1 million pounds of gunpowder for his Eleutherian Mills, Irénée du Pont, in Philadelphia to negotiate a business loan to make possible the necessary expansion, fell dead of a heart attack outside his hotel. Succession at the mills was passed on to his son, Alfred, although Irénée's seven children—three sons and four daughters —became owners of the company in a simple partnership. But each of Irénée's children was to own his or her share in the company only during his or her lifetime. Shares would not automatically devolve upon the children of shareholders; instead, each partner would choose a new partner from among the younger Du Ponts who worked in the mills. The effect of this arrangement was to place a high premium on remaining near the Brandywine, and it ensured that the Du Ponts would retain control of the Eleutherian Mills for generations to come.

Soon after Alfred took over the leadership at the mills, the United States went to war against Mexico, and the Du Ponts were faced with an ethical issue that would recur: whether or not to sell their gunpowder to both sides in a war. The family chose to declare their loyalty implacably on the side of their own government, and never, over the years, faltered in this decision. Later, during the Civil War, Du Pont gunpowder was provided only to the Union side, and the Eleutherian Mills, guarded by a garrison of some 2,500 Union soldiers, became a prime target of the Confederacy.

Tightly strung by the pressure of running the mills, Alfred's nerves came near being shattered by a particularly hideous explosion on the Brandywine. Eighteen powdermen had

been killed and more than that number severely injured. Flesh
hung from the branches of the Brandywine's trees. Business,
nonetheless, continued to improve. The discovery of gold in California created a demand for gunpowder there. Increased coal
production in the Pennsylvania fields heightened the demand for
Du Pont blasting powder. The tension accompanying these new
business possibilities was not easily handled by Alfred, who was
never completely to regain his composure after the great explosion. The responsibility of running the mills having proved too
much, at the age of fifty-one he stepped down from the senior
partnership to be replaced by his brother Henry. Henry was
fourteen years his brother's junior, and his reign over the Eleutherian Mills, though long and profitable, would be divisive.

Henry du Pont, a short man with a full red beard and a rigor
of bearing acquired at West Point, was a more daring businessman than any of the Du Ponts thus far to come along. In the
Crimean War, for example, once assured of United States neutrality, Henry supplied both sides, Russia and England, with Du
Pont gunpowder. Profit-minded above all, he was ready to sacrifice all to profit: the quality of the product for the better price,
his workers' safety to increased production. Henry was the first
of the Du Ponts not to be admired by his workers. Within the
family he earned a respect that stopped far short of affection. So
firm was his hold on the company and family reins that a number
of the members of the next generation bridled, and for the first
time Du Ponts left the Brandywine to make their way outside
the mills.

When his younger brother Alexis was killed in an explosion,
the death left Henry du Pont the last of the remaining sons of
Irénée and hence in complete control of the Eleutherian Mills.
He began to buy up much of the land surrounding the mills. With
the outbreak of the Civil War, Henry raised the American flag
over Du Pont property, and drove off to Washington to assure
Lincoln that E. I. du Pont de Nemours & Company was squarely
on the Union side. Henry was made a major-general of the Delaware militia. One of Henry's nephews, Lammot, son of Alfred,
a chemist like his father and grandfather, had simultaneously
improved the product and cheapened its cost by substituting

sodium nitrate for potassium. Profits could only rise. And they did: first, as usual, from the war, then, as usual, from the peacetime expansion and rebuilding that invariably followed the war.

But profits from without could not allay strains of dissension from within. A decisive step making for internal turmoil was the marriage of Lammot du Pont to Mary Belin, daughter of the company bookkeeper and (herein lay the problem) a one-quarter Jewess. One quarter was sufficient to cause Mary Belin du Pont to be ostracized among the Du Pont women, who had pretensions to aristocracy on the Brandywine, and Lammot to be ostracized along with his wife. Aware of the whisperings going on behind his wife's and his back, Lammot nevertheless remained on the Brandywine, at least long enough for his wife to bear him two daughters and then a son, whom he named Pierre Samuel, after the founding Du Pont father. Eventually Lammot and his family would leave the Brandywine over a dispute about whether the Eleutherian Mills ought to manufacture dynamite, the new explosive recently discovered by Alfred Nobel—Lammot being in favor, Henry opposed.

Like so many other capitalists of the front rank, Henry du Pont had not much use for free enterprise, at least insofar as it meant wretched scrambling, price-cutting, and cutthroat competition that minimized profits. Control was the name of his desire; and to have control over the gunpowder industry in America, Henry formed among the various gunpowder manufacturing firms an organization called the Gunpowder Trade Association, with his nephew Lammot as its first president. Hungering for control over the Du Pont family as well, Henry, after a number of early deaths and strange illnesses within the family, ordered an end to the Du Pont habit of intermarriage. It was a rule that Henry's own son William was soon to break, when he married his cousin, from the line of Victor, Mary Lammot du Pont. His other son, Henry A. du Pont, looked to be a failure; certainly he did not have anywhere near the business acumen required to run what by now could fairly be called the Du Pont empire. His capable nephew Lammot, meanwhile, had been killed in a nitroglycerine explosion in his own dynamite manufactory away from

the Brandywine. The question of succession seemed bleak as
Henry, the last living grandson of Pierre Samuel, approached his
eightieth year and death.

When Henry died, Eugene du Pont, son of Henry's
younger brother Alexis, took over as senior partner in the company. But his reign was to be on the order of an interregnum.
Alexis kept the mills running at a high profit, modernized them
in different ways, but could do nothing about the general divisiveness and decline among the Du Ponts. Ostentation and
scandal crept into the family, whose name began not to creep
but to leap into the headlines. One Du Pont bought a lavish
yacht; another married a barmaid in Ireland; yet another took
up his seat in an armchair at the Wilmington Club, placed a
revolver to his temple, and killed himself. Divorce became
more common among them. Factional squabbling broke out
over profits and over control of the mills. The family harbored
Young Turks, anxious to challenge Eugene's ideas and indeed
his supremacy in the mills. Others began to leave: a chronicler
of the family notes that around this time for every Du Pont
who remained on the Brandywine, five Du Ponts left to seek
out brighter prospects elsewhere. Tradition among the family,
which had grown multitudinous and wealthy, began to lose its
hold.

When Eugene du Pont died in 1902, E. I. du Pont de Nemours & Company was without a leader, although there were
three strong contenders: Alfred I., the elder grandson of the
elder son of Irénée; Thomas Coleman Du Pont, who had long
lived away from the Brandywine in Louisville; and Pierre Samuel, son of Lammot and of the quarter-Jew Mary Belin. Each
of these three cousins had a substantial chink in his armor.
Alfred I. suffered (though not for long) a bad marriage, and
sought relief in the love of a cousin, which caused further family dissension; Thomas Coleman had enormous ambition with
vanity to match, the two combining to form a boundless ego;
Pierre suffered under the blight of resentment, thinking himself the unwanted Jew among the Du Ponts. After the death of
Eugene, these three cousins, to prevent the sale of the Eleu-

therian Mills to outsiders, joined together to take over the business. But so different were their temperaments, characters, and desires that the partnership guaranteed contention and permanently rivalrous feelings.

Although they had expanded and diversified and everywhere laid down and maintained important connections, until the twentieth century the Du Ponts were not great speculators, money men shuffling precious paper, but instead devoted their energies to running a single large business. This now began to change. Where courage and persistence were the qualities that once won through on the Brandywine, now a fast pencil and a talent for manipulation weighed in more heavily. Of the three cousins, Alfred I. was in some ways the most traditionally Du Pont, at any rate in the family's heroic strain. While a student at M.I.T. he became a friend to the great John L. Sullivan. Working the mills on the Brandywine, he flew in the face of the danger of the work by bringing his two young daughters along with him. Thomas Coleman du Pont, Coly, as he was called, had political ambitions, not stopping shy of the White House. He later built a road for the people of Delaware, in effect a prone monument to himself stretching nearly the length of the state. A large man, he had a grandiose style, a booming voice (he would eventually die of throat cancer), and a nervous stomach that, when it acted up, could bring tears to his eyes and bend him double in pain. Pierre, who looked most the part of the bookkeeper (later photographs show him, commercial-ascetic, in rimless spectacles), was by far the most careful calculator, planner, organizer, and finagler of the whole "god-damned tribe," as one of the family's enemies called the Du Ponts. While his cousin Alfred was entangled in domestic sordidness (among other things he attempted to have the last name of his own son by his first wife changed so that he would no longer be a Du Pont), while his cousin Coly was off cultivating other fields (politics, the building of skyscrapers, high-roller corporate finance), Pierre gradually took over E. I. du Pont de Nemours & Company. Not, to be sure, without much family squalor involving the three cousins and their allies within the family—open confrontations, backbiting, embarrassing intrafamily litigation, bad feeling all around. But when the ruckus was over and the dust had cleared, Pierre emerged supreme.

As the Du Ponts began with a Pierre Samuel, so in effect would the family end with a Pierre Samuel. Not literally, of course, for there would be further generations of Du Ponts, but what Pierre had accomplished was to make the family richer than it had ever been before, yet while doing so to extricate it from the business that had been its prime reason for being. The first of the large-scale speculators among the Du Ponts, Pierre early invested in, then eventually took over control of, a young firm calling itself General Motors. He had meanwhile put E. I. du Pont de Nemours & Company into a number of highly profitable subsidiary businesses that would eventually eclipse the gunpowder business: chemicals, paints, synthetic rubber and leather, and much else beside. Although he lived on the Brandywine after marrying rather late in life, Pierre ran the business for the most part from Wilmington. Company growth affected company character. After World War I, Pierre had to dismiss thousands of Du Pont workers from the Eleutherian Mills, where to keep them on would been ruinous. Such a dismissal would have been unthinkable in the old paternalistic days.

Pierre Samuel du Pont had turned his family's company's profits from the millions to the billions. But in an essential way the Du Ponts had been changed; once powdermen, they were now financiers. After yet another explosion, in 1921, it was decided that the Eleutherian Mills on the Brandywine were not worth rebuilding. Pierre, who would live into his eighties, had himself installed as president of General Motors. He had no children to whom to pass on the family business. The battle of the cousins for control left casualties of bad feeling everywhere within the family. In time the majority of the Du Ponts would leave the Brandywine, until the control of E. I. du Pont de Nemours & Company passed into the hands of strangers.

In 1970, Lammot du Pont Copeland, the son of the chairman of the board, went bankrupt as the result of bad investments, having been found to have assets of $26 million as against liabilities of nearly $63 million. His father resigned the chairmanship, becoming the last member of the family to head E. I. du Pont de

Nemours & Company. Now a modern corporation, as opposed to a family business, it was led, after the departure of the last family member, by a career executive named Shapiro. The Du Ponts would always be rich, exceedingly rich, but paper rich—rich in money rather than in land, or in having a business, a tradition, something living and to be continued by sons and by the sons of sons.

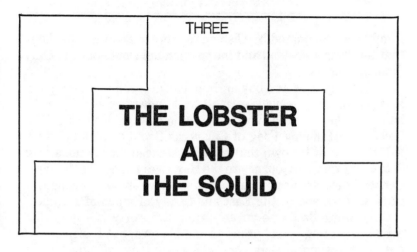

THREE

THE LOBSTER
AND
THE SQUID

The Man in the White Suit

Mark Twain, the Lincoln of our literature, as William Dean Howells called him, landed not in the White House but in a white suit. He was the first American writer to attain national celebrity, to be everywhere read and recognized and to turn a big buck off literature, and the white suit was part of his act. He it was who affixed the label Gilded Age to the time in which he flourished, and he not only labeled it but lived it. He was brilliant at marketing, his product being himself, often first-class goods. But he was not much at detail. With one eye on literature and one eye on business, he developed a cross-eyed talent. To excoriate your time yet revel in its luxuries, to proclaim the virtues of the simple life yet complicate your own life beyond imagining—you can't have it both ways, but neither can you blame a man for trying. Mark Twain tried, and failed.

"Poor gentry" describes the condition into which Samuel Clemens was born in Missouri. The accent, however, has to fall upon the word *poor*, the gentry deriving not so much from financial fact as from his father's pride in his Virginia heritage and the ownership of 70,000 useless acres of land in Fentress County, Tennessee. His father, a lawyer who was called Judge Clemens, was a bust-out not in one but in several kinds of endeavor: farming, trading, storekeeping, land speculation. The family was dominated by Clemens's mother and by hope: hope that the Tennessee land and the son Samuel would pay off. Only Samuel ever did.

His early days as a boy in Hannibal, as a cub riverboat pilot, as a journalist in Nevada, are all well known, enshrined in the legend of the rise of the writer and national sage. He wrote "The Celebrated Jumping Frog of Calaveras County," a story which led to jumps of his own that far outdistanced that famous frog —to California, to a journey to the Hawaiian Islands, to the West Coast lecture circuit as a humorous speaker, and to the conquest of New York and of the East and finally of much of Europe.

As Mark Twain he wrote: "Honest poverty is a gem that even a King might feel proud to call his own, but I wish to sell out. I have sported that kind of jewelry long enough. I want some variety. I wish to become rich, so that I can instruct the people and glorify honest poverty a little, like those good, kind-hearted, fat, benevolent people do." High jocularity, but of a kind that was at bottom no joke. Part of his act, as lecturer and writer, was to play the bad boy, the cigar smoker, the drinker, the user of mild profanity, admitting to laziness, small dishonesties, petty lies. But his true vices were the greed normal to his time: insecurity, social climbing, and a perhaps unparalleled craving for attention. "The secret source of humor itself," he wrote, "is not joy but sorrow." That is not the kind of remark for which he is best remembered.

A case could be made that Twain married into wealth and respectability and in doing so eluded the vast potentialities of his talent. He married the beautiful Olivia Langdon, of Elmira, New York, the daughter of Jervis Langdon, who was in the coal business; the family was new money and of the rising minor plutocracy in America. He sought not merely the hand of Olivia but the respect of the upper-middle class in which she lived; the price of both was the taming of Mark Twain, the smoothing out of the rough bohemian he was into the solid citizen of property and probity. In later years Olivia, along with his friend William Dean Howells, combed his manuscripts to expunge material that might be deemed off-color, coarse, or otherwise insufficiently civilized. Almost unfailingly he accepted their deletions.

The trapdoor opened when Twain's father-in-law, as a wedding present, provided him with a house for which he paid $43,000, no small sum for that day. Later he would buy a house in Hartford, Connecticut, in the exclusive Nook Farm section, of an opulence unknown to any previous American writer: a $70,000 turreted house on a $31,000 lot, stocked with $21,000 in furniture, attended by no less than six servants. His neighbors were uniformly high-rollers. Twain called the Congregational Church at Nook Farm the Church of the Holy Speculators. Another of his double-edged jokes.

Twain scored a solid commercial triumph early with the publication, by subscription, of *The Innocents Abroad*. The effect of this triumph was to give him a taste for the big money and to sell him on subscription publishing. He would not only sell his own books by subscription but would eventually become a subscription publisher himself. "The publisher who sells less than 50,000 copies of a book for me has merely injured me," he wrote, "he has not benefited me." Subscription books were sold by canvassing salesmen; they were best long, roughly 600 pages; and to publish by subscription meant one sought a popular and commercial rather than a select and distinguished literary following. The 600 pages was sometimes a problem; Twain ruined at least one book, his *Life on the Mississippi*, by stuffing it with dross to get it up to the desired—that is, the salable— length. He attempted, without success, to industrialize the production of his writing, joining with collaborators, hiring men to do research for him. He had a high nut, as the small businessmen put it, his expenses for the year 1881, including investments, coming to roughly $100,000. His dreams of wealth were mightier than his pen.

Mark Twain suffered, as Howells once remarked, "excesses of enterprise." Although he had no talent for business, he had a taste for the plunge. The list of inventions, investments, and deals he entered into shows him to have had a keen eye for the bad thing. Some of the bad things he went in on, according to Justin Kaplan, one of his biographers, were: Mark Twain's Self-Pasting Scrapbook; a domestic still for desalinating water; an improved generator for tugboats; Kaolotype, a chalk-plate process for making printing plates and casting brass stamping dies; the Mark Twain Memory-Builder, A Game for Acquiring and Retaining All Sorts of Facts and Dates; a perpetual calendar; a bed clamp, to be used to prevent children from kicking off their covers when having bad dreams; a fire extinguisher that worked like a hand grenade; a spiral hatpin; a cash register of a new type; a stock promotion called the Book-Lover's Library; and Plasmon, a granulated high-protein food concentrate. Though of differing magnitudes, nearly every one of these was a loser.

The unmitigated disaster among Twain's investments, though, was the infamous Paige typesetter, in which he was slowly inveigled—slowly inveigled himself—into owning full rights. A hemophiliac of a deal, it eventually bled Twain into bankruptcy. At one point becoming a publisher himself, he had made a great deal of money bringing out General Grant's *Memoirs*, but most of it went into the Paige typesetter. This same machine, with its 1,800-odd movable parts, forced him back on the lecture circuit, which he despised, and away from his family, which he adored. He had hoped, through his investment in the Paige typesetter, to cut out one of the historic American fortunes—he was, during this time, friendly with Andrew Carnegie and H. H. Rogers of Standard Oil—and to be free at last of all interest in money by going over the top in securing more than he could ever possibly need. Instead of going over the top he nearly went under, and was forced to sell off many of his family's possessions, find jobs for his servants, and retreat to Europe.

If it hadn't been for H. H. Rogers, a Rockefeller partner and rapacious businessman but a loyal friend, Mark Twain would probably have gone permanently under. (Many years earlier, in 1866, he had thought of suicide, going so far as to put a pistol to his head. "Many times I have been sorry I did not succeed," he remarked many years afterward, "but I was never ashamed of having tried.") Rogers took Twain's finances in hand, organized his repayment of debt, invested his earnings carefully, and allowed Twain and his family, after an absence of nearly ten years, to return to America in the pride of solvency.

Although his commitment to writing was never for long

more than partial, Mark Twain had become America's most popular writer. His was a natural talent, but it was at least matched
by his talent for publicity and self-promotion. His interest in
business usually overshadowed his interest in writing. About his
writing there was much confusion—confusion abetted by the
time in which he lived. *Huckleberry Finn,* for example, rightly
thought to be his single best book, even though flawed in its
ending, was banned for what was thought to be its coarseness
and removed from the shelves of the library in Concord, Massachusetts; it was a book that was never well thought of by the
genteel critics in American letters of its time and their word
seems to have been good enough for him. His own tastes in
literature tended toward the anti-intellectual, almost the anti-
artistic. Of the works of Henry James, who thought no better of
Twain than Twain did of him, he said: "I would rather be damned
to John Bunyan's heaven than read that." Among the ironies
clustering around the idea of success itself, about the time that
Mark Twain had returned from Europe virtually to wallow in
unsurpassed national admiration, Henry James suffered one of
the great disappointments of his life when the New York edition
of his fiction had a perfectly dismal reception.

It was after his return from Europe that Mark Twain took
to wearing his white suits. He would stroll down New York's
Fifth Avenue of a Sunday afternoon, unmistakable to his admirers. Banquets were organized in his honor. Tributes came in
from around the world. His income, under the careful management of H. H. Rogers, rose to about $100,000 a year. Yet Twain
the public conscience had become that very different thing,
Twain the public figure. He voice was silent during the great
muckraking era of exposing the trusts and large corporations;
he was silent again when Maxim Gorky scandalized Americans
by arriving in the United States with a woman who was not his
wife. "By the goodness of God," he said, "we have those three
precious things: freedom of speech, freedom of conscience, and
the prudence never to practise either." Often it was difficult to
tell whether Mark Twain was the satirist or the spokesman for
his age.

This much is known: he was split down the middle, his energies diverted every which way, scampering off like a dog in heat after money and fame. Had he been able to concentrate his energies on his natural talent as a writer, would that prodigious talent have bloomed into a truly great rather than a much flawed genius? Hard to say. He once told his wife that his friend H. H. Rogers had remarked to another business associate that "other people's successes in this world were made over broken hearts or at the cost of other people's feelings or food, but my fame had cost no one a pang or a penny." The question remains: What did it cost Mark Twain?

Although they are not often spoken of thus, novels are among the world's greatest instruments of personal education. People, and especially the young, take from novels a great many things, not all of them what the novelists themselves may have originally intended. Like the movies, novels teach small things: how to order a drink, how to conduct oneself in intimacy with someone of the opposite sex, the nature of repartee. But unlike the movies, novels are better in teaching what might be called general ideas. Part of the greatness of the novel as a form, surely, is that there is scarcely any general idea with which it cannot, at the hands of an expert practitioner, deal. Ambition, in its multifacetedness, has traditionally been a subject that novelists have warmed to; and, until fairly recently, American novelists above all. It would be naïve to assume that many of the notions that Americans hold about ambition do not originate in the novels they have read.

In his novel *The First Circle*, Alexander Solzhenitsyn has a young woman, a minor character who is a graduate student in literature, remark: "Have you ever noticed what makes Russian literary heroes different from the heroes of Western novels? The heroes of Western literature are always after careers, money, fame. The Russians can get along without food and drink—it's justice and good they're after." Careers, money, and fame have indeed been among the great subjects of Western novels—and perhaps in no other country has this been truer than in the United States. Sometimes careers, money, and fame—in short, ambition and success and their ambiguities—have seemed the only subjects of American literature.

Certainly no major American literary figure has failed to get in his word on the subject of success, and most have not spoken kindly of it. James Fenimore Cooper, Nathaniel Hawthorne, Edgar Allan Poe, Herman Melville, William Dean Howells, Mark Twain, Robert Herrick, Frank Norris, Henry James—through the nineteenth century, from Cooper's distrust of the self-made man to James's deliciously sneering reference to his country-men's "grope of wealth"—viewed success in America in terms ranging from equivocation to condemnation. In the twentieth century, the terms have been closer to those of unrelieved contempt. Antisuccess has been perhaps the strongest strain in American literature of the past half century. And to be against success is to put ambition itself in grave doubt.

English literature has nothing comparable to American in the way of the latter's argument with ambition and success. Why should this be so? Why haven't ambition and success been a problem for English writers to the extent they have been for American? English writers might strike out against patriotism, imperialism, the culture and society made by their fathers, but they did not turn against ambition or success as wrong, as intrinsically foul, in themselves. Has this to do with the way classes have traditionally been organized in England? Has it to do with the fact that an elite—with its underlying assumptions of achievement and worldly rewards being linked together—has always been taken for granted in England as it has not in America? Has it to do with the pretensions and promises of democracy being greater here than there? Writers in revolt in England might turn to dandyism, or the wasteland vision, or (as in the 1930s) to communism, but for the greater part they have not turned against the mainstream values of their own society with anything like the same intensity as their American counterparts.

The intensity of the attack against ambition and success shown by American writers has been often of a kind akin to a grudge. "Some misunderstanding must always take place," Henry Adams wrote, "when the observer is at cross-purposes with the society he describes." "Cross-purposes" is to put the case very gently indeed. "It is a complex fate to be an American," wrote Henry James, who found it sufficiently complex to prefer to deal with it for much of his adult life by putting an ocean between himself and his native land and moving to England. So often the relation of American writers to the notions of ambition and success in their own land was adrench with distrust and irony. The irony is that by and large they never seemed so distrustful of the American ideal of success as when they themselves had realized their own ambitions and succeeded —and on their countrymen's terms. At his estate in Sonoma County, California, the yield of years of turning out stories and novels that mixed Marxist and Rotarian ideas, Jack London dreamed of escaping the American rat race, having just built Wolf House, a mansion intended to be "the greatest castle in the United States." From this most splendiferous rat trap, London in 1916 took an overdose of morphine sulfate and departed the scene. Stephen Crane, a writer haunted by money problems largely the result of an appetite for high living, worked himself to death before his thirtieth year. William Dean Howells, earning in the 1890s the rough equivalent in current dollars of $120,000 a year, felt himself riven by success in America, torn between the demands of business and the demands of art, which forced upon him a personal crisis.

A lesser known writer than any of these, Robert Herrick, illustrates the inability of American writers to come to satisfactory terms with ambition and success. They are at the center of nearly all Herrick's fiction, where they lodge like bones in the throat. Born in New England, educated at Harvard, Herrick betook himself to the Middle West, settling in Chicago, where he taught at the University of Chicago, remaining for thirty years in a state of unrelieved loathing for the society in which he lived. As he remarks in *Memoirs of an American Citizen* (1905), one of his better-known novels, "Whatever was there in Chicago in 1877 to live for but success?"

Memoirs of an American Citizen purports to be the autobiography of one Van Harrington, the chronicle of his ascent from a rural and bedraggled youth in Indiana to mastery in the meat-packing business in Chicago. "No one, I suppose," Harrington remarks, "ever came to Chicago, at least in those days, without a hope in his pocket of landing at the head of the game." Harrington wants to catch "that tide of fate," to wind up one of the winners, and through industry, cunning, and luck, he does, going from the sausage business to a seat in the United States Senate. A conventional enough story for the most part, *Memoirs of an American Citizen* is distinguished by the verisimilitude of its detail, the high quality of its throw-away insights ("I have noticed that women find it hard to reconcile themselves to a rich man's early taste in women"), and above all by its author's extremely unclear feelings about his hero. Although Harrington at one point lapses into unethical behavior, and is everywhere a main-chancer, it is, as Herrick creates him, difficult altogether to lose sympathy with him. Part of the reason is that he, Harrington, is telling the story, and so his point of view dominates the novel; but part has to do with the fact that there really is no one else in the book worthy of claiming our sympathy. True, there is some talk about an older generation of businessmen, purer, principled, without their hands in the pot; and one character, an older banker from Maine (Herrick's native New England), is meant to stand as representative of the type. But this scarcely offsets our—and Robert Herrick's—interest in Van Harrington's adventure, his attempt to rise to the top in a situation where everyone was "fighting for what only a few could get."

Floyd Dell once remarked apropos of Robert Herrick that "there is Ambition which even if it be directed to purely commercial ends yet retains a certain human dignity, if not a romantic beauty." Dell went on to say that Herrick nonetheless refused to respect ambition of this kind—the ambition of the businessman. "It is to him a dirty affair." Although later students of Herrick's work have gone along with this judgment, one wonders if it is not in fact askew. Even in the grubby meat-packing business, even in nineteenth-century Chicago, an intrinsic fascination resides in the subject of the man of ambition; it is the fascination of the struggle, the brawl, the jungle. Not for nothing has a city such as Chicago produced so many splendid novelists; in that city inheres a splendid novelistic subject. Not even Robert Herrick, who went on record time and again as despising commercial civilization, loathing Chicago, detesting business, could finally resist it. In others of his novels he did resist it, through the cumbersome—and, for a novelist, deadly—machinery of moralizing. But in *Memoirs of an American Citizen* he did not; and the book, whatever its author's true feelings, is better for it.

The subject of novels such as *Memoirs of an American Citizen* is essentially the subject of *Robinson Crusoe,* itself an irresistible book which has been called, not with injustice, "the primary textbook of capitalism." It is the story of the fight for survival and beyond that of accumulation. At the hands of Daniel Defoe, true, the story has a happy ending; whereas at the hands of a Robert Herrick, and so many novelists to follow him, the ending is deliberately dampening: success is hollow, accumulation does not bring happiness, the struggle of ambition finally was not worth it. But the ending, whether happy or unhappy, somehow does not take away from the natural interest inherent in the story.

If Robert Herrick displays unconscious ambiguity toward ambition and success in American life, in the work of Theodore Dreiser, a much superior novelist, the identification of a writer with the aspirations of most of his striving characters is near complete. A bumbler as a prose stylist, often muddleheaded as a thinker, difficult at best as a human being, Theodore Dreiser is thought by some to be the best, because the most powerful, novelist to have written in twentieth-century America. If this is so, it is because Dreiser took on the subject of ambition in America with a directness and complex understanding of all that it involved and surpassed all other writers of our time. Whatever else he did not know, whatever was closed to him in the way of elegance and grace and subtlety, Dreiser knew all about ambition: about its excitement, about its heartbreak, and, above all, about the desire behind it.

Dreiser knew these things so well because he lived with them all his days. The son of a failure, a man whipped about in the strong winds of destiny, Theodore Dreiser was born poor and ugly and with outrageous appetites. Craving and living were synonymous in his life. Nobody felt desire more keenly than he: for distinction, for sex, for rising out of the mass. Other writers might *know* these things; Dreiser *felt* them. That is why there have been better writers than Theodore Dreiser—subtler minds, cooler technicians, better organizers—but none more potent.

In one way or another all of Theodore Dreiser's novels are about ambition and success in America. *An American Tragedy* is about the heartbreak of success, for its main character, Clyde Griffiths, who eventually is executed in the electric chair as a result of his own pitifully overheated ambition, is one of those (thousands? tens of thousands? hundreds of thousands?) who attempt the climb but lose their grip and crash on the rocks below. *Sister Carrie* is about the ruthlessness of success, with its heroine, Carrie Meeber, playing on through as the sad figure of Hurstwood, once her lover and patron, goes under. A *Trilogy of Desire,* as Dreiser's three novels about Frank Cowperwood are called, is about the excitement of ambition: the heat and pull and seductiveness of the urge to control one's own destiny. *"Emma Bovary, c'est moi,"* said Flaubert; but Clyde, Carrie, Hurstwood, Cowperwood—*all* were Theodore Dreiser.

If Dreiser was intoxicated by success, he was by no means, as a novelist, swept away by it. He had a vision which he worked out in his novels. Early in *The Financier,* the first of the Cowperwood trilogy, the ten-year-old Frank Cowperwood, already pondering the question of how life is organized, one day along the wharves of the Delaware Bay, notes a lobster and a squid put into a tank together, with the lobster offered no food "as the squid was considered his rightful prey." Day after day Cowperwood returns to find small portions of the squid torn from its body and left in the claws of the lobster. The slow dismantling of the squid by the lobster fascinates the boy. When the lobster is about to close in for the kill, the boy Cowperwood plans to return, in the hope of seeing it. Dreiser writes:

> He returned that night, and lo! the expected had happened. There was a little crowd around the tank. The lobster was in the corner. Before him was the squid cut in two and partially devoured.
>
> "He got him at last," observed one bystander. "I was standing right here an hour ago, and up he leaped and grabbed

him. The squid was too tired. He wasn't quick enough. He
did back up, but that lobster he calculated on his doing that.
He's been figuring on his movements for a long time now.
He got him today."

Frank only stared. Too bad he had missed this. The least
touch of sorrow for the squid came to him as he stared at
it slain. Then he gazed at the victor.

"That's the way it has to be, I guess," he commented to
himself. "That squid wasn't quick enough." He figured it
out.

This is, one need scarcely add, a vision that offers cold comfort. But Dreiser abided by it unrelievedly. Although in the
Cowperwood trilogy Dreiser endows Frank Cowperwood with
many of his own ideas and aspirations, the book does not have
anything resembling a happy ending. Recognition of the irrationality of unslakable ambition is paid throughout: "That frail
little lamp, the human mind," Dreiser notes, "that wholly unrea-
soning force, the human will." Elsewhere he refers to human
beings as "poor wind-blown sticks of unreason." "I satisfy myself," says Cowperwood throughout all three novels in the trilogy, and it is clear that Dreiser is, along with his hero, "thrilled
by a dream of activity and possession." Business is not glorified
but seen through for what it can be: "those most religious of all
American institutions, the bank and trust companies." The
world's injustice is not skirted: "The world is like that, unfair,"
remarks Cowperwood toward the end of his life, "full of gifts for
some and nothing for others." Yet at the trilogy's end, after
Cowperwood has died, there is almost nothing left of his efforts,
most of his money is eaten up in expenses, his art collection is
sold off, his estate fought over and divided up by middlemen.
Cowperwood's is one of the "dramas which produce either failure or success"; he was not one of those "dragged along at the
chariot wheels of others." But to what end? Dreiser does not
pretend to know. Nor can he be said to be very much interested
in making final judgments. More important for the instinctive
artist that he was, he was faithful to his vision: to show life, "its
tangles of desire and necessity."

Theodore Dreiser was the last first-class novelistic talent among American writers to take the drama of ambition head on, to confront it directly, to contemplate the moth that is man hovering around the flame that is desire. Other American novelists who followed him dealt with it—ambition and the struggle for success were too much a part of the American emotional landscape to be ignored—but almost inevitably through the squinting eye of irony, disdain, or outright contempt. The pursuit of ambition and its attainment in success, in their view, was a cheat, a sell, a shuck, a trap—in all, a grand and grandly stupid illusion. From the 1920s onward, ambition and success have had a terrible press from our novelists.

Sinclair Lewis was one of the first, and certainly among the most energetic, to go to work on them. In novel after novel, he remained on the attack. Born a small-town boy in Minnesota and himself later a student at Yale, Lewis, in his commercially successful novels, spewed vitriol in the face of business civilization and, by extension, into the face of the idea of success. In *Main Street,* he took on small-town and middle-class life. In *Babbitt,* he worked over the businessman, stripping back his skin after a thorough flogging to reveal the pretensions, hypocrisy, and pitiful aspirations that lay underneath. The words *Babbitt* and *Babbittry* entered the language as synonyms for the conventional—and pitiable—striving after success. In *Dodsworth,* a novel in which Lewis expended some sympathy on his hero, the emptiness of ambition and the delusion of success were laid bare. When he was done, marble from shattered idols was strewn everywhere.

Disfigurement of a similar kind was carried on in the early novels of John Dos Passos. In these books, and particularly in Dos Passos's trilogy *U.S.A.,* society itself was shown to be an instrument that was organized to twist and crush human personality, and of course it did this chiefly through a principal malefactor: business. To have truck with business in any of its forms was to be trodden down, face first, into the slime. To enter business was to have one's character distorted, one's personality twisted and rendered ruthless. To oppose business, as many of Dos Passos's Wobbly characters or the historical figures in his novels did, was to come out worse: to be an outcast, to be imprisoned, sometimes to be killed. Men of the greatest integrity could not stand up to business villainy: it stole from science, it brought good people down, it squirted a dominating stink over all of American life. Later in his life Dos Passos very nearly reversed himself on these views; big labor and collectivistic liberalism became the enemies. But it was too late; the job had been too effectively done; no one was listening.

In *The Great Gatsby*, F. Scott Fitzgerald dealt ambition a stylish blow. In this elegantly constructed novel, the illusions of success, the forfeiture of promise from the promised land that is America, were nailed down with great thoroughness. "They're a rotten crowd," Nick Carraway calls out to Gatsby, in what are nearly his last words to him in the novel. "You're worth the whole damn bunch put together." But how much, really, is that worth? Poor James Gatz, with his ample ambition, his belief "in the green light, the orgiastic future that year by year recedes before us," is finally a pitiful creature. Success cannot bring back the past for him, cannot return to him his Daisy, whose voice "is full of money"; it can only bring him a drawer full of silk shirts and a tragic and stupid death. No threnody so exquisite has ever been sung over a dead ideal than that of *The Great Gatsby* over the dream of success.

Elsewhere ambition and success seem simply to have departed from the American novel. In the novels of Hemingway almost no work is good work—or, much the same thing, manly work—unless it confronts danger; one is permitted to be a bullfighter, a fisherman, a soldier, and of course a novelist, but all other work is trivial. In the work of a more rounded novelist, Willa Cather, especially in such novels as *A Lost Lady* and *The Professor's House,* success is admired, but only success in the past: the new men that have arisen to seize it are grubby, narrow, without vision, unlike the heroic pioneer generation with its integrity, honor, heroism. William Faulkner turned in a similar performance in his trilogy about the Snopes family as well as in others of his novels, whose point was often that in contemporary life only the swinish succeed, that the day of the men of character is past. In *The Late George Apley,* John P. Marquand set out to do in the established Brahmin class of Boston, which had consolidated the commercial triumphs of earlier generations through its exclusive clubs, careful schooling and marrying, and the social enclosure of tradition, and did a stinging good job of it. (Later the men extolled in Willa Cather's and William Faulkner's novels, the pioneer and cavalier generations, would be charged by revisionist historians and left-wing critics with raping the land, dispossessing the Indians, trading in slaves, and as traitors generally to every American ideal; but the historical memory in the United States is mercifully short.)

It was not so much that these novelists preached failure but that they impugned success, and thus debunked ambition. They brought down the house but erected nothing in its place. They left appetites but without the old justifications to satisfy them. These appetites are nowhere more evident than in the lives of many of the novelists themselves. The Fitzgeralds, so slavish in their imitation of the rich, loved the Plaza Hotel, Rolls-Royce automobiles, the French Riviera. Their friends Gerald and Sara Murphy took for their motto the Spanish proverb, "Living well is the best revenge"; but what did they, heirs to the Mark Cross luggage fortune, have to revenge themselves against? Hemingway also took pains to live supremely well: with houses in Cuba and Idaho, large advances, commissions from *Life* magazine, he seems, after fame arrived, never to have traveled less than first-class. With his hunger for equipment, his love of guns and boats and fishing gear, he seems preeminently the house writer for Abercrombie & Fitch. When he failed to win the Pulitzer Prize for *Main Street*, Sinclair Lewis sulked in a way that a man not elected to the presidency of his Rotary Club would never think of doing. John Marquand, that grand attacker of snobbery and tradition, and commercial success, used to call his publisher nearly daily to obtain fresh sales figures for his novels, married an enormously wealthy woman whose sister had married John D. Rockefeller III, and was perhaps never so delighted as when accepted as a member of the Somerset Club in Boston, the most exclusive club in the most snobbish city in America. John O'Hara, frustrated his life long over not having gone to Yale, lived in a most exclusive suburb outside Princeton, drove a Rolls, and worked in a study that, as described by his biographer Finis

Farr, seemed to resemble nothing so much as the gift section of Dunhill's. More recently, Norman Mailer has said that he requires at least $200,000 a year to keep his ample ship—three ex-wives being among the passengers—afloat.

But the point here is not that on the subjects of ambition and success American novelists have tended to write one way and live quite another. Instead it is that their preponderant views on these subjects have come to dominate American life. These views have been taken up by, and found support in, sociology and other academic disciplines. *The Status Seekers, The Lonely Crowd, The Organization Man, The Culture of Narcissism* are only a few of the successful books of recent decades that have colored in the drawing originally limned by the novelists succeeding Theodore Dreiser. Rightly or wrongly, it is the better part of what is nowadays taken for a good education to question the point of ambition and success with the most intense, even ferocious, scrutiny. The successful are, given this background—a background learned in college where greater and greater numbers of Americans have come to learn about the world—guilty until proven innocent. Lionel Trilling once remarked that "there has grown up a populous group whose members take for granted the idea of an adversary culture." Success itself is one of the things the adversary culture is adverse to. Proving innocence, for those who have attained some share of success, is difficult to do. Thus there has reigned in this country for many years now the paradoxical situation in which the children of the successful have been sent off to the best schools, where they are taught to despise their parents' own aspirations and achievements.

How well the lesson has been learned is everywhere in evidence. Exhibit A was put forth in the middle of the 1960s when Norman Podhoretz, the writer and editor of *Commentary* magazine, published a book entitled *Making It*, openly avowing the virtues of ambition and success; or how at least he for one, and most people along with him, would rather be boss than employee, a success than a failure, have power than not. Podhoretz claimed that this rather rudimentary knowledge was something of "a dirty little secret" among the educated classes in America.

The book was greeted with a furor of criticism, a rancor of reception, far in excess of its demerits. These demerits were real, some of them literary, some of them strategic: the book promised much more than it delivered, for example, about the squalid behavior of certain intellectuals who had become celebrities; strategically, it is always a mistake to claim oneself, as Norman Podhoretz did in *Making It*, a success.* But Podhoretz's true sin, it seemed apparent from the reviews, was in saying that it is all right to want to succeed, there is nothing wrong in enjoying the emoluments that flow from success— nothing to be ashamed of about either of these things. The artillery fired away at the fragile vessel that was *Making It*. Norman Podhoretz's secret, an article in *Esquire* noted, may not be "very dirty, but it sure is little." Podhoretz had broken the ban, gone against the grain of one of the most strongly held bits of conventional wisdom of our time, and he was made to pay in the coin of public humiliation.

Those who have upheld the conventional wisdom, on the other hand, have not been made to pay but have received—and in coin not of metaphorical minting. A case in point is the novel *Something Happened* by Joseph Heller. A loose, rambling, and repetitive work, this novel is about modern despair in various of its forms, but chief among them the despair that comes with the climb toward success in American life. The novel's hero works for a large corporation; what he does for the corporation, what the corporation does for its profits, are all left vague nearly to the point of mystery. What isn't left vague is the quality of life in the corporation, which is hell itself, nothing but intrigue, backbiting, pettiness, and heartbreak. What is interesting here is that, as a novelist, Joseph Heller does not have to work very hard to prove any of this—it is merely assumed. *Something Happened* is a novel built upon, and trading off, years of assumptions about the emptiness of ambition and success. More

---

*A mistake more patently successful men, among them Benjamin Franklin, Andrew Carnegie, and John D. Rockefeller, did not make. Measured modesty is the winning autobiographical tone of the success story—the formula, however phony, for a successful book of this kind.

interesting still, this novel, offering so little in the way of pleasure either in plot or character or ideas, was itself a considerable success. Nowadays one road to personal literary success in America has come to be through attacking the idea of success itself.

Betwixt the uplifting spirit of the boosters (the Napoleon Hills, the Dale Carnegies, the Norman Vincent Peales) and the debunking spirit of the novelists, the novelists have won the day. The former are viewed as clownish, the latter are read like Scripture. The boosters are in fact clowns, but are the novelists so deserving of respect? Although they might wish to disclaim the role, novelists are great teachers—of personal style, of conduct, of world views. Is what they teach about ambition and success true?

Curiosity Shop ◻ Benjamin Franklin's *Autobiography* being the text for the day, the professor asks his class for definitions of success. It is one of those large and lumpy questions to which students are never eager to respond. With prodding, however, they do. Success, says a young woman, is attaining the goals you set out to attain and the contentment you realize thereby. Success, says a bearded young man, is peace of mind, being at one with yourself. Success, says another, is probably indefinable, each person has to define it on his own. Success, says yet another, is putting it all together. The professor is antipathetic to such language, and tells the last student that he will accept his answer if he can tell him what "it" is and how it looks when assembled. Then he adds that he doesn't wish to seem vulgar but he notes that in all the definitions offered by the class the words "money," "fame," and "power" seem curiously absent. Is there no one in the class, he asks, who would not like the freedom that money sometimes provides; or to be well known, if not necessarily in a blatant, movie-star way, at least for being a distinguished person; or to have power, perhaps not over other people, which might (who can say?) be interesting, but certainly over one's own destiny? The class unanimously agrees that all of these things would be very agreeable indeed. Why, then, did it not occur to any of them to include such things in the definition of success? They are students of literature, most of them, and perhaps they have learned their lessons too well.

The Guggenheims

And Simon begat Meyer. And Meyer begat Isaac and Daniel and Murry and Solomon and Benjamin and Robert and Simon and William. And these among them begat Harry and Eleanor and Edmond and Harold and Peggy and more yet. . . . And Peggy begat Sinbad. From Simon to Sinbad in three generations; here, obviously, is a real American story.

Simon Guggenheim, founder of the Guggenheim family, had lived in Lengnau, in the canton of Aargau, in Switzerland under the restrictions Jews had suffered for centuries. "Tolerated homeless persons," their papers read, "not to be expelled." But not to be quite accepted, either. Simon was a tailor, a widower with a son and four daughters. The son, an enterprising boy named Meyer, was twenty, and worked as a peddler in Germany selling clothes and odds and ends door to door. Things could have been worse: pogroms were no longer common, some old restraints had been lifted, certain qualified freedoms expanded. But they also could have been better. Simon Guggenheim learned, from letters and from other Jews of Lengnau who had emigrated to America, that there things were better. No gold in the streets, to be sure, but, more important, freedom in the air. One day in 1847 Simon and his family boarded a boat for Hamburg, and thence secured passage on a ship to Philadelphia.

In Philadelphia Simon was remarried, to a widow also from Lengnau, and he and his son Meyer began work as peddlers. Simon worked the city of Philadelphia, Meyer the outlying districts of the Pennsylvania anthracite region. One of Meyer's hot items was stove polish. He quickly saw that serious money was not to be made in peddling but in manufacturing. So Meyer hired a chemist and learned how the stove polish was made. Simon began making it at home, while Meyer continued to peddle it from a pack upon his back. Then he bought a machine that would produce the polish more efficiently and in larger quantities. He next started to manufacture and sell an essence of coffee, made from cheap coffee beans and a strengthening agent. In four years in America he had earned and saved enough to marry and set up house for himself in the then somewhat shabby suburb of Roxborough.

Before the activity had acquired the name, Meyer had the habit of diversification. From stove polish and coffee, he next went into general merchandise, imported spices, dealt in groceries. He bought the patent rights from an English firm to a formula for manufacturing lye and, with partners, opened a small factory. He undersold the competition, and so to eliminate his nuisance value Pennsylvania's principal lye manufacturer bought him out—Meyer's end of the purchase being the handsome figure of $150,000. Out of lye, Meyer went into lace, which he imported from an uncle of his wife's in Switzerland. Once again, from importing he went into manufacturing: producing a less expensive product for which there was a large demand. Still in his forties, hopping from one business to another, with only the glue of hard work and his native acumen holding his various activities together, Meyer Guggenheim had earned $1 million. For a rolling stone he had gathered much moss.

A million was nice but not nearly enough, at least as Meyer viewed it. He had eight sons (one, Robert, would die young) and three daughters. Dowries for the daughters had to be given; a substantial helping hand for each of his sons, though not strictly required, seemed desirable. Good, Meyer Guggenheim felt, if he could manage before he was done to bequeath $1 million to each of his boys. Why not? It was not after all impossible, given what he had accomplished already. Although Meyer was less religious a Jew than his father, and his sons would be less religious than he, he was nonetheless a patriarch in the Jewish manner. When the boys had done a mischief, he laid on the strap. He liberally dispensed advice to them. In an alien world, he taught his sons, money could be a friend.

As soon as possible Meyer installed his boys in his prospering lace business. Isaac, the eldest, a careful man with details, a necessary plodder, worked for the firm in New York. Daniel, the second born, a more debonair and daring fellow, was sent to oversee the firm's factories in Switzerland. The next two brothers, Murry and Solomon, followed Daniel to Switzerland. Meyer, meanwhile, having a taste for absolute control, bought out his partner in the lace business and changed the name of the firm to M. Guggenheim's Sons. Each of the boys was to enter the firm with an equal partnership, even though some had worked at it longer than others. Meyer hoped to eliminate discontent and divisiveness of the kind that follows from inequality. United, he told his sons, you are impregnable.

For all his ambition, Meyer Guggenheim was not a plunger. He preferred situations where the variables were few, and in which he, about whom there was nothing whatever variable, could exert control from the center of things. Yet he had bought some shares in a small railroad, the Hannibal & St. Joseph, which Jay Gould needed for one of his complicated stock market shenanigans. Meyer refused to sell, holding on until exactly the right moment, then clearing what some claim to have been a $300,000 profit on the transaction. In 1879, a man named Charles D. Graham, whom Meyer had dealt with in the grocery business, came to him for a loan on two silver mines in California Gulch, outside Leadville, Colorado. For $5,000 Meyer was able to obtain a half interest in the two mines. Then both mines flooded, and more money was needed to pump them out. Not one to throw good money after bad, Meyer boarded a train to Leadville to look the matter over for himself. He hired a mining engineer to supervise the pumping out and running of the mines. One of the partners, tapped out, sold his shares in the mines to Meyer, giving the Guggenheims controlling interest. Not long afterward one of the two mines struck it rich—but very rich!

Before a decade was out the two Guggenheim mines had produced 9 million ounces of silver and 86,000 tons of lead. Meyer's son Benjamin, who had studied metallurgy at Columbia on his father's advice, worked summers at Leadville. So, soon, did William, the youngest son, who had gone to the Wharton School of Business, then switched to study metallurgy as well. Two flies, however, spoiled Meyer's enjoyment of this otherwise rich Colorado soup: one was labor trouble, the other the exorbitant cost of smelting the ores extracted from the mines. About the former he could do little; about the latter, he could do a great deal. He could—and soon did—go into the smelting business himself. As John D. Rockefeller made his fortune in refining, so the Guggenheims would make theirs in smelting—aboveground where the risks were less, the profits as great.

The smelting business was the first Guggenheim venture in America that didn't take right off. The preliminary arrangements were worked out with masterful touches. As usual, they hired the best technicians. In order to be selected as the site of the Guggenheim's Philadelphia Smelting and Refining Company, the town of Pueblo, hungry for industry, supplied the land on which the smelter was to be built, came up with $25,000 as a token of earnestness, and waived all taxes for a decade. But labor problems and fluctuations in the prices of refined ore brought early losses. Although Meyer had invested his own money in the smelting business, having turned his other businesses over to his older sons, they now joined him in this Western venture. Some of the boys—Murry, Simon, Benjamin, and William—settled in Colorado permanently. Daniel, the most savvy of the brothers Guggenheim, remained in New York, but soon began to interest himself in the possibilities of the mining industries—possibilities he viewed as limitless.

The Sherman Silver Purchase Act of 1890, which required the U.S. Treasury to purchase 4.5 million ounces of silver each month, steadied the market and saved the day for the smelting industry. The Guggenheims, restless as always, now went international. Daniel worked out an arrangement with the Mexican government to set up Guggenheim smelters in Mexico, where the labor was cheaper and less troublesome. The family planned expansion, hoping to do as much as possible of the total smelting business in North America. Before long these plans to expand would themselves be expanded to include large segments of South America as well.

Meyer and his wife had meanwhile moved to New York, into a solid town house off Central Park on the West Side. It qualified as a mansion, but was nowhere near so grand as the homes that his sons Daniel and Simon had set up on Fifty-fourth Street off

Fifth Avenue, then the preserve of such American Medicis as the
Vanderbilts and the Astors. The boys had also built stately
pleasure domes in Long Branch, on the shores of New Jersey.
Meyer had sent his daughters off to be educated in Paris at
Madame Bettlesheimer's finishing school for Jewish girls. One
of his daughters, Rose, married a Loeb. Yet the Guggenheims
were never altogether accepted by the American German-Jewish
aristocracy of the nineteenth century, the Loebs, Schiffs, Selig-
mans, Kuhns, Lehmans, and Lewisohns. These great banking
and investment families found something harum-scarum, perhaps a bit scruffy and jumped-up, about the way the Guggenheims had come into their money. For his part, Meyer Guggenheim apparently could not have cared less.

Photographs show the Guggenheim boys in the 1890s to
have begun to grow puffy with prosperity. But whatever their
exteriors, within they remained hungry—and savvy. They
opened new smelters, went into iron mining, began to smelt
copper, extended their operations to Bolivia. Until now they had
excluded all partners outside the family. When they formed the
Guggenheim Exploration Company, or Guggenex as it was
called, they took in a Gentile partner, William A. Whitney, to
swing the deal. Division now tore the family. The two youngest
sons, Benjamin and William, in disagreement over taking in an
outsider, dropped away, although they retained an interest in all
Guggenheim investments outside Guggenex. In a momentous
and complex stock battle, the Guggenheims took on the industry
giant, the American Smelting and Refining Company, led by
such tigers as the Rockefeller lieutenant H. H. Rogers, Leonard
Lewisohn, and August Meyer, and emerged triumphant, gaining
ownership and control over the larger company. The reward for
this coup was a near monopoly over the smelting of ore in the
United States.

Having begun to sour, relations among the Guggenheim
children did not grow sweeter. The daughters married and
moved away. Benjamin and William no longer shared fully in the
family enterprises. Benjamin, who had married a Seligman, emigrated to Paris, where he indulged his taste for high living, a
penchant for well-born mistresses not excluded. He is noted for

a bit of avuncular advice: "Never make love to a woman before breakfast for two reasons. One, it's tiring. Two, you may meet someone else during the day that you like better." William, also a bit of a womanizer, married a Gentile, a divorcee from California. The Guggenheims were never very serious about their Judaism, but this was going too far, at least as brother Daniel construed it. Before their father could find out about the marriage, Daniel sent William abroad, like a child being sent to his room for misconduct, arranged a divorce, and paid off the woman with a settlement of $150,000. (Years later she would return for a second helping of Guggenheim money, though unsuccessfully.) Although he went off docilely enough, William bore his family a lifelong grudge.

Not that this impeded business as usual. Daniel, at the helm, sailed the family back into mining. The Guggenheim practice was to hire the best man at the highest price and give him plenty of leeway. To scout out new mining properties, they hired a man named John Hays Hammond for $250,000 a year plus a one-fourth share in all new mines he discovered—and he proved to be a bargain at the price. The son of Meyer's doctor, a young man named Bernard Baruch, was hired to negotiate buying out the last of the serious smelters in the Northwest. The Guggenheim boys had in the meantime become more than adept at the paper games of high finance—creating new corporations, floating stock, shuffling assets, liabilities, and profits. The Guggenheim name was now a widely respected one in international finance. In 1905, after three operations, at the age of seventy-seven Meyer Guggenheim died. He left a personal fortune of only $2 million, to be divided among his daughters and favorite charities. But he left seven sons each worth many millions more than he.

And they were to become richer still. Intercontinental in scope now, the Guggenheims had investments in rubber, gold, and diamonds in the Belgian Congo and Portuguese Angola. They had a hand in copper in Utah and gold in the Yukon. They were said to control as much as 80 percent of the world's silver mining. (Later they would go into tin in Southeast Asia.) In Colorado, Simon, the brother born between Benjamin and William, through supporting the state's Republican party, strategic philanthropy, and (as was the custom of the day) buying the state legislature, was elected to public office. Excluded from the Denver Country Club, he thus worked his way into a more exclusive club: the United States Senate.

It was not all onward and upward, however. As money men, the Guggenheims felt the pinch of the Panic of 1907. In connection with their Yukon holdings, for the first time ever they promoted a stock, not to expand their enterprises, but to profit from sheer stock promotion. Heretofore treated respectfully by the press, they now came in for the kind of criticism dealt out to Rockefeller and J. P. Morgan. And nowhere more so than in their dealings in Alaska, where they were accused of attempting to steal the state and, by Gifford Pinchot, of being a menace to conservation. In politics, Senator Simon Guggenheim was ridiculed as a man who not only bought his Senate seat but was himself bought by his own family's interests. Increasingly the Guggenheims became a favorite target of progressivist writers and politicians. Meyer Guggenheim's grandchildren began to hear stories about their uncles' being public nuisances.

In political cartoons Daniel Guggenheim was shown, as all big capitalists were, as a predator but—an added anti-Semitic touch—with a big nose. The family was blamed for monopolistic practices, for labor troubles with the I.W.W.; even Henry Ford chipped in with criticisms. The hatred of the Guggenheims was, as much as anything else, symbolic of their power, for they were now viewed second only to the Rothschilds as the most powerful Jewish family in the world. Or so at least they were seen from the outside.

From within, things had begun to look different. The Guggenheims had spread themselves thin; true, there was a lot of them, and their money, to spread. But their tendency in business dealings had shifted from control through ownership (a principle of Meyer Guggenheim's) to control through manipulation (a principle of the House of Morgan). A thinning out of the family ranks was also under way. By 1910 Isaac, the oldest of the brothers, had gone into semiretirement. Benjamin died aboard the *Titanic* (the mistress with whom he traveled having survived in a lifeboat). William sued his brothers over money he felt himself entitled to and, because he threatened to have the family books looked into, won a settlement. Rich in all else, the Guggenheims were poor in male descendants. In 1919 Daniel, so long the family leader, retired. A new partnership under the name Guggenheim Brothers was formed, into which Harry (Daniel's son) and Edmond (Murry's son) were inserted. But these two Guggenheims of the third generation left the partnership in a family schism of 1923, when the other partners, against the younger men's wishes, decided to sell Chuquicamata, the family's Chilean copper mine.

Other third-generation Guggenheims were at best uninterested in the storm and stress of business careers. Daniel's other son, Robert, the family playboy, married a woman of the Pennsylvania horsy set and promptly converted to Catholicism. Harold Loeb, the son of Meyer's daughter Rose, lived as an expatriate and wound up being the model for Hemingway's cruel portrait of Robert Cohn in *The Sun Also Rises*. Solomon's daughter Eleanor May, engaging in that traditional pastime of the daughters of American millionaires, married a titled Englishman. Isaac, having no sons, before he died asked his daughter to name his grandson Isaac Guggenheim II, in exchange for which he would leave the boy a large inheritance, but as the boy grew older he took up his father's name of Spiegelberg. Hazel, one of the three daughters of Benjamin, lost two sons (ages four and one) off the roof of a Manhattan penthouse apartment, and later had to be put in a mental institution.

Then there was Marguerite, known as Peggy, another of Benjamin's daughters, and perhaps the most indefatigable of the third-generation Guggenheims. As soon as she was old enough, Peggy fled to Europe, where much of her girlhood had been spent. She had plastic surgery (botched) to alter her Guggenheim nose. She married a man named Laurence Vail, who called himself king of the bohemians. He beat her up, once kicked her down the stairs, another time tried to rip her dress off in a bar, and gave her the child she named Sinbad. Peggy lived the bohemian life, but first-class all the way: nomadic but invariably with cooks and other servants in tow. Isadora Duncan called her Guggie Peggleheim. She pursued Samuel Beckett across Europe. She opened a gallery in London; Marcel Duchamp aided her with his advice. She gave shows for the work of Kandinsky and other avant-garde painters, always buying at least one work by each artist she exhibited. Later she would be similarly hospitable to the Abstract Expressionists in America, Jackson Pollock chief among them. Not altogether without the Guggenheim touch, her collection of paintings would one day be estimated as worth millions. In the 1970s she owned the last private gondola in Venice. In the 1930s she wrote an autobiography entitled *Out of This Century;* among her relations and behind her back the book was known as *Out of My Mind.*

People have theorized that the behavior of the Guggenheim grandchildren could be chalked up to the guilt that comes with possession of great and unearned wealth. Certainly the money made possible yachts and race horses, divorce and scandal. If their fathers felt any guilt, before their deaths the brothers Guggenheim—Daniel, Murry, Solomon, and Simon—made several strokes at assuagement through philanthropy. Daniel created the Daniel and Florence Guggenheim Foundation, for aiding hospitals and medical institutions, and the Daniel Guggenheim Fund for the Promotion of Aeronautics, which, along with much else, paid for much of the research on Robert H. Goddard's work on rocketry. Simon founded the John Simon Guggenheim Foundation, named after a son who had died in adolescence, which has given out more than $1 million a year, the income on its endowment, to artists, academics, and scientists. Murry, the least flashy of the brothers, set up the Murry and Leonie Guggenheim Dental Clinic to provide free dental care for poor children. And Solomon, through the auspices of the foundation named after him, left $5 million for the Solomon R. Guggenheim Museum in New York, which houses his own extraordinary collection of modern paintings.

Before they died the third-generation Guggenheims had one last fling at extraction, one final dip into the earth, when they went into nitrates, principally for their use in fertilizers and munitions and their valuable by-product of iodine. But toward the end the brothers had become less entrepreneurs than coupon-clipping capitalists. An exception was Daniel's son Harry, a free spender like others of the third generation of Guggenheims but with a conscience and energy for work. He was avid for aviation, and the presiding force behind his father's Fund for the Promotion of Aeronautics. With his third wife, Alicia Patterson, Harry began, and made a success of, the Long Island newspaper *Newsday*. Cain Hoy, his horse-breeding and racing stable, turned out a winner as well. Late in life Harry Guggenheim attempted to reestablish the old family business, inviting his nephews and grandnephews into a new partnership, which he accomplished with only partial success.

Although the Guggenheims would not want for money, things would never be quite the same with them. They held assets, which they managed artfully, but they were no longer explorers or producers. Perhaps the primordial hunger was gone; perhaps the joy had left the game; perhaps the family allotment of ambition had been used up. Whatever the cause, however they may have felt about the effects, by its fourth generation the Guggenheim family had passed the dice.

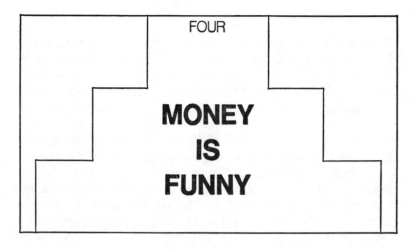

FOUR

MONEY IS FUNNY

The Car Humanitarian

In the nineteenth century one of American agriculture's bumper crops was extraordinary technologists. The revolution that made possible America's great cities was begun on farms. Elias Howe, Eli Whitney, Thomas Alva Edison, Alexander Graham Bell, George Westinghouse, Orville and Wilbur Wright, the American geniuses of invention, manufacturing, transportation, were farm boys all. And not altogether surprisingly. Whatever its limitations as a teacher of culture or sociability, the farm was a superior forcing house of technical ingenuity and mechanical skill. Henry Ford, another American farm boy, born on a farm outside Dearborn, Michigan, in 1863, was the most famous mechanic the world has known. Strictly speaking, Henry Ford invented nothing, but he tinkered with nearly everything. Years later, recalling his early days on his father's farm, Ford said: "My toys were all tools—they still are."

Henry Ford was the first of six children, and he grew up without hardship, luxury, or trauma. William Ford, his father, had come to the United States sixteen years before his son's birth, from Cork County, as did so many other Irish immigrants, because of the potato famine. Henry's mother, Dutch and Belgian by descent, was early orphaned and raised by a family named O'Hern. Protestant by religion, hard-working by nature, the Ford family quickly became American by temperament, at home among their neighbors and in their country. Henry was not at all religious, nor did he make a religion of work. He had no appetite for drudgery. Of the work on his father's farm, he said: "My earliest recollection is that, considering the results, there was too much work on the place." Farming, he decided early, was not for him. From childhood he was averse to horses; in his maturity he did as much as anyone to get them off the streets.

Henry was trained in the common virtues. At school this meant the *McGuffey Readers*, with their featured selections from the great authors and an admixture of moral instruction. At home there were no whippings. Wrongful acts received the silent treatment, the shame paid to bad conduct. This was his mother's way, and Mary Litogot Ford, a solid woman with strong good looks, ruled in the Ford home. She was a sensible woman as William Ford was a tolerant man. At thirty-seven, she lost a baby at childbirth, and twelve days later she herself died. Henry was then thirteen. A man for mechanical metaphors, Henry Ford said of his family after his mother's death that the house was like a watch without a mainspring.

Henry's mechanical skill did not take long to reveal itself. Given a watch as a boy, he immediately took it apart—and then put it back together without a hitch. Soon he was doing watch and clock repair for neighbors; and doing it for nothing. When his father told him to stop, he continued to do it behind his father's back. He sighted his first mobile steam engine at thirteen, and was swept up with fascination. While still a schoolboy, he directed a project setting up a water wheel and fiddled with a steam turbine. "Machines," he said, "are to a mechanic what books are to a writer."

How're ya gonna keep 'em down on the farm? was a practical question for William Ford, who wanted Henry to be, like himself, a farmer. But the boy wanted to work among machines, and so he let him have his head, hoping he would one day soon return to the farm. At seventeen Henry's first job, at the Michigan Gas Company in Detroit, paid $1.10 a day. After six days on the job he was fired for too great efficiency. A piece of machinery had broken down, according to one account, which the com-

pany's regular mechanics were unable to repair after spending
the better part of the day on it; when everyone else left for
supper, Henry went in and fixed the damned thing without any
trouble. He was fired for interfering where he wasn't wanted.
His next job, at apprentice status, paid $2.50 a week. His room
and board cost $3.50 a week. To keep above water he worked
four nights a week, at fifty cents a night, repairing watches for
a local jeweler. At one point he thought about manufacturing
inexpensive watches in great numbers. "Even then," he said, "I
wanted to make something in quantity."

Henry Ford kicked around, from this job to that, but always
his work had to do with machinery. When he courted his future
wife, Clara, he built a special sleigh for the purpose, with steel-
cut wheels and cushioned shocks. When they married, Henry
took his father up on an offer to live on forty acres of timberland
adjoining the Ford farm, an offer made with the proviso that he
give up his ambition to be a machinist. Rather than farm the
land, though, he built a sawmill upon it. Days were spent at the
sawmill, nights in his work shed at the hobbies that were the
passion of his life: making a copy of the famous Otto engine,
building a double-cylinder engine he planned to mount on a bicycle, experimenting with steam engines. His wife he called The
Believer—what she believed in was Henry Ford. More than believing in him, she complemented him and understood him. When
he wished to pull up stakes—as he did when, in 1891, he took a
job in Detroit with the Edison Illuminating Company so that he
could learn more about electricity—she offered no argument.
When he kitchen-tested his two-cylinder engine—literally in the
kitchen, over the sink—Clara Ford poured the gasoline for him,
fearful that the fumes might poison their infant child. When he
took his first home-built car out for a spin, Clara and Edsel, their
only child, were in the front seat with him. She disagreed with
him on only two known occasions in the fifty-nine years of their
marriage, and in both instances he backed down: she threatened
to leave him if he did not settle in a 1941 dispute with his workers; and she persuaded him, when he was eighty-two, to turn the
presidency of the Ford Motor Company over to his grandson
Henry Ford II.

A long time was to pass, of course, before there was a Ford Motor Company. In the 1880s and 1890s, Henry Ford was only one of scores of men who dreamed of a motor-powered vehicle. In Europe, among such men were Gottlieb Daimler and Karl Benz; in the United States, Ransom Eli Olds and Charles Duryea, Hiram Maxwell Perkins and Alexander Winton. The motorcar was indubitably an idea whose time was coming. Auxiliary industries had developed to pave the way: steel, oil refining, bicycle manufacturing, rubber production, gasoline engines, electrical services. Pipes, cylinders, pistons, crankshafts, cams, valves, carburetors—the parts, like so many pieces of a jigsaw puzzle, were all there; the question was who would best put them in place.

In the race to build a sound motorcar, Henry Ford had no running start. He was a proficient mechanic and an operational engineer, but he had no laboratory experience, no mathematical background, no theoretical grounding; better-trained men than he doubted if he could read a blueprint. One early employee described his methods as those of a "cut and try man." What he did have was inexhaustible energy ("No work with interest is ever hard"), perseverance ("The man who has the largest capacity for work and thought is the man who is bound to succeed"), and wondrous organizational powers ("I never saw Mr. Ford make anything," a blacksmith who worked for him said. "He was always directing."). In 1896, working in a garage—it was not yet called that—behind his house in Detroit, Ford completed work on his first motor-drawn vehicle, or, as he then called it, his "quadricycle." It worked, and such was the curiosity it aroused in Detroit that, when he left it on the street, he had to chain it to a lamppost. He was then thirty-three years old, and still a long way from success.

Encouragement was not wanting. At a meeting in New York of Edison Company engineers, Ford, on the back of a menu, drew for Thomas Alva Edison himself his idea for a motorcar. "Young man," Edison exclaimed, "that's the thing! You have it—the self-contained unit carrying its own fuel with it! Keep at it!" Ford sold his quadricycle for $200. He was able to acquire backers to work on a second car, under the name of a firm calling itself the Detroit Automobile Company, of which Ford was superintendent and a small stockholder. In 1899 he left the Edison Company to work full time on automobiles. Between 1896 and 1903 he claimed to have built twenty-five cars—and was dissatisfied with all of them. By 1900, when the Detroit Automobile Company went out of business, there were already fifty-seven different American plants engaged in making automobiles. The auto had in the meanwhile acquired the cachet of fashionable society: August Belmont's son drove about in a French automobile and so did the Vanderbilt boys, William K. and Alfred, and Harry Payne Whitney; Edith and Teddy Wharton were also early automobile addicts. In 1901, Henry Ford, the man who for years would be the nation's greatest car manufacturer, still did not own his own home.

Unsophisticated in many ways, Ford wanted no instruction from anyone when it came to publicity. He may have been an even greater publicist than mechanic. His sense for the value of publicity caused him to turn his attention to racing. Going into his own money he built a racer, and driving it himself beat Alexander Winton at the Grosse Pointe racetrack outside Detroit. Back in his garage, he built two additional racers, "The Arrow" and "999." Barney Oldfield, a champion bicycle racer, after taking a week out to learn how to drive a car, drove "999" for Ford, again at Grosse Pointe, in a record time, for five miles, of 1:06 per mile. Although Ford-built cars would race again, Henry Ford's new preoccupation, with fresh financial backers behind him, his new dream, was to put (as he called it) "a family horse" on the market.

Life begins at forty: the old bromide, in the case of Henry Ford, needs to be revised to read, Success began at forty. For in 1903, riding the wave of publicity from his racing ventures and with the aid of an astute and tightfisted business director named James Couzens, the Henry Ford Company began to manufacture automobiles in earnest. And with profit. Directing its marketing attack on the medium- and low-price buyer, in its first nine and a half months the company sold 658 cars, grossed $354,190, and showed a profit of $98,851. Contracting parts from outside—cushions, tires, engines, bodies, wheels—the Henry

Ford Company was able from the very beginning to finance its operations from revenues.

Henry Ford came down to his plant on Mack Avenue in Detroit sometime before 8 A.M., worked until supper, then returned most nights to work until 10 or 11 P.M. The Mack Avenue plant then employed roughly forty workers. Henry Ford's style in those days was that of the backslapper, very much one of the boys, a practical joker not above nailing a man's shoes to the floor or his hat to a chair or electrifying a doorknob. With all this, there was never any doubt that he was boss. When it served his purposes he could be ruthless. Later he eased James Couzens, to whom his company owed so much, out of his management position over something as trivial as an argument about a pacifist editorial that he, Ford, wished to run in the Ford *Times*. He could also be wily for his own good. Once in later years he threatened to leave the company, at a time when his name was perhaps greater than the company's, as a ruse to gain control of its stock.

Henry Ford's modest reputation as an automobile racer and low-priced manufacturer grew after 1903, and it was helped along through litigation. In 1879 a Rochester, New York, attorney named George B. Selden filed a patent application for a "road carriage" he designed but never built. The patent, received in 1895, was to cover all gasoline-fueled vehicles and to run until 1912. He had thus tied up automobile manufacturing in the United States; rather than fight the Selden patent, by 1903 twenty-six American automobile makers banded in an association—the Association of Licensed Automobile Manufacturers (ALAM)—and agreed to pay the patent holder a royalty of 1.25 percent of the price of each car they sold. The advantage of the ALAM was that it could also be used to keep other manufacturers out. When Ford applied to join the association, he was denied entry, on the bogus grounds that his cars could not meet ALAM standards for licensing. An aggressive advertising campaign began on both sides, and the upshot was that Ford forced the ALAM to litigation. Forty-three other automobile makers joined Ford in his fight against the ALAM, but they eventually dropped away, especially after 1909, when the Federal District Court in

New York sided with the ALAM. Ford, alone now against the combine, appealed, and won his appeal decisively. It was the Progressive Era, the time of concern for the little man and hatred of the trusts. Henry Ford emerged, in this context, as the David who slew Goliath—a man of courage, a battler, the man of the people, the symbol of the revolt of the independent against the monopoly. No better public relations could have been staged for Henry Ford, the common man who asked only to be allowed to make cars for other common men.

The populist aura about Henry Ford never faded. "I will build a motorcar for the great multitude," he announced, "constructed of the best materials, by the best men to be hired, after the simplest designs that modern engineering can devise ... so low in price that no man making a good salary will be unable to own one—and enjoy with his family the blessing of hours of pleasure in God's great open spaces." The car in question, of course, was Ford's Model T, which first appeared for sale in 1908. A family car, utilitarian, sturdy, plain (it was available in any color the customer wanted, Ford joked, "so long as it's black"), and inexpensive. When first produced, the Model T sold for $850. But beginning in 1910 Ford consistently reduced its price, claiming, no doubt rightly, that he sold at least another thousand for every dollar he cut from the customer's cost. By 1915–16 he had brought the cost of the basic Model T down to $360. The result was that the Ford Motor Company dominated car sales in the United States for eighteen years. In 1918–19 and from 1921 to 1925 Ford produced more than half the cars in America; and from 1911 to 1915 and in 1918 and 1921 the company earned more than the rest of the automobile industry in the United States combined.

More than a commercial success, the Model T, also known as the Tin Lizzie, began to take on the proportions of a legend. Each of Ford's price reductions was reported in the press. Indian princes and European noblemen took to driving it; show-business figures posed in it. Books of jokes about it were published. Dozens of songs were written about it, "The Little Ford Rambled Right Along" being an unenticing example. "Hunka Tin," a parody after Kipling's "Gunga Din," appeared. The Ford dealer in Nashville drove a Model T up the sixty-six steps of the Tennessee capitol building; the owner of another Model T won a race against more expensive cars up Pikes Peak in 1922. All this, of course, to the accompaniment of the maximum publicity.

Henry Ford's fame rose with that of the Model T, with which he was thoroughly identified. The magazine *Motor World* called the car "a credit to the genius of Henry Ford." For all his publicity skill, Ford was, at least initially, a shy man, and capable of egregious faux pas on public occasions, as when he told an audience of convicts at Sing Sing: "I'm glad to see you all here." Great already, Ford's fame grew greater still with his advent of the five-dollar day, and then that refinement of industrial organization, the assembly line. Ford inaugurated the five-dollar day in 1914. Along with doubling the wage—before, workers at Ford received a minimum wage of $2.34 a day—he lowered the hours in the working day from nine to eight, and added modest profit-sharing into the bargain. The response to the five-dollar day was so great that a riot took place at the Ford Highland Park plant, when more workers showed up than there were jobs for and the police turned water hoses on the men who refused to leave. Industry despised Ford for raising wages; the press covered him with flowers. The Cleveland *News* referred to him as "the Car Humanitarian." "I think," Ford told reporters after his five-dollar day announcement, "it is a disgrace to die rich."

Under the weight of the many bouquets thrown at him, Henry Ford caved in. As a result of the Selden suit, he was the champion of the individual; as a result of the price cuts in the Model T, he was the champion of the family man; as a result of the five-dollar day, he was the champion of the workingman. Newspaper interviews by the score were requested of him; letters by the bagful came to his desk telling him what a great man he was. His modesty melted, his shyness departed; he came to believe all the extravagant things said about him. The men who worked for him began to note a hunger on his part for endless attention. Profit-sharing the company might have; publicity-sharing, never. The press was interested in anything Henry Ford had to say, and he fed it with pronunciamentos on all subjects: the gold standard, the single tax, evolution, alcohol, foreign affairs, capital punishment. His own ignorance on any of these subjects was not allowed to impede his supreme confidence that what he had to say was of grave importance.

World War I was Henry Ford's first setback. He entered it on the side of pacifism, when he began, as a former Detroit *Free Press* reporter he hired as his "secretary for peace" put it, "a worldwide campaign for universal peace." "Men sitting around a table, not men dying in a trench," Ford said, "will finally settle the differences." When someone suggested that Ford charter a ship—a "peace ship"—to take a special American mediation board to Europe to plead for peace, Ford, sensing its publicity value, latched onto the idea instantly. An unvarnished disaster followed. At the docks at Hoboken, as William Jennings Bryan made his bon voyage speech to the departing ship, someone handed him a squirrel in a cage. The cage under his arm, Bryan finished the speech. Someone else let loose a number of squirrels into the crowd. Half the clowns and cranks on the Eastern seaboard seemed to be on the Hoboken docks that day; and a goodly share of them were on board the *Oscar II* for the peace voyage. At sea the delegates—characterized by the press as "nuts, fools, and maniacs"—argued madly among themselves. Seeing what he had gotten himself into, Henry Ford took to his cabin. He alone among the delegates was spared the press's obloquy. "Ford is a white man," the *New York Herald-Tribune*'s correspondent wired his paper, "and most emphatically sincere."

Fiasco though it was, the peace-ship venture did not seriously damage Henry Ford's reputation. Such was his popularity with the masses that between 1916 and 1924 his name was regularly bandied about as a possible presidential candidate. In 1918 he was put up for the United States Senate, and, though ultimately defeated, won the Democratic primary without making any speeches or spending any money on his own behalf. Meanwhile, when the United States entered the war, Henry Ford, the pacifist, turned part of his company's efforts toward making warships. He promised to turn back any war profits he might make; and while there is no evidence that he did so, the promise was better publicized than the failure to deliver on it.

Ford's reputation was further enhanced when he was taken

to court by his stockholders—chief among them the Dodge brothers—for suspending dividends to enlarge his company's facilities while further cutting prices on the Model T. On the witness stand Ford made all the correct moves. "Business is a service," he remarked, in defense of his paying high wages and asking only moderate profits, "not a bonanza." The plaintiff's attorney quizzically put the following statement to him. "But your controlling feature . . . is to employ a great army of men at high wages, to reduce the selling price of your car, so that a lot of people can buy it at a cheap price, and give everyone a car that wants one." Here was Ford's strategy exactly—and, as it proved, an immensely profitable one.

The truth was that Henry Ford was not interested solely in money. ("No successful boy," he once said, "ever saved any money.") He was already a millionaire many times over. His principal pleasure was neither accumulation nor expenditure on art or the fleshly pleasures. What did interest him was the curious mélange of notions that spun continually through his mind. Sometimes his hobbies, like that of cultivating soybeans and promoting them for both health and industrial uses, developed into passions. Passionate, too, could his crotchets become. He hated, for example, the city, felt cities were a thorough mistake: "Farm and factory should have been organized as adjuncts one of the other, and not as competitors." He loathed government interference. After buying a railroad, the Toledo & Ironton, he remarked: "I learned you could own a railroad, but you couldn't run it. The Interstate Commerce Commission did that for you." He was a great booster of self-help. At the Henry Ford Hospital workers recuperating from illness or injury were given, if they wished, work to do in bed to earn additional income. Ford hired an inordinately large number of handicapped employees—in 1919, they made up nearly 20 percent of the Ford work force. He was also one of the first large-scale industrialists to hire blacks in large numbers. "Help the Other Fellow" was another of his mottoes. "Henry Ford," the San Francisco *Star* noted, "was a businessman with a heart."

Yet in that heart Henry Ford kept a cold spot for the Jews. In the muddledness of his mind, Jews were confused with bankers, whom he hated, cities, which he hated, and stockholders, whom he hated, saying of the last that they were "people who gave nothing to an enterprise but money." In the Dearborn *Independent,* the organ for his views, Ford in 1920 ran a series of ninety-one articles on the Jews, not missing an anti-Semitic cliché. Anti-Semitism has always been the ugly side of populism, the xenophobia of the farm-reared, and Ford, until he was silenced, showed this side without shame. The Jews were out "to destroy Christian civilization." The Jews were "mere hucksters, traders who don't want to produce, but to make something out of what somebody else produces." As for Jews at the Ford Company, Ford allowed that they were hired, but added "we see that they work, too, and that they don't get into the office."

Ford alienated the Jews as later he would alienate organized labor through the works of his lieutenant Harry Bennett and his goon squad. Jews refused to buy Ford products. His son and grandson worked for years to undo the old man's work on both the Jewish and the labor fronts. Ford at one point published a public apology for his statements about the Jews, but the taint of anti-Semitism clung to him his life long. Publication of *The International Jew,* a book drawn from the articles in the Dearborn *Independent,* was brought out without his permission in Germany, Spain, and Brazil in the 1930s. The American edition of *Mein Kampf* mentioned Ford by name. As late as 1938, Ford, along with Charles Lindbergh, accepted the Grand Cross of the Supreme Order of the German Eagle from the Nazi government. Robert E. Sherwood denounced Ford and Lindbergh as "bootlickers of Hitler." Oswald Garrison Villard more coolly remarked: "I honestly do not think that Mr. Ford has the mentality to understand actions like [accepting the medal from the Nazis] . . . a boy of twelve would do better."

Foxy though he could be at business, clever though he was at garnering publicity, Henry Ford was at his best at his workbench or in one of his giant plants. His work on refining the design for the Model A, which in 1928 replaced the Model T, and on the V-8 engine, developed during the Depression, bears this out. Not that these were finally separable from his showmanship. The suspense awaiting the arrival of the Model A was as big a newspaper story in 1928 as the Lindbergh flight, the Sacco-Vanzetti and Scopes trials, and the Dempsey-Tunney fight—one of the glorious media binges of the 1920s. For the quick starts and power of his V-8 engines Ford received thank-you notes from John Dillinger and Clyde Barrow. He could draw a huge crowd with an exhibition—more than 25 million of his country-men came out to see the Model A the week it was released—or grab a headline with a fast comment. At the height of the Depression, a small Massachusetts newspaper looked to Ford as "an American Moses leading his people out of the Land of Depression Bondage into a new Economic Land of Promise." Still, Henry Ford's real world was the world of the workshop.

After 1934 the Ford Motor Company lost its lead in the automobile industry to become, instead of its leader, one of the Big Three, and it would eventually slide to third among the Big Three at that. By then Henry Ford was in his seventies, and his hobbies dominated his days. Apart from his anti-Semitism, his reputation with the public remained high. Resentment over his immense wealth—which had been estimated to be more than $700 million—was nowhere near so great as over that of the wealth of the Du Ponts, the Morgans, the Rockefellers; the feeling being that Henry Ford had acquired his money through hard work and without the aid of monopoly, stock manipulation, or war profiteering. He was also viewed—as he felt himself to be—as an enemy of Wall Street. At the outset of World War II, Ford, who had been an isolationist with a hatred of the British perhaps equaled only by his hatred of Franklin Delano Roosevelt, nonetheless turned his Willow Run plant over to the production of B-24 bombers. In the process the former pacifist became the fighting patriot.

For all his popularity, for all he had achieved, Ford, as exhibited through his antiquarian interests, hungered for the American past of his boyhood. Perhaps Oswald Garrison Villard was more right than he could have known when he referred to Henry Ford being, in some matters, not different from a boy of twelve. His creation (or rather re-creation) of Greenfield Village, his village industries, his schools where no foreign languages were taught and "no art but the utilitarian and no literature for its own sake"—all were emblematic of Henry Ford's hunger for the past he had known. His passion for old-fashioned dancing, his favorite music (he used to fiddle "Turkey in the Straw" on a $70,000 Stradivarius), the sermonettes on his company's "The Ford Sunday Evening Hour" radio show, spoke to the same nostalgic yearnings. The man who had done as much as any other to change the topographical character of his country from rural to urban, from back road to highway, seems finally not to have been pleased with the results of his own work.

Henry Ford's last years were scarcely crowning ones. His son Edsel, who loved and insofar as he was able protected his father while largely being neglected by him, died at forty-nine, of cancer thought to result from bleeding stomach ulcers— preceding by four years Henry Ford's own death. (His neglect of their son Edsel was the one thing Clara Ford never forgave her husband.) Ford took over the company's presidency once again at his son's death; now in his eighties, his value to the firm was chiefly that of a figurehead. He suffered strokes. He went about in public in carpet slippers. He grew irascible, suspicious; his faculties drifted away. Wizened and slightly crazed is the look upon his face posing with his wife for a photograph in his first automobile before a house in Greenfield Village in 1946. At his death the following year his company, the largest privately owned firm in the United States, was valued at $466 million, his personal estate at $80,319,455. Although he had succeeded beyond any possible dreams he could have had as a boy, he dreamed, in the success of his later years, of returning to the world of his boyhood. In his trouser pockets at his death were a comb, a pocketknife, and a Jew's harp.

Two kinds of people, and two kinds only, affect to despise money: those who have more than they need and those who secretly believe, if they have not already had it proven to them, that they are unable to obtain enough of it. Much the greater part of mankind, whose reactions to money range from an open obsession with it to a pretense of uninterest, live in various states of thrall to this extraordinary invention. Although it is easy to forget that money is an invention, Tacitus among others has remarked, speaking of the warlike nation of Germans of the first century A.D., that they were without cities, letters, arts, or money, and in the process reminds us that money marks an advance toward civilization. As with most such advances, ironic side effects tag along. Gibbon, that supreme ironist, has put it best: "The value of money has been settled by general consent to express our wants and our property, as letters were invented to express our ideas; and both these institutions, by giving a more active energy to the powers and passions of human nature, have contributed to multiply the objects they were designed to represent."

The objects money was designed to represent—what a list that might make! The history of whole civilizations might be writ on it. At a minimum its palpable items would include property in all its various forms—palaces, country houses, and estates, rare works of art, jewels—titles and rights, and the full range of pleasures, aesthetic, physical, and perverse. Its abstract, but no less real, items would at a minimum include respect, security, and power; this last for good, for evil, or for the sheer simple exercise of it. Money makes possible charity but also oppression; it can add refinement but as often encourages coarseness. In the hands of some it is viewed as carrying sober responsibilities; in the hands of others it is viewed as placing its possessors well outside the pale of responsibilities. Not least among its values is that owning a large sum of money can place one—sometimes but not very often—above the need to think constantly about money itself, although Epicurus declared that being rich was not an alleviation but merely a change of troubles.

If ambition be the fuel of achievement, money is often its octane. Like octane, money can remove the knocks. Or so it is generally conceded. Certainly, almost every dream of achievement—for founding a university, curing a disease, composing a symphony, getting a useful invention out into the world, reforming public life—eventually wakes to the necessity of money for its realization. For some ambition starts and ends with money; for others money is the great stopper, the substance without which even dreams do not seem possible. Although the majority doubtless do view money as a means to other, perhaps never finally formulated ends, money and ambition are nonetheless bound together—inextricably.

Yet to think long about money is to be forced to concentrate on the general indignity of the human species. Much that is vicious, more that is squalid, has been done for money. Is there anything that has not been done for it? Extortion, kidnapping, murder by contract, these supposedly passionless crimes have in common the very real passion for money. Which is morally more repulsive—to murder because of hatred, or because of money? Most people, if pressed, would be inclined to say the latter. But why should this be so? Is it that hatred is understandable but the pursuit of money for its own sake is not? Is the one motive somehow human, the other obscene? In its way the passion for money is a more logical passion than that of vengeance. But the passion for money is also a passion about which there is a necessary hypocrisy.

Without this necessary hypocrisy, the stitches that make it possible for society to cohere would come unraveled and life in all its appalling rawness would spill out. Thus, money becomes the subject of much psychologizing, while it also becomes the object of manifold discriminations: old money and new money, clean money and dirty money. Unwritten though seriously enforced rules are established governing economic behavior: certain ways of earning money are deemed vulgar as are certain ways of spending it. ("There is nothing more ill-bred," says Thomas Apley to his son George, in *The Late George Apley*, "than the over-lavish spending of money.") Too great wealth often needs be disguised to appear less, too little wealth must be gussied up to appear more. Fine lines are drawn everywhere when it comes to money, and most people tiptoe most carefully around them.

Without this necessary hypocrisy, the awareness of what an immense advantage money is becomes too glaring. The always clear-minded David Hume remarks of money: "It was a shrewd observation of Anacharsis the Scythian, who had never seen money in his own country, that gold and silver seemed to him of no use to the Greeks, but to assist them in numeration and arithmetic. It is indeed evident, that money is nothing but the representation of labour and commodities, and serves only as a method of rating or estimating them." Hume here speaks of money as an instrumentality, but of course it is—it does—so much more. Money may not buy happiness, but it can set the conditions necessary for achieving happiness: an absence of economic worry, material want, petty desire. Through the purchase of the best diet and climatic conditions, money can improve health; through the purchase of the best medical care, money can prolong life. Money can build confidence. Money can give one a high opinion of oneself. Many are the things that money cannot buy or do, but when one is without money often few of these things seem of any significance. "Blessed money!" wrote George Gissing, a novelist part of whose personal tragedy was the lifelong absence of it, "root of all good, until the world invents some saner economy."

"I call people rich when they're able to meet the requirements of their imagination," says a character in Henry James's *The Portrait of a Lady.* As a novelist engaged in a lifelong struggle to earn his own keep through his writing, Henry James never thought money either a trivial or a vulgar subject. No writer had a clearer sense of the liberating power of money, and none knew better its limitations. What money could and could not buy were continual Jamesian questions, worked out with the greatest care in his novels. Henry James, this most cerebral of novelists, never for a moment underrated the importance of money to the human drama.

Curiosity Shop □ An intelligent man who has only recently become wealthy claims that one of the benefits of his recent wealth is the ability it confers to look in the eye—to spit in the eye, if it comes to that—of other wealthy men, and (in effect) say: "You have money, and I have money. You with all your money are still a swine and so, for that matter, am I with all of mine. Whatever else your money may do for you, it can no longer allow you to include me within the circle of those for whom you are secretly—and, sometimes, not so secretly—contemptuous." His having wealth, he explains, robs inferior men who also have wealth of even the illusion that they are better than he. "It is a bit complicated," he says, "but, please believe me, very comforting."

Few stories give so much pleasure as those about either a man or a woman who has succeeded in his or her quest for money, or someone who has inherited great wealth, but who ends in grave unhappiness. Literature and the movies are filled with such stories. "The victor belongs to the spoils," a line F. Scott Fitzgerald gives to his character Anthony Patch in *The Beautiful and Damned,* can stand as the epigraph to all such stories, in life and in letters. *Citizen Kane* is essentially this story. Howard Hughes, whose reclusive life exerted so considerable a fascination in his last years, is another version of the same story. Ivan Goncharov, the nineteenth-century Russian novelist, treated the theme in a novel aptly entitled (in English translation) *The Same Old Story.* "Money," John Jacob Astor once remarked, "brings me nothing but a certain dull anxiety." J. Paul Getty, too, sounded the note everyone wishes to hear: "I hate and regret the failure of my marriages. I would gladly give all my millions for just one lasting marital success." The need to believe that money does not bring happiness—that quite the reverse is true—runs very strong. And why not? It is so very solacing.

Strong as well is the need to believe that a concentrated interest in money—its acquisition, the saving and the spending of it—is abnormal. One of the things his money cannot any longer buy a millionaire of any prominence is freedom from being publicly psychoanalyzed. When the acquisition of a fortune is not accompanied by an omnipresent state of glee—as in the case, for example, of John D. Rockefeller—the assumption is that the motive for acquiring the money in the first place cannot have been other than as the result of a twisted psychological development. In the case of John D. Rockefeller, one writer, Ferdinand Lundberg in *The Rockefeller Syndrome,* has not suggested but declared that Rockefeller's tight financial rein can be traced to the young John D. Rockefeller's strict toilet training. Because Rockefeller was born some 135 years before this pronouncement was made, it has to be assumed that the writer who made it was not seated on the edge of the bathtub in the Rockefeller home, and therefore does not speak out of direct observation. But, then, the amateur psychologist's work is never done.

What Mr. Lundberg does speak from is doctrinal assurance —the doctrine, in this instance, being (roughly) that of Sigmund Freud. What, specifically, did Freud say on the subject of money? Many things, it turns out, and some of them, it can be argued, contradictory. The most famous among the things he said, certainly, has to do with his connecting money and feces. In "Character and Anal Eroticism" (1908), Freud remarked: "It is possible that the contrast between the most precious substance known to man and the most worthless, which he rejects as 'something thrown out,' has contributed to this identification of gold with feces." In the same essay, he notes: "The original erotic interest in defecation is, as we know, destined to be extinguished in later years; it is in these years that the interest in money is making its appearance as something new which was unknown in childhood. This makes it easier for the earlier impulse, which is in process of relinquishing its aim, to be carried over to the new one." (Sandor Ferenczi, Freud's early associate, in "On the Ontogenesis of the Interest in Money," also equates money with body wastes: "Nothing other than odorless dehydrated filth that has been made to shine.") Often it is difficult to be certain whether Freud is talking about universal or neurotic behavior; often it is difficult, in the same way, to determine if, in Freud and others, neurosis isn't assumed to be universal. For elsewhere, in "Anal Eroticism and the Castration Complex" (1918), Freud notes: "We have accustomed ourselves to trace back interest in money, insofar as it is of a libidinal and not of a rational character, to excremental pleasure, and to require a normal man to keep his relations to money entirely free from libidinal influences and to regulate them according to the demands of reality."

On the demands of reality, Freud is especially worth attending to when he comes to discuss—as he does in his paper "Further Recommendations in the Technique of Psycho-Analysis" (1913)—the question of the physician's fee. "The analyst," he writes, "does not dispute that money is to be regarded first and foremost as the means by which life is supported and power is obtained, but he maintains that, besides this, powerful sexual factors are involved in the value set upon it; he may expect, therefore, that money questions will be treated by cultured people in the same manner as sexual matters, with the same inconsistency, prudishness, and hypocrisy." Freud cautions analysts not to be equivocal about fees. Straightforwardness is best: "By voluntarily introducing the subject of fees and stating the price for which he [the analyst] gives his time, he shows the patient that he himself has cast aside shame in these matters." But, more important, for Freud "the absence of the corrective influence in payment of the professional fee is felt as a serious handicap; the whole relationship recedes into an unreal world; and the patient is deprived of a useful incentive to exert himself to bring the cure to an end."

There is a theoretical Freud and there is a practical Freud—and the practical Freud can almost always be counted upon to be the more impressive. So it turns out to be with Freud on money. That money and feces are somehow connected is possibly brilliant but certainly arguable and uncertainly helpful; that the payment of a fee is likely to hasten cure is solidly commonsensical and immediately persuasive. The reason has to do with the very demands of reality Freud himself postulates as necessary for one's own healthful relations to money. Money itself, Freud is saying, has a reality of its own; and it is, one might add, greater than the reality of much high-blown theorizing about it.

An instance of such theorizing is found in the work of Melanie Klein, a psychoanalyst whose work has thus far enjoyed greater popularity in England than in the United States. Dr. Klein has linked money to what she has termed the "phantasy of the inexhaustible breast." In her scheme of things, those who seek money with inordinate energy are in reality seeking the contentment that they may have known only in infancy or, prenatally, in the womb. They seek, in other words, a condition of nirvana. Thomas Wiseman, a Kleinian at least on money matters, in his book *The Money Motive* writes: "Because of its interest-bearing aspect, money is the nearest thing to such a source [the inexhaustible breast] that we can put our hands on. Untouched capital can give us income and never be exhausted. Only in the psyche can we find something that comes closer: a bountiful and loving internal object created out of the image of the mother."

Freud, who referred to money as "the most precious substance," nevertheless was in no doubt about its inability to bring happiness. "Happiness," he wrote in a letter to Wilhelm Fliess, "is the deferred fulfillment of a prehistoric wish. That is why wealth brings so little happiness; money is not an infantile wish." Why then, Doctor, one can hear the gruff voice of a reasonably prosperous businessman respond, if wealth brings so little happiness, does poverty bring so much misery?

Gold and feces, the most precious substance, the inexhaustible breast, prehistoric wishes—even if all this were demonstrably true, would the mystery of the value of money be finally explained? Decidedly not. "The question as to what value really is," Georg Simmel noted, "like the question as to what being is, is unanswerable." What is left is to determine what might be the appropriate attitude toward it.

Curiosity Shop □ To an audience of wealthy men, a fund-raiser for a charity tells the following story:

"In Kracow, in the bitter cold of a January blizzard, an aged beggar discovers a newborn child wrapped in a thin blanket left in a snowbank. The old man clutches the child close to him; the child cries out in hunger, the old man recognizing in the desperation of the cry the nearness of death if the child is not soon fed. Having no place else to turn, the beggar raises his eyes to the heavens and asks the help of God. No sooner does he do so than he notes that, *mirabile dictu,* God has given him the breasts of a woman, from which the child is able to take sustenance and thus survive."

A man in the audience asks: "But wouldn't it have been

easier for God simply to have given the beggar a few coins with which to buy food for the child?"

"Ah," the fund-raiser replies, "God is not stupid. Why, after all, spend money when you can have miracles for free?"

Part of the mystery of money has to do with the fact that it is both (and simultaneously) symbolic and real. It is also both (and simultaneously) a means and an end. Money is a means of, among other things, facilitating trade, measuring value, condensing and making portable wealth. Its behavior as a means—its regulation and supply, its fluctuations through inflation and deflation, its performance amid the currencies of other nations, its volatile reaction to the impingement of national and international events—all this and inexhaustibly more is the domain of the economists. But money as an end—what it can buy, what it does to people well supplied with it or to those deprived of it, its contribution to human happiness and human misery and thus to the formation of human character—this is the province of everyone.

Money as an end is not least interesting in being the sole begetter of a number of special vices: avarice, miserliness, and spendthriftness chief among them. More fascinating vices may exist but none more tenacious. David Hume thought avarice incurable, and on the subject wrote that "none of the most furious excesses of love and ambition are, in any respect, to be compared to the extremes of avarice." It is a point upon which Georg Simmel, in his *Philosophy of Money*, concurs, noting that "compared to [avarice] the most intense other passions seem to have only a partial hold over the emotions." Gibbon weighs in by remarking: "Avarice more properly belongs to ministers than to kings, in whom that passion is commonly extinguished by absolute possession." Which may be another way of saying that avarice visits everyone but kings. Balzac thought that "avarice begins where poverty ends."

Passion about the acquisition of money (avarice) is one thing, but equal passion about its sheer possession (miserliness) or its utter waste (spendthriftness) are, it would seem, two very different things. The three are, it turns out, intertwined, and no one of them could have come into existence in an agricultural as opposed to a money economy. The product of agriculture could not, for example, be hoarded because of its perishability. Short of setting fire to it, neither could it be wasted in the grand spendthrift style. With both these possibilities precluded, avarice itself, in an economy based on agriculture, had natural limits: the amount one's family, guests, or community could eat and safely store.

The first, and most obvious, difference between an agricultural and a money economy is the built-in absence of limits of the latter. As money itself seems to exist in a state of infinitude, such seems the state of dreams it makes possible: infinite. "Money in modern times," David T. Bazelon noted, "is a contract with parties unknown for the future delivery of pleasures undecided upon." A man can wear only one pair of trousers at a time, runs a maxim meant to counsel moderation in the pursuit of money. But it is a maxim that says nothing of what stocks and certificates and cash can be carried in the pockets of those trousers, of what gems might be sewn into the seams. A dreamy substance, money, bringing with it the dream of security, the dream of independence, the dream of winning love, the dream (even) of immortality.

In perhaps no other areas of life can irrationality come so near to be counted upon than in those having to do with money. In money matters one meets nearly everywhere with madness, both petty and grand. The philanthropist who gives millions to charity yet is a niggardly tipper. The beggar who dies with more than $300,000 stuffed into shoe boxes on a shelf in his closet. Who has not read or heard or known such stories? Less exotic if not less irrational tales, though, regularly show up where money is at stake. Inheritance is a prime example; given any room for it, strange, if not vicious, behavior is bound to result. Parents of a practical bent have been known to alert sons or daughters that, when they die, they, the sons or daughters, are to go directly to the bank vault, and only afterwards worry about grieving. "Everybody," wrote Gertrude Stein, "has to make up their mind if money is money or money isn't money and sooner or later they always do decide that money is money."

Money throws up odd types. There is the type of the hustler, who cannot seem to derive much pleasure from making money in a conventional way but must have an angle, a chance to sink the knife in, so that one is left to conclude that his delight isn't found in money so much as in the methods of attaining it. There is the type of the already wealthy saver, who not merely refuses to go into capital but even into interest, choosing instead to live off the interest earned by his interest. There is the type of the perennially financially jealous, who combines greed with envy and who cannot himself ever have enough money and sorely resents anyone who has more than he. (A high percentage of cases of tax fraud are said to have first been brought to the attention of the Internal Revenue Service by the business associates, friends, and even relatives of those reported for fraudulence.) There is the type who acquires through money a taste for the more potent narcotic of power.

Of the various types created by money perhaps no two are more interesting—because no two are more extreme and hence more pure—than the miser and the spendthrift. The man who cannot let money go and the man who refuses to hold on to it are special types, exhibiting as they do something of the mystery of money in high relief. The miser—not simply the man who is cheap, niggling, tight, "a little near," as used to be said in Victorian England—but the true miser is a figure who is among the most imaginative in the world, concentrating his imaginings upon a single subject: what his money might buy. Schopenhauer, in this connection, wrote: "Money is human happiness *in abstracto;* consequently he who is no longer capable of happiness *in concreto* sets his whole heart on money."

Georg Simmel has put it neatly when, noting the psychological tone of joy in the mere possession of money common to the miser, he writes: "The strange coalescing, abstraction, and anticipation of ownership of property which constitutes the meaning of money is like aesthetic pleasure in permitting consciousness a free play, a portentous extension into an unresisting medium, and the incorporation of all possibilities without violation or deterioration of reality." Although Simmel later talks about miserliness being one of the abstract joys, and hence "one of the furthest removed from sensuous immediacy," he implies nevertheless that the miser is, in effect, an onanist over property. He is the fantasist par excellence, doing endlessly and concentratedly what many without money do occasionally and dreamily: thinking about the possibilities of money. What distinguishes the miser, however, is that he cannot bear consummation. What excites him about money is strictly its potentiality.

The spendthrift, who is interested in consummation only, cannot abide the foreplay aspects involved in dealing with money. The planning of how money might most efficaciently be spent, the thought that goes into the expenditure itself, the consideration for the future—for none of these has the spendthrift the least patience. A distinction need be made between the spendthrift and the big spender, and the best distinction is, again, Simmel's, who notes that the spendthrift "is not someone who senselessly gives his money to the world but one who uses it for senseless purchases—that is, for purchases that are not appropriate to his circumstances." More important still, the spendthrift derives his excitement from the sheer pleasure of waste—as opposed to the pleasures of ostentation, or the enjoyment of objects, or the delight of entertaining others—wherein, according to Simmel, "the attraction of the instant overshadows the rational evaluation of money or of commodities."

Of the two types, the miser is traditionally credited with a meanness of character, the spendthrift with a largeness of character. Not to be concerned about money, to be distinctly unconcerned about it, has almost everywhere been a mark of worldliness. The sport, the spender, the high-roller, these are usually admired men. The gesture that says, in effect, I spit on money, is the one that gains admiring attention. Robert Evans, the movie producer, is said to walk out of restaurants in Los Angeles without paying his bill or leaving a tip, but is later billed for food and service—probably, as he concedes, overbilled. "At the end of the year," he has remarked, "if it costs me a thousand dollars more, so what? To me it is a great luxury not to wait." Why, when most people at least superficially examine their bills in restaurants, would many people find this gesture, if not worthy of admiration, at least amusing?

The chief reason is that it is a gesture that announces a freedom from concern with money. Here surely, such a gesture says, is a man not enslaved by the pettiness of money—a man for whom it is worth a thousand dollars a year to walk out of a restaurant when he damn well feels like it. A thousand dollars: once enough for a two-week holiday in London; braces for a child with crooked teeth; bail for a crime of fairly serious magnitude; three very good men's suits; an Edward Hopper print of limited edition; many splendid books; food sufficient to last a family in India several months. But to think this way is to think of the potentiality of money; to think, no less, in the way of the miser. Yet even the gesture of paying an extra thousand dollars a year to walk out of restaurants is itself dependent for its grandeur upon the potentiality of money. It is a grand gesture only because money itself is actually treasured—by the spendthrift fully as much as by the miser as by all who fall in between the two types. When it comes to money, no one but monks, very young children, and the insane are entirely free from its influence.

Curiosity Shop □ Money, it is said, talks. Sometimes it has a rasp, sometimes a lisp. It speaks in various accents and inflections. Its tone can be cultivated or coarse. It does often tend to go on. Almost always it earns a hearing: occasionally grudging, more usually respectful. The possession of large sums of money even unaccompanied by small sums of knowledge lends a speaker authority. Note that in many a room across the land the person doing the most talking is the person earning the most money. Having money often inclines people to the belief that they have something to say, and on—you name it—any subject: politics, sex, childrearing, religion, and above all on money itself, which, none too surprisingly, frequently turns out to be the number-one subject of the monied. Money talks, no question about that, but if it is always worth attending to, it is less because of what it has to say on any particular subject than because of what it tells about human nature. The puzzle is not why money talks but why other people, on the edge of their chairs, are listening so intently.

Why is it so difficult to acquire a clear perspective on money? Even casual references on the subject sound forced: glib, insincere, seeking for effect not truth. Money is like a certain kind of woman, one such bit runs. Nice to have but not worth running after. Clever though it is, this does not ring quite true. It is closer to the truth to say that money is one of those subjects—perhaps *the* subject—about which people can be depended upon not to be candid. Sooner expect candor about a person's sex life than about his or her financial life. Sooner expect as well hypocrisy —the Communist with the expensive summer home, the church member systematically selling everyone else in the congregation real estate—over financial than over any other matters. Why should this be so?

It is chiefly so because money is a subject whose moral code —those Morse-like blinks of approval and disapproval—has not over the centuries spelled out a clear message. If money has a moral history, the tendency of that history has been for money to be condemned in principle yet honored in practice. In religious as in secular history, the message is no less mixed. The Old Testament admonishes against worshiping the golden calf, yet everywhere virtue is rewarded with plentiful crops, fatted herds, beautiful wives, and other of the treasures of this earth. The New Testament reminds to "lay up for yourselves treasures *in heaven,* where neither moth nor rust doth corrupt, and where thieves do not dig through nor steal" (italics added); Judas sold information about Jesus for thirty pieces of silver; and Saint Leo remarks: "There is not a trace of justice in that heart in which the love of gain has made a dwelling"; and upon such truths so vast a treasurehouse as the Vatican is built.

If religious views about money offer a field filled with obfuscation, political views about money offer, more simply, a minefield. The leading modern political religion, Marxism, is about little else. As Freudianism has induced self-consciousness about sex, so has Marxism induced self-consciousness, often shading into guilt, about money. Here, for example, is Marx himself sounding the note: "The less you eat, drink, and read books; the less you think, love, theorize, sing, paint, fence, etc., and the more you *save*—the greater becomes your treasure which neither moth nor dust will devour—your *capital.* The less you *are,* the more you *have;* the less you express your own life, the greater is your *externalized* life—the greater is the store of your alienated being" Wide has been the influence of Marxist doctrine, and not in Eastern Europe or the countries of the Third World alone. So wide indeed has it been that capitalism today has come to be a word with a built-in bias, denoting sweat shops, child labor, and money grubbing of an almost lascivious kind. Not that capitalism, mixed, pure, and even cruel, lacks defenders; yet at the level of the individual man or woman a certain element of guilt frequently attaches to having large sums of money. Large gain, the inherent logic of Marxism implies, must be ill-gotten. While such a thought might give comfort to the less-than-well-off, very often it turns out that the rich believe it, too; or at least their children tend to.

"Nobody," a Russian proverb runs, "ever died of having too many rubles." But many have, metaphorically at least, gagged on them, though few to the point of coughing up enough so as to seriously inhibit their own style of living. Much philanthropy, in the low view, is seen as a balm to the wounds of guilt involved in ample acquisition; a form of "didomania," in Ferdinand Lundberg's phrase, the reverse of kleptomania, the guilt-ridden putting back in return for all one has taken. It is scarcely a coincidence that the politics of so many men and women in Hollywood in the 1930s took a sharp leftward turn; they were earning, many of these members of the Communist party and its fellow travelers, $3,000 and $4,000 a week in the Depression, when their countrymen were so patently doing without. From money to guilt to politics is not an uncommon transition in American life. Where once the result was the fairly innocuous charity work of society women, it now more usually takes a political turn, a dabbling at the fringes of revolution. Witness the little evening Leonard Bernstein put on in his home for the Black Panthers in January, 1970.

Whether it be through sheer irresponsibility, or irresponsibility fueled by guilt, the squandering by sons and daughters of fortunes earned by fathers is another common story. "I suppose we must allow for the swing of the pendulum," Sir Robert Hart, the nineteenth-century Englishman who built up a fortune as head of Chinese customs remarked, "I have done the work and the gathering, and he [my son] can enjoy the leisure and the scattering." Much energy has gone into the scattering of fortunes, and the inheritance of large fortunes has tended, in its effects on the sons and daughters of the rich, to leave an endowment perhaps as significant as that of any genetic one. Doris Duke, Barbara Hutton, Huntington Hartford, James Gordon Bennett, Jr.—are these, one wonders, instances of sons and daughters paying (or, rather, paying out) for the sins of fathers? On the other hand, Quentin Bell, in his brief book on John Ruskin, reports what Ruskin did with his father's fortune:

> During the 1860s and 1870s there were few extravagances and fewer charities that he could resist. He bought diamonds and gave them to museums, missals and cut them up for friends, he put a tenth part of his fortune into a scheme for establishing an English Utopia, he purchased slum property and placed it in the firm yet charitable hands of Octavia Hill, he set the unemployed to sweeping the streets and his family retainers to dispensing tea to the poor in packets, he tried to buy an Alp, he did buy a supposed Titian, he established a drawing school at Oxford, he gave away collections of pictures and minerals, he subsidised a girls' school, he made C. A. Howell—who was a scoundrel—his almoner and through this agency disbursed money to anyone who could tell a sufficiently affecting story of undeserved misfortune. On one occasion, finding a little girl who had nowhere to

play, he promptly bought her a field. Altogether, he probably got better value for his money than do most very rich men.

Immense wealth need not be necessarily accompanied by either guilt or irresponsibility. The late Lucius Beebe, the chief chronicler of the rich in America, our Livy of the lavish, in *The Big Spenders* and other of his books, has provided a megillah of untrammeledly enthusiastic spending by the wealthy. Beebe wrote history that was pure anecdote, which he loved, and much of what he records would dazzle the most pinch-mouthed Leninist. More than a bit of a snob,* Beebe had a taste for the stylish gesture, such as Benjamin Guggenheim's supposedly changing into dress clothes for the sinking of the *Titanic.* But he also appreciated the gaudy if done on a sufficiently grand scale. Michael Arlen, the novelist and author of *The Green Hat,* once remarked, "All I want in the world is very little. I only want the best of everything, and there is so little of that." Not true, at least to judge by Lucius Beebe, whose pages overflow with what he termed "spacious gestures of material satisfaction."

Accounts of dinners at Rector's, Sherry's, Delmonico's, the great lobster palaces of the turn of the century, are lovingly given at menu length in Beebe's pages; "expensive cheerfulness," he calls such dining. He recounts the famous parties, such as that given by the Bradley-Martins in 1897 at a cost of $369,200; or Diamond Jim Brady's more intimate gathering for fifty at a cost of $105,000, with $60,000 of this sum going for mementos for his guests. Unlike the great balls, parties, fêtes of our own day, such affairs, as Beebe is pleased to report, were not diluted by the cause of charity; their only reason for being was to have a damn good time. Beebe fondly chronicles the eccentricities of the toweringly solvent, among them Ned Green's Packard with indoor plumbing; a Mrs. Crocker, of San

---

*A delicious anecdote records Beebe's snobbishness. Once, when he was to go into the hospital for exploratory surgery, one of his female acquaintances is said to have remarked to another: "Well, I do hope that the surgeon has the common good taste to open Lucius at room temperature."

Francisco, who regularly sent her dry cleaning off to be done in
Paris; and the man who paid Paderewski $3,000 to play for his
guests behind a screen. Beebe's most striking single anecdote
has to do with James Gordon Bennett, Jr., the inheritor of the
old New York *Herald,* who, when unable to get a table at his
favorite restaurant in Monte Carlo, bought the place on the spot
for $40,000, had another patron ejected, and sat down to his meal
—at the end of which, in what must be the largest single tip on
record, he gave the deed to the restaurant to his waiter.

Champagne, in Lucius Beebe's pages, always pours in
Niagaras. Men and women walk into Daimler automobiles built
high enough off the ground so that stooping is not required upon
entry. The trophies of the rich—houses, stables, cars, yachts,
titled sons-in-law—are handsomely displayed. At a lesser level
of expense, so is the 4-H club of spending: on horses, hounds,
haberdashery, and horticulture. Brand names are exultantly
brandished: Rolls-Royce, Tiffany, Cunard, Corona, Peal, Poole,
Dom Perignon, Revillon, Huntley and Palmer. Lots of the best
of everything might stand in as Beebe's motto. A lifelong railroad buff, he was especially keen at describing the lavish private
railroad cars that were once the badge of the very rich—a badge
that, as he puts it, "can never be downgraded by common availa-
bility or middle-class patronage." Coming away from Lucius
Beebe's chronicles of the wealthy one may still believe that the
meek shall inherit the earth, yet it is difficult not to believe that
the earth has already been picked clean.

Curiosity Shop □ Although no one has ever succeeded in solv-
ing for long the economic problem—the problem of bringing economic life under control, reducing scarcity, increasing
economic justice, and avoiding drastic fluctuations and dislo-
cations—economists exude a confidence that seems well beyond
the palpable results of their lucubrations. They are to money
what physicians are to health—the sole authority on a subject of
absolutely vital importance. Yet unlike the generality of physicians, whose thoughts about health tend usually to form a rough
consensus, economists are, intramurally, a hotly contentious lot.

Perhaps it is the disputatiousness among them that provides them separately with so thick an air of authority. By the main force of confident utterance they hope to banish contending claims to the truth about the behavior of markets and money. Two economists, existing in a state of perpetual and total disagreement, cannot both be right. Yet why is each so cocksure?

The confidence of economists extends to their clothes. Take their suits. Excepting only Lord Keynes, who was something of a dandy, the suits of economists are not notably fashionable. But they seem very solid. Something there is in the weave and cut of these garments—something a bit dull, a bit out of it—that nonetheless recommends them as quality goods. Bought right. Possibly half a dozen of them at a shot. Where do they buy them? Wherever they might have been purchased, one senses that the price was right, that value for the dollar was obtained. Economists think and talk and write about nothing but money all the day long. They must know something—something the rest of us do not know. Proper vestments, these suits, for a priesthood who preach not so much to the converted as to the desperately interested and permanently puzzled.

Wealth of the kind that attracted Lucius Beebe, gaudy and noisy and free-spending, appears in our day to have gone out of style if not altogether out of existence. Many a multimillionaire had lived with eccentric modesty before—Daniel Drew, who wore his suits threadbare; Hetty Green, whose household economies nearly destroyed her son's health; Russell Sage, who walked to work to save streetcar fare—but in time certain serious crimps were put not so much into the accumulation as into the retention of great wealth. Chief among these has been taxes: income taxes, capital gains taxes, inheritance taxes. Because primogeniture has never been the custom in the United States, as it was for centuries in England and on the Continent, great fortunes often tended to be dispersed at death. True, this did not prove to be the case for the Rockefellers or the Fords, but it did for the Guggenheims, Singers, and Vanderbilts. Inheritance itself often could be a drag on enterprise. "I would as soon leave to my son a curse as the almighty dollar," said Andrew Carnegie. "It [inheritance] is as certain as death to ambition," wrote William K. Vanderbilt, the grandson of the Commodore, "as cocaine to morality."

Not that big new money ceased to be made; or ceases yet. Howard Hughes at his death is said to have left an estate valued at $1.5 billion. Ray Kroc, of McDonald's, started in his fifties when the current century was already in its sixties. Bob Hope and Lucille Ball—he through real estate, she through astute television production—are reported to be worth in the hundreds of millions. An occasional hustler, such as Bernard Cornfeld, wins through (though in his case not for long). Millions are made by movie stars, athletes, authors. Inventions rationally marketed—such as Edwin Land's Polaroid cameras or Thomas J. Watson's International Business Machines—can still ring the gong. Salesmanship, as always and in its various forms, provides a continuing avenue to wealth. Real estate, retailing, and publishing continue to produce multimillionaires. Yet something has changed. In *Looking Backward* (1888), Edward Bellamy likened society to a coach being dragged along through mud and over rocky terrain by the enslaved many while the comfortable few rode atop. Today there are fewer doing the dragging and many more people atop—but none riding quite so high as formerly.

What has changed is the nature of the game itself. Government regulation, for one thing, has substantially altered the rules of the game. The advent of the Securities and Exchange Commission would today prevent the stock-watering practices of old pirates like Daniel Drew and Jim Fisk. Jay Gould's manipulation of railroads could not be brought off under the current supervision of the Interstate Commerce Commission. Antitrust legislation precludes the emergence of a contemporary John D. Rockefeller. Let the public be damned, the repeated war cry of the roughhouse generation of the robber barons, is no longer met with impotent silence.

The field on which the game is played, for another thing, has been considerably constricted. The frontiers have closed (though not yet all the byways). Fresh fortunes in land acquisition—such as the King Ranch or Henry Flagler's large holdings in Florida or Bob Hope's in Southern California—seem unlikely to recur. The extractive industries of mining, oil drilling, gas, and steel, though scarcely exhausted, have become too expensive to be open to the type of the Carnegies, Mellons, Morgans, and Guggenheims. Useful inventions and innovations in manufacturing, while they continue, are often swallowed up by already settled industry in the form of conglomerates. Where once the dream of businessmen was of empire building, now it is more often that of being bought up and taken out of the business wars. For those who stay in the wars various taxes, despite the Byzantine methods devised at high cost to elude them, appreciably lessen the spoils.

None of which ought to be construed as a cry for pity and relief for the modern businessman, nor as nostalgic yearning for the good old days of let-'er-rip capitalism. As of 1972, the number of millionaires in the United States, according to Professor James D. Smith of Pennsylvania State University, was estimated to be 133,400—an increase of 44 percent over the number of American millionaires of a decade earlier. Millions there are to be made, but not, as once, hundreds of millions. What is more, much of this new money is earned at the periphery rather than at the center of life. Advertising, television, real estate, show business, sports, these are where the glamour of money making now is, whereas once it was in building railroads, extracting ore and minerals from the earth, revolutionizing technology through invention and advancements in organization. Deplorable and self-centered though much of the conduct of the robber-baron generation was, ruthless and rueful though many of its leading figures have come to seem, after all that is bad has been said about them, it needs to be said yet again that they built up the country. The more recent generations of millionaires—lawyers, organizers of conglomerates, franchisers, real estate developers, advertising men, cosmetics manufacturers—less harsh though they be, have not built up but lived off the country.

Cutting deeper, though, is the fact that business is no longer generally revered, nor does it absorb the country's best minds as it once did. In the 1860s, in England, John Stuart Mill complained that "there is now scarcely any outlet for energy in this

country except business." In America the same plaint was
lodged well into this century. The young Van Wyck Brooks, in
America's Coming-of-Age, moaned that in the United States
business "occupied the center of the field": "the highest ambition of young America is to be—do I exaggerate?—the owner of
a shoe factory." Business then had glamour, held excitement;
many a young man whose family could have afforded to send him
to college forbore going, impatient to get down to business. In
an earlier generation men like Rockefeller and Carnegie began
in business in their adolescence. The prospect of business was
enticing—and dangerous in the bargain. Men's careers could be
quickly crushed, their ambition snuffed out—Van Wyck
Brooks's father was a casualty of business—but business was
where the action was, and the brightest young minds, unless
deterred by artistic temperament or radical political visions,
hurled themselves into it with enthusiasm.

The appetite for business was enlivened by religious en-
dorsement. William Lawrence, the Episcopal bishop of Massachusetts, pronounced that "material prosperity is helping to
make the national character sweeter, more joyous, more un-
selfish, more Christ-like." Reverend Russell Conwell, a Baptist
minister of Philadelphia, in a famous sermon entitled "Acres of
Diamonds," exhorted: "Money is power. Every good man and
woman ought to strive for power, to do good with it when obtained." At Yale a spirit that George Santayana characterized as
one of "muscular Christianity" held success in business to be the
duty of the best young men; and many of the most energetic of
its students in the second and third decade of this century—
Chester Bowles, Henry Luce, William Benton—went forth, one
might say, and did likewise. Humbler clergymen, less grand
institutions than Yale, may have continued to admonish that "it
is easier for a camel to pass through the eye of a needle than for
a rich man to enter the kingdom of heaven," but theirs was far
from the dominant voice.

In the kind of bald statement one rarely any longer hears,
Lord Beaverbrook, himself a throwback to the type of the self-
made man, announced: "The money brain is in the modern world
the supreme brain. Why? Because that which the greatest number of men strive for will produce the fiercest competition of the

intellect." Perhaps the reason one rarely hears such statements any longer is that they are no longer true. The striving continues, all right, the competition remains in some respects as fierce as ever, but in a way that is qualitatively different from what it once was. Business schools flourish, law schools are inundated by applications, young men and women pay their fees and take their degrees—but there often tends to be something mechanical and a bit hopeless about the entire procedure. The law student proclaims he intends to specialize in civil liberties, the business student hopes to make use of his business training as a springboard to involvement in international trade in the foreign service. Idealism, in short, desperately searches for an outlet. Others attend business and law schools shorn of idealism. They go, they shruggingly allow, because they have nothing better to do—and one has, after all, to make a living. Excitement at the prospect of a career devoted to making money, even if it is felt, cannot be openly admitted.

The reason it cannot is that it has been systematically downgraded for a number of decades now, and these students, often the best among them, have learned their lessons well. What are these lessons? Business, to begin with, is hypocritical and sterile (see *Babbitt*). Ambition is unseemly and everywhere suspect (see *What Makes Sammy Run, The Great Gatsby*, and, for nonreaders, the movies *Citizen Kane* and *The Apprenticeship of Duddy Kravitz*). Middle-class life is essentially boring (see modern literature); upper-middle-class life, worse (see, these students say, their own families). Affluence is a sham, a greedy affair bringing no happiness (see Galbraith et al.) This chiefly applies to the sons and daughters of the middle classes, who, as a result of their parents' business, ambition, and affluence were enabled to go to college in the first place. (It does not yet appear that those who have had no direct experience of affluence, such as the children of the working classes, are so disdainful of it.) Most of them will nonetheless next go into business of one sort or another—even a healthy economy can afford a limited number of writers, forest rangers, professors, classical guitarists, and social workers—but with a clouded mind and less than half a heart.

In *The Rockefellers: An American Dynasty*, Peter Collier

and David Horowitz devote a good deal of attention to the great-grandchildren of John D. Rockefeller, only a small number of whom have gone into the family businesses or any other business. While none among them qualifies as a ne'er-do-well—one is governor of West Virginia—a high proportion of the young Rockefeller cousins have become teachers or social workers, or have gone into politics or administration. One, married to a graduate student in California, spends her summers in a converted railroad caboose, where, as a family of four, she and her husband and children claim to live on $700 a month. Many find the name Rockefeller an encumbrance; and at least one has changed her name. Another, disavowing her background, remarks: "There is no way to justify the money." The need for justification, either for the way he earned his money, or for the philanthropic endeavors upon which he spent so much of it, would not have even remotely occurred to her great-grandfather.

Curiosity Shop □ It is arguable that every man has his price, as the cynical claim, but certain that there is a price at which every man balks.

Small-claims court in Chicago. A chaotic scene in a dim room. A man with a lawyer in tow is here to collect an $80 business debt from another man, whom he had earlier served with a subpoena at his, the latter man's, expensive address. This is their second appearance in court, the case having previously been granted a continuance. Two mornings away from work, the lawyer's fee, the cost of having a subpoena served, all rather expensive to get back $80. The judge, a black, finds on behalf of the plaintiff. The defendant has to pay over the $80. When the judgment is rendered, the plaintiff announces, "Your honor, I'd like to donate this money to the United Negro College Fund," and strides triumphantly from the room. It was, he maintains, the goddamn principle of the thing.

A sum of $35 is owed, a simple error in bookkeeping, which can be rectified by a telephone call. But is it worth making the telephone call to collect the money? He is not a mean man but a neurotically nervous one. There will be his little misfired quips to hear; false jollity will be required in response to them. The pretense of a friendship that doesn't actually exist will have to be upheld. The usual hypocrisies will have to be observed: How's the wife? How's business? No, it is not worth calling him. Very well, but for how much money would it be worthwhile to call him? Not less than $50. No, it is clearly not worth less than $50 to make that phone call. Definitely not worth calling for $35.

It's not the principle of the thing; it's the amount of money involved.

"Let me tell you about the very rich," said F. Scott Fitzgerald in an often quoted remark. "They are different from you and me." Hemingway, in an equally famous riposte, is said to have replied, "Yes, they have more money." With this rejoinder Hemingway is usually conceded to have won the day, earthy common sense winning out over naïveté. But it is evident that Hemingway was quite wrong; and the reasons that he was wrong can perhaps be adduced to explain why he was in some ways a lesser novelist than Fitzgerald. Hemingway had not, if this response be taken as representative of his imaginative sense of the way society works, the least inkling of the transformative power of money on character and human relationships.

A brief anecdote told by Heine is instructive. Heine was a friend to James Rothschild, of the House of Rothschild in Paris, and took an inordinate pleasure, "as a philosopher," in viewing the reactions of others to Rothschild's wealth. He especially enjoyed doing so from the vantage point of Rothschild's offices, where "I can observe how people bow and scrape before him. It is a contortion of the spine which the finest acrobat would find difficult to imitate. I saw men double up as if they had touched a Voltaic battery when they approached the Baron." Heine's best moment in this connection, though, came when he "saw a gold-laced lackey bringing the baronial chamber pot along the corridor. Some speculator from the Bourse, who was passing, reverently lifted his hat to the impressive vessel."

If not everyone is ready to tip his hat to a Rothschild chamber pot, many are prepared to go nearly as far in their reverence for money. Fortune hunters, for example, stand prepared to overcome physical repugnance for money. Others muffle their true opinions in the presence of money—chiefly in the hope of acquiring money of their own. Money can call forth subservience to the point of groveling and beyond. Money can command attention where true merit goes unannounced. Money can buy a great deal of a nonmaterial kind, including respect, love, obeisance, and hatred. Envy over money brings to the fore a gallimaufry of associated emotions, among them feigned disdain. Gibbon relates: "But it is always easy, as well as agreeable, for the inferior ranks of mankind to claim a merit from the contempt of that pomp and pleasure which fortune has placed beyond their reach."

As for those not so placed, money can have the most extraordinary effects on personality. The possession of that "mysterious entity," money, notes the novelist Anthony Powell, "can become as much part of someone as the nose on the face." The adjectival phrase "rich-looking" has entered the language, used not alone in advertisements in *Vogue* and *Town & Country*. Novelists write of "the creamy cheeks" of the rich, men and women alike. "One can never be too rich or too thin," Babe Paley, the late wife of the chairman of the board of CBS once announced. Money can lend a glow, not solely purchasable at Elizabeth Arden. Money can carry different, and quite special, looks that extend beyond the matter of habiliments and grooming: the pinched look of the wary rich; the ebullient look of fresh opulence; the confident look backed up by solid assets; the wretched look of having paid too high a price for one's winnings. All of these are brought about by the special dispensation of money—and they are different from those of people without money.

The story of men and women and money is many-tiered. On one level there is the struggle to acquire it; on another, there is the struggle to hold on to it. Meanwhile there is the interior drama involving the effects on character of these other two struggles. "Hanging on to money is hard, of course," reports Saul Bellow in *Humboldt's Gift*. "It's like clutching an ice cube. And you can't just make it and then live easy. There's no such

thing.... When you get money you go through a metamorpho-
sis. And you have to contend with terrific powers inside and out."

"It's only money," an old saying has it, and perhaps none
was ever more false. Money is a universal incitement: to acts
good and bad, grand and trivial. Money, said Gertrude Stein, is
funny. Its possession in abundance can enervate or enliven natural energies. Lord Keynes thought the love of money "a somewhat disgusting morbidity, one of those semi-criminal, semi-
pathological propensities which one hands over with a shudder
to the specialists in mental disease." Keynes wished to distinguish the love of money as a possession from the love of money
for "the enjoyments and realities of life." But the distinction is
not always so readily drawn. Keynes himself had an unflagging
appetite for the enjoyments of life, which, as an astute player in
the stock market, he was able to make accessible to himself in
amplitude. He spoke then, as they say at the racetrack, as one
who was "holding." But what might be the "realities of life"
mentioned by Keynes? One supposes them to be love, art, truth,
and beauty. Yet is not money, in ways direct and devious, entangled with each of these? Might not money itself, such is its
pervasive influence, qualify as yet another of life's realities?

Yet such has been the reality of money that most utopian
visions begin by dispensing with it altogether. Oscar Wilde, in
"The Soul of Man Under Socialism," dreamed of a time when,
without money and its invidious social divisions, the soul of man
"will be a marvellous thing.... It will have wisdom. Its value
will not be measured by material things. It will have nothing.
And yet it will have everything, and whatever one takes from it,
it will still have, so rich will it be." Norman O. Brown, in *Life
Against Death*, holds the acquisition of money to be a positive
perversion, for at the root of the need to have money he finds the
compulsion to work:

> This compulsion to work subordinates man to things.... It
> reduces the drives of the human being to greed and competi-
> tion (aggression and possessiveness) . . . the desire for
> money takes the place of all genuinely human needs. Thus
> the apparent accumulation of wealth is really the impover-

ishment of human nature, and its appropriate morality is the renunciation of human nature and desires—asceticism. The effect is to substitute an abstraction, *Homo economicus*, for the concrete totality of human nature, and thus to dehumanize human nature.

Visions such as Wilde's and Brown's no longer command the appeal they once did. In part, this is owing to the unencouraging examples of socialism now extant. Wilde's and Brown's visions are of a socialism for artists and a socialism for the psyche. But fresh definitions of socialism, as Jean-François Revel has put it, are not what is needed; fresh *examples* of socialism are. The Wildean socialist utopia seems a fit place only for artists, or at least a certain kind of artist, but for few others. Brown's moneyless utopia is a sexier affair. Freed from a money economy, from the compulsion to work, mankind will be free—to do what? Give vent to its full human nature, frolic in the sun, draw beautiful pictures, engage in polymorphous sex.

For better or worse, money is an inducement to human industry. Without it perhaps much scheming, unsocial aggressive behavior, and artificial distinctions would disappear, but so would most good works, many conveniences, and much art. The tendency of the very rich businessman, from the merchant Medicis through the mining Guggenheims, to become patrons of the arts is to the point. It is as if such men knew that the treasures they have shored up in their lifetimes are transient, ephemeral, and that if they are to leave a niche it will have to be through something more durable—art and philanthropy. Whether they do this out of bad conscience or out of an urge to gain immortality is beside the point. The hospitals and museums and foundations stand.

As for the artificial distinctions that money brings, whatever may be said against them—and much has been said, accurately and devastatingly—they are nonetheless in the end more merciful than any other arrangement one can think of. If life is a game, money is one way of keeping score. Fortunately, it is not the only way. If one chooses to teach, for example, behind such a decision is the tacit assumption that one has agreed to forfeit the more opulent material pleasures for the pleasures of the mind: indulging one's intellectual curiosities, writing out one's opinions, having the leisure to follow the mind's wanderings. Something similar holds true for artists of various kinds, who, with luck, might also strike it rich. Other professions offer similar trades: politics, social work, scientific research. If they bring in less money, they bring in greater prestige—and the added psychic benefit of feeling oneself removed by conscious decision from the fray. Exhilarating though it may be, moneymaking is not the only game in town.

Men and women who make a great deal of money are, it is now better understood, not necessarily the most intelligent people. They are merely the most intelligent at making money, which is a special and distinctive kind of intelligence that does not automatically carry over to other aspects of life. Drive and prescience, with an admixture of luck, all concentrated on accumulation are what allow them to win through. For those who do win through, certain freedoms and distinctions can become available. Often enough, it is true, they are unable to avail themselves of these freedoms—the habit of concentration upon moneymaking, once formed, appears not easily broken, enduring long after any reasonable need. ("Exclusive concentration on the acquisition of wealth," Edward Shils has written, "is baseness.") And such distinctions as they accrue—easier entrance to better schools for their children, say, or clubs for themselves—are deplorable only to the extent that these are closed off to the less-than-rich. Although they are being gradually ameliorated, these distinctions remain. But the question is, under what other system would distinctions of this kind be lessened? To make social distinctions by intelligence, for example, would be much crueler. Money, after all, regularly changes hands; new money is always arising, old money petering out. Unlike intelligence, which is often an inheritable and hence permanent possession, money, except in unusual cases, is ephemeral. In a recent survey of the new rich, *Time* magazine notes that a high proportion come from poor families.

Puzzling inequalities in income do endure, and will doubtless continue. Income in the United States remains top-heavy and bottom-light: as of 1975, the best-paid fifth of the population earned 43.4 percent of all income, while the lowest fifth earned only 4.3 percent. A man gets $250,000 a year for reading the news over television; another, a lawyer, earns more than $4 million for winning a class-action suit; yet another (Marlon Brando, to be specific) earns $2.25 million for twelve days' acting in a movie. One could throw in the towering earnings of a Muhammad Ali, a Johnny Carson, a Henry Kissinger, to make such inequalities seem even more extravagant. Other income figures seem quite fair. One might wish to put the best possible face on this by arguing, for example, that Marlon Brando's $2.25 million for twelve days' work represents a good share of the money unearned by all the actors who, for whatever reasons, are standing in unemployment lines. But it won't quite wash. It would be marvelously convenient if people were paid salaries commensurate with the importance of their work to society. (Arguments about this would be endless.) Economic justice, where it exists, is very rough justice indeed. Possibly the best that can be hoped is that the edge of economic injustice does not cut deep against any single group. The former basketball player Oscar Robertson, asked by a congressional investigating committee whether he thought he was worth the high annual salary he was paid, answered, fittingly enough, that the man who paid it to him must have figured he was, else he would not be getting it.

Meanwhile, disparagement of money continues, with the usual contradictions in full force. Evidence of hypocrisy is, as usual, not wanting: authors of books deploring affluence who regularly call their editors for up-to-the-minute royalty statements; Marxist professors with two Volvos in the driveways of their summer homes. *Esquire,* whose pages spill over with advertisements for cars, clothes, travel, and other worldly treasure, runs an article on the pleasures of downward mobility. In England the magazine *New Society* ran a survey that discovered little interest among respondents in becoming rich; most people queried felt they wished to work only as much as they needed to have a pleasant life. Neither Americans nor Englishmen seem any less materialist than formerly; yet both seem to be undergoing something of a small revolution of falling expectations.

Is there, then, finally a correct attitude about money? Apart from a measured realism, knowing what it can buy and what it cannot, what its influence is on people who have it and on people who do not, perhaps no useful detailed advice is possible. Yet William Faulkner offered useful general advice. In *The Mansion*, the last of the novels in his Snopes trilogy, Faulkner's narrator, a Mississippi sewing-machine salesman on a trip to New York, has ordered two neckties that he does not realize sell for $75 apiece. Having ordered them, he insists upon paying for them, although the woman who owns the shop refuses his money. He, in turn, refuses to accept the ties for nothing.

"So," she says, "You cannot accept the ties, and I cannot accept the money. Good. We do this—" There was a thing on the desk that looked like a cream pitcher until she snapped it open and it was a cigarette lighter. "We burn it then, half for you, half for me—" until I says,

"Wait! Wait!" and she stopped. "No," I says, "no. Not burn money," and she says,

"Why not?" and us looking at each other, her hand holding the lit lighter and both our hands on the money.

"Because it's money," I says. "Somebody somewhere at some time went to—went through—I mean, money stands for too much hurt and grief somewhere to somebody that jest the money wasn't never worth—I mean, that aint what I mean . . ." and she says,

"I know exactly what you mean. Only the gauche, the illiterate, the frightened and the pastless destroy money. You will keep it then. You will take it back to—how you say?"

"Mississippi," I says.

"Mississippi. Where is one who, not needs: who cares about so base as needs? Who wants something that costs one hundred fifty dollar—a hat, a picture, a book, a jewel for the ear; something never never never anyhow just to eat—but believes he—she—will never have it, has even long ago given up, not the dream but the hope— This time do you know what I mean?"

"I know exactly what you mean because you jest said it," I says.

"Then kiss me," she says. And that night me and Lawyer went up to Saratoga.

Curiosity Shop □ For more than a decade they appeared each Sunday evening, dressed to the nines and prepared to play their game. The men were in dinner clothes, the women often in gowns, usually bejeweled. The moderator, also in dinner clothes, was suavity itself: cosmopolitan, carefully accented, slightly effeminate. Dorothy and Bennett, Arlene and John, the moderator, and a guest filling out the fourth place on the panel, sometimes Steve but almost as often Martin, who was Arlene's husband.

Oh, they had their little jokes, especially Bennett, who specialized in puns. You know how it is with puns, the worse the better. Everyone would moan and then smile. Bennett was intractable: a man in his sixties, a famous publisher, with the mischievousness of an eight-year-old boy. These puns sometimes threatened to get out of hand, but John, a stern parent, kept Bennett well in control.

Dorothy was something else again. She was tight-lipped and stiff-necked and more than a little humorless. The camera never panned over to her when Bennett committed his puns; she may, for all we know, have registered a look of disgust, as if asked to pick up a dead and hairy rat. She was a columnist, Dorothy was, and not noted for dispensing mercy. People had clearly been coming to her, not the other way round, and for a long time.

The game was to guess odd occupations. They would discover what everyone else's line was. Every Sunday night for years they did it. It would be quite a moment when, after they had either guessed or been stumped by one of the guests with a zany occupation (a tattooed man, say, or a hula-hoop salesman, or a manufacturer of toupees), the guest passed before the panel to shake hands with each of the panelists before leaving to resume his rightful obscurity. Best of all was the mystery guest, who was someone well known and usually from show business. When the mystery guest came on, the panelists wore masks of the kind worn at balls at the court of the Sun King but with the eyeholes covered. When he or she was revealed, the mystery guest was usually on first-name terms with the panel. Kisses and hugs and handclasps all round. Even Dorothy proffered her cheek.

As they asked their various questions, made their jokes and puns, chattered their chatter, it became clear how isolated and padded in silk their lives were. Their least intonation spoke to the assumption that everyone had weekend homes, friends in show business, a quarter of a million or so a year in income. Had they ever had a bad meal? Was any door ever closed to them? Did they know any of the common griefs? Of course they must have, but it all seemed unlikely that they had. Unlikely, too, does it seem that they could have known that they were despised by a large portion of their audience—that great numbers of people turned on the show to fume at their frivolousness. The part they played, although they could scarcely have been aware of it, was that of the idiot rich. They performed in this role something of a public service, for one of the oldest and most enjoyable sports in a democracy is taking ample note of the stupidity of the rich.

The True Believer

He spoke with something of a stammer, which psychologists used to say was a certain sign of not-so-secret rage or a hidden injury incurred in childhood. In his own lifetime he stirred a not-at-all-secret rage in thousands and many claimed open injury from his publications. Henry Luce—mere mention of his name could explode a room into divisiveness. He was one of those subjects about which it was impossible to be neutral. Gardner Cowles, of Cowles Communications, said of him: "Henry Luce was a true journalistic genius." Norman Mailer thought Luce's mind no less than exquisitely and subtly totalitarian. By no means striking the golden mean, for which he was never noted, Henry Luce said of himself: "I am a Protestant, a Republican, and a free-enterpriser, which means I am biased in favor of God, Eisenhower, and the stockholders of Time, Inc.—and if anyone who objects doesn't know this by now, why the hell are they still spending thirty-five cents for the magazine!"

For a man who had made room for himself at the top so early—Henry Luce was a self-made millionaire at thirty—and who managed to stay at the top so long, Luce showed little in the way of personal presence. Nothing of the magical "chemism" that Dreiser spoke of, that concentrated magnetism that clung to men of power, adhered to Luce. Blue-eyed, beetle-browed, and balding, as *Time*, the magazine in his publishing empire fondest of alliteration, might have put it, Luce had an oral delivery that was machine-gun-like in its rapidity. His public appearances, which were many, were generally disappointing: his official utterances lacked the vibrant flashiness associated with his magazines; his writings, when not banal, were dull and tended toward the pompous. People could be found who had seen him smile but few ever heard him laugh. "Shy and guarded" is how he was often described—but with an iron will to power. He was for the most part content to wield the spotlight rather than bask in it. In American magazine publishing, he was the nation's first and possibly last towering figure.

Henry Luce was born in 1898, in Tengchow, China, where his parents were missionaries at the Presbyterian mission compound, ardently bringing word of Jesus Christ to the heathen Chinese. In preparation for the Hotchkiss School in America, Henry was put to a year at the Chefoo School in China, modeled after English public schools in its employment of birching, caning, and fagging. At Hotchkiss, where he prepped for Yale, he edited the school's literary monthly; there, too, he met Briton Hadden, later to be, along with himself, co-founder of *Time*. At Yale he contributed stories, poems, and essays to the *Literary Magazine;* he became editor of the *Yale Daily News.* He ended up Phi Beta Kappa and in his senior year was tapped for Skull and Bones, the most revered of the school's secret societies. After a brief stint in the army—he was not called upon to serve overseas—he returned to Yale, graduating in the class of 1920. He next spent a year at Oxford reading history, thence plunged into the workaday world of journalism, first on the old *Chicago News*, then, with his friend Briton Hadden, on the *Baltimore News*.

In 1922, having managed through loans to scrape up $86,000 between them, Luce and Hadden quit the newspaper business for good, and set out to bring to fruition an idea they shared for a weekly newsmagazine that they hoped would be peppery and entertaining and, as they dreamed, indispensable in a country that had no real national newspaper. At first they planned to call the magazine *Fact* but then decided instead on *Time*. The first issue appeared on March 3, 1923. Much of the copy for the early numbers they wrote themselves. They cut economic corners wherever possible—Hadden for the most part handled editorial chores, Luce took responsibility for the business side—weathered stormy financial days, and watched circulation rise until, in 1927, *Time* went into the black. As a parodist was later to write, with *Time*'s then famous inverted syntax as his target, "Where it will all end, knows God."

Briton Hadden died of a streptococcus infection in 1929, but under Henry Luce, Time Incorporated was fated to go a very long way indeed. Under Luce, *Time* begat *Fortune* (which originally was to be called *Power*), the two begat *Life*, and other offspring followed in fairly orderly progression: *Architectural Forum*, "The March of Time" newsreels, *House & Home*, *Sports Illustrated*, Time-Life Books, et al. At Henry Luce's death in 1967, Time, Inc.'s four major magazines—*Time, Life, Fortune, Sports Illustrated*—in their national and international editions printed more than 14 million copies. The corporation's revenue was $503 million; its net earnings, $37.3 million. The market value of its 6.9 million shares of stock was $690 million, of which Luce, as the largest single shareholder, owned 16.2 percent, at a market value of $109,862,500. Time, Inc. had, moreover, diversified admirably. According to *The New York*

Times, the impressive rate of the appreciation of the stock's market value "is a measure of the success and profitability of the company's magazines, its expansion into other businesses, such as book publishing, radio and television broadcasting, pulp and paper manufacturing, and a variety of other interests, including developments in the graphic arts, information storage and retrieval, and marketing information." This growth, these financial figures, were an accomplishment Henry Luce brought off almost singlehanded. A public corporation, Time, Inc. was a highly private concern: a near perfect reflection, in both its virtues and vices, of Henry Luce himself.

Henry Luce was a most astute businessman. But he was also a journalist and a self-confessed propagandist. The three roles—businessman, journalist, propagandist—meshed nicely, in his view, and together the three conjoined to make of Henry Luce one of the most powerful men of his time. Part of the secret of his success was an absence of cynicism. He believed in everything he did: he believed in business, he believed in his magazines, he believed not only in America but also that he knew what was best for it. All this was reinforced by an unshakable belief in God, with a humility that did not preclude the belief that God was on Henry Luce's side.

Although a religious man, Henry Luce was not in the least a contemplative or reflective one. He chain-smoked; he filled up the rare open half-hour toward the end of his life with work on jigsaw puzzles. *"Life* Goes to a Party" used to be a regular feature of his prodigious enterprise in photojournalism, but there was little of the party spirit in the boss. In his spasmlike notes to employees, usually *Time* bureau chiefs in cities he was about to visit, he would instruct: "Arrange small dinner party, interesting people." Why he required interesting people is something of a puzzle, for, from most reports, he was a monologist, who tended to lecture his guests; an autocrat of the dinner table. When he took up bridge, he had the great expert Charles Goren, then a columnist for *Sports Illustrated,* teach him the game. Because he was a duffer of a golfer, at the course he regularly played in quasi retirement in Arizona, the traps were filled in especially for him with hard-packed sand, so furious would he

become with frustration when attempting to thwack his way out
of the traditional soft sand.

No one could accuse Henry Luce of thinking small. One of
the items on his agenda was to reverse the communist revolution
in China. He had a special attachment to the country in which he
was born, and to which his parents had devoted the better part
of their lives—to the country and to Madame and Chiang Kai-
shek. He, Luce, had been the driving force in founding the
United China Relief in America, which had not only funneled a
great deal of money into China but into the China lobby in
Congress. In the pages of his magazine, no wavering on the line
of China was tolerated. The line was: Chiang was heroic, and our
man; Mao devilish, and our enemy. The former's return to the
Mainland was inevitable. Whoever thought Luce in the pay of
Chiang Kai-shek had only to visit Formosa when Luce did to
wonder if he had not gotten things the wrong way round. Pomp
of the most splendiferous kind greeted Luce at the airport; state
dinners fit for visiting royalty were held; the toast between the
old friends was, invariably, "Back to the Mainland!" Chiang's
inability to bring off the great revanchist coup was one of the
few—though assuredly one of the major—disappointments in
Luce's life.

"I like Luce," John F. Kennedy remarked after a lunch with
him and his editors in New York. "He is like a cricket, always
chirping away. After all, he made a lot of money through his own
enterprise so he naturally thinks that individual enterprise can
do everything. I don't mind people like that. They have earned
the right to talk that way. After all, that's the atmosphere in
which I grew up. My father is the same way. But what I cannot
stand are all the people around Luce who automatically agree
with everything he has to say."

Did Luce know he was feared and even hated by many
among his employees? He must have known. The number of
writers and intellectuals who worked for Henry Luce's magazines over the years, at large salaries, was myriad: Edmund
Wilson once declared that, because of this, Luce was one of "the
two great enemies of literary talent of our time" (Hollywood was
the other). But then Luce never seduced these writers into work-

ing for him. They came for the money, and after they left, he
could usually count upon their ingratitude, which was generally
made public. They would write novels in which he, in fictionalized
form, was put upon the rack of excoriation, or they would score
a point against him in their memoirs. But while on the payroll
they agreed with him, hewed the current line with only brief
demurrers, and he, so seldom did he meet with it, was frankly
startled by disagreement. The extent to which Luce was hurt by
this is not known. When it came to the crunch, he would tell them
who was boss—as if anyone could harbor serious doubt about
it—yet he was not personally able to fire anyone himself. He
would kick them upstairs, or have someone else do the firing, or
put them to planning another project that he was not altogether
in earnest in expecting to come to fruition. T. S. Matthews, who
was the managing editor of *Time* for so many years, when he
became politically and editorially troublesome, was sent to London to plan a new Luce magazine in England, which never came
off. Why did you keep me so long on tiptoe, Matthews at one
point wired Luce, if you were not going to kiss me? Yet the
wonder is why Henry Luce didn't fire such men flat out.

Another wonder is why they stayed on—many of them, like
Matthews, for a quarter century or more. For some it was the
money, for some the glamour, but for many what kept them
going was the feel of power—even toward ends they did not
particularly believe in. In the United States alone Luce's magazines were said to have been read by as many as 50 million
people. Robert Hutchins, who went to Yale at the time that Luce
did, once noted: "Mr. Luce and his magazines have more effect
on the American character than the whole educational system
put together." Abroad, at the height of his power during the
years of the Eisenhower administration, Luce's magazines were
felt to be, in effect, the house organs of the United States government; and Henry Luce, in foreign countries friendly to America, was treated as something akin to a minister without port-
folio. The distinction between Luce's publications and the United
States itself was never blurrier than in 1959, when, enraged by
a story about Bolivia in *Time*, 10,000 Bolivians stoned the
American Embassy in La Paz.

In the United States, Luce drew more fire than perhaps any other American of his time; and surely more than any American who did not hold public office. Herblock, the political cartoonist, said of *Time* that it was "yesterday's newspaper and today's garbage homogenized into a single package." Jacques Barzun called *Time* "misinformation trimmed with insult." Almost an entire issue of a short-lived magazine called *Fact* was given over to invective against Henry Luce and his magazines. After Luce died, his biography was written, chillingly, by W. A. Swanberg who detested his politics, and hence Luce himself. Luce was a great grey eminence whom everyone, with a tar brush in hand, painted black.

The problem—as well as the reason behind Henry Luce's success—was one of belief. Other great press lords—Hearst, Beaverbrook, in our own day Rupert Murdoch—believed in making money, and if it took a roll in the gutter (or, more precisely, the gutter press) they were not in principle opposed. But Luce believed absolutely in what he did. His magazines were an extension of his interests, politics, personal philosophy, religion—himself. Somehow it all finely meshed in his mind. His publications —and *Time*, the keystone magazine, especially—were to be entertaining yet instructive, lively yet in earnest, moneymaking yet missionary, products yet profound. Success and virtue and business acumen and right thinking and the national purpose were all of a piece to him. "Impartiality," he held, "is often an impediment to truth." And again: *"Time* will not allow the stuffed dummy of impartiality to stand in the way of telling the truth as it sees it."

Such views earned him many enemies. Among the left in American political life he was uniformly viewed as evil incarnate, the journalistic equivalent of, say, the CIA or the FBI. Yet politically he had his own rightward limits: he came out fairly early against the depredations of Senator Joseph R. McCarthy and he could not bring himself to support Senator Barry Goldwater for the presidency in 1964, even though his wife, the actress, playwright, congresswoman, and later ambassador to Italy, Clare Boothe Luce, was solidly in the Goldwater camp. Dwight David Eisenhower was the great figure in Luce's own political pantheon, and another of the great disappointments of his life was not being asked to serve in the Eisenhower Cabinet.

Luce and his magazines were inextricably one. In the public view he was his magazines—a view he would not himself have argued against. When he had a heart attack in 1958, for example, it was reported as influenza that had developed into pneumonia, for he feared that news of his own fragility might lower the price of Time, Inc. stock. Of the upper-middle class himself, through his magazines he had for years guided the middle and upper-middle classes in America, instructing them on how to think and what to do. In the 1920s and 1930s the great American magazine was the *Saturday Evening Post*—great in the sense of being influential, of seeming to speak for, while incorporating, the values of the mainstream of national life—but in the 1940s and 1950s it was, in combination, *Time* and *Life*. After Henry Luce was dead, his corporation's book division would bring out books, plucked from the files of *Life* magazine, with such titles as *Life Goes to the Movies* and *Life Goes to War*. For *Life* one could substitute the word *America* and for America, in turn, one could substitute the name Henry Luce. "No one man," the German newsmagazine *Der Spiegel*, itself a rough copy of *Time*, noted in 1961, "has, over the last two decades, more incisively shaped the image of America as seen by the rest of the world, and the American image of the world, than *Time* and *Life* editor Henry Robinson Luce."

Henry Luce died in a hospital bed, of a coronary occlusion, on February 28, 1967. His last years were not his best. Not that, for all his triumphs, he had ever been notably happy. But now his dream of the American Century, as he entitled a slim volume he wrote prophesying that the twentieth century was to mark the emergence and supremacy of America as a civilization, had begun to go sour—to the point where even he, who tended to see in history an enactment of his own desires and opinions, could not fail to have noticed it. His dream of his friend Chiang Kai-shek one day returning to the Mainland had shriveled to hollow wistfulness. The country was rent by protest, college campuses had gone berserk, his own reporters had outraged him with their reporting of the war in Vietnam, everything he had preached upon and propagandized about and prayed for now was in doubt, if not actively ridiculed. He kept up his old round of busyness: traveling about, grilling as always *Time* bureau chiefs in each city he visited, having attentions lavished upon him, chain-smoking, golfing, the full agenda. But it could not have been quite the same. The world was not going his way.

In the end, judging his own accomplishments, Henry Luce fell back upon the standards of profit and public opinion. "All our publications, all our activities are successful," he told his assembled editors. "They are successful not only at the box office, but they are successful also in the opinion of a large part of mankind. This is a considerable consolation for our efforts over the years." *Consolation* is an interesting word to appear in such a summing up, especially from a man for whom irony was not a habitual mode. Consolation, perhaps, for disappointments, for efforts that had not brought about desired ends.

The week he died Henry Luce's picture appeared between the red borders of his own *Time* magazine. But since his death, *Life* went under, to return as a pale version of its old self as a monthly, and *Time* has changed its political tone and point of view to the extent that it is no longer recognizably Luce's own. Were Luce able to read *Time* in its current incarnation, he would doubtless spin in his grave. He would not have mistaken the fact that no one is left to carry on the mission that he had devoted his life to. The result has been to make Henry Luce seem smaller in death with each passing year. Like the emperor Ozymandias of Shelley's poem, Luce might have had engraved on his modest four-foot tombstone, in the small cemetery attended by Trappist monks in Mepkin, South Carolina, where he owned a 7,200-acre estate, *"Look on my works, ye Mighty, and despair!"*

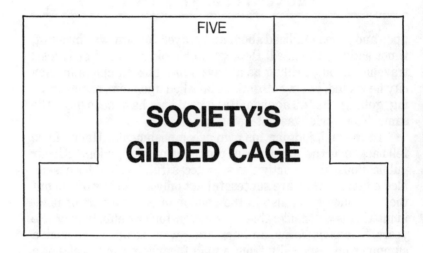

FIVE

SOCIETY'S GILDED CAGE

Edith Wharton

Edith Wharton entered the world with every possible advantage
—breeding, money, a secure place in the inner circle of New
York society—except encouragement from her family in her
chosen career of writer; and this, too, she would later decide, was
an advantage. She was born, in 1862, Edith Jones. The Joneses
were major stockholders in the Chemical Bank and owned many
blocks of real estate in New York. Her ancestors were mainly
merchant shipowners, of Dutch and British middle-class families. Her mother was a Rhinelander; and her mother's sisters
married Newbolds and Skinners and Edgars; earlier generations
of Rhinelander girls had married Schermerhorns and Gallatins.
If the family had bothered to form a cousins club, this cousinage
would have had to be called Society.

George Frederic Jones, Edith's father, did not work but
lived off income derived from real estate. He served on this board
and that commission. Along with their cousins, the Joneses did
charitable works. The family and its social circle, the closest
thing to an aristocracy nineteenth-century America would ever
know, were upstanding, virtue-minded, correct. At twelve years
old, Edith, already feeling the stirrings of the incipient writer,
showed her mother a story she was working on, which began,
" 'Oh, how do you do, Mrs. Brown,' said Mrs. Tomkins. 'If only

I had known you were going to call I should have tidied up the drawing room.' " Her mother handed back the story, remarking icily, "Drawing rooms are always tidy."

"Authorship," Edith Wharton recalled, in the view of the social set of her youth and young womanhood "was still regarded as something between a black art and a form of manual labor." It was not, clearly, a thing to be encouraged, especially in a young lady. Even years after she had become an established writer, few people in her family or among her old New York friends ever mentioned her books. Literature was too closely associated with bohemianism; Herman Melville, a cousin of the Van Rensselaers, was ruled out, for example, and as a girl Edith never heard his name or books mentioned. Yet thinking it through over the years Edith Wharton concluded that she was "no believer in pampered vocations," having seen too many young people of artistic temperament, whose families coddled them, go stale and grow ineffectual in maturity, while "more and more of the baffled, the denied or the ignored . . . have fought their way to achievement." In her own instance, she felt that the drawbacks of her family's indifference were outweighed by the advantages. Early flattery, local celebrity, having her way made smooth from the cradle—none of this in the end, she concluded, would have made her a better writer.

No very cogent case can be made for Edith Jones as a poor little rich girl. Her advantages were very real, and she herself never gainsaid them. She was brought up in an atmosphere of probity, and among people who, however chary they may have been about living writers, nonetheless respected education and good manners. Good food was a tradition; so was European travel. Unliterary though the family might otherwise be, they had a reverence for the English language, and used it precisely. "One was polite," Edith wrote, "considerate of others, careful of the accepted formulas, because such were the principles of the well-bred." The other side of this polished and valuable coin was a fear of innovation and a dread of public responsibility: none of the men in the family circle considered entering national or state, let alone city, politics.

"A little world so well-ordered and well-to-do does not often produce eagles or fanatics," Edith Wharton noted. Especially, one might add, among its women. This self-enclosed world was hard enough on its men, in the sense of delimiting their possibilities. Edith felt about her own father that he was a lonely man, "haunted by something always unexpressed and unattained." Cultivated many of these men were, and capable into the bargain; yet few among them found objects worth lavishing their abilities upon. Edith's own husband-to-be, Teddy Wharton, seems to have been raised for nothing more pressing than horsemanship and the knowledge of wines. As for the women, the traditional toast, "the ladies, God bless 'em" seems to sum up their position among the families in which Edith grew up.

Yet, oddly, given all that was to follow, Edith Wharton may have been fortunate in her feminine birth. As a young girl, she was under less constraint than a young boy might have been, at least insofar as her education was concerned. Left to her own devices, she found imagination her one great device. Before she could read she began making up her own stories. Pretending to read a book, sometimes holding it upside down, she would make up a story out of its to her still incomprehensible pages. Once she had learned to read she gravitated directly to adult fare, preferring, for example, stories drawn from mythology to fairy tales. Later her education was taken in hand by governesses; from her account of it, this education was chiefly instruction in foreign languages: French, Italian, German. Traveling with her parents in Europe—she was an early cosmopolitan; between the ages of five and twenty-five, eight years of her life were lived abroad—she contracted typhoid, and as a result was not pressed to study hard. She was thought to read altogether too much as it was. She afterwards regretted that she knew no Greek or Latin. But a natural curiosity such as hers, allowed to range in her father's somewhat old-fashioned library of classics of world literature, was probably the best possible training for the novelist she was to become. Had she been a boy, the young Edith might have been thought too dreamy, not sufficiently concentrated, a time-waster who needed to be taken in hand. As a young girl, though, her intellectual development seems not to have been of great interest, and she was left to develop on her own.

The adolescent Edith Jones was notably shy, anxious, as she once put it, to please only God and her mother. She was erect in carriage and retreating in disposition. "There was in me," she later noted, "a secret retreat where I wished no one to enter, or at least no one whom I had yet encountered." Her coming out, at seventeen, at a ball at the Fifth Avenue home of Mrs. Levi Morton, she described as a sheer agony of shyness. Summers the Jones family spent at Newport, where older women paid calls upon one another and younger women shot archery and, later, played lawn tennis; and where everyone took part in the regular round of watering-place mundanities. Although Edith knew no other kind of life, she nonetheless never quite warmed to this one. General society, she would remark often, was not something she found congenial. Bashful and undemonstrative, but with her own intellectual resources, she was a young woman who felt lonely only in company.

Yet it would be a mistake to suggest that Edith Wharton was utterly at odds with her environment. She was instructed never publicly to mention money but she well knew that it could round off the rough edges of life, making possible the hundreds of small but cumulatively essential comforts and elegances she had grown up with: fine clothes, picnics in Cannes, the best hotels in Europe, chartered yachts. Nor was she opposed to her family's social conventions, including those regarding marriage. Her own engagement to an attractive young man named Harry Stevens was broken off, not—as the Newport *Daily News* reported—because of "an alleged preponderance of intellectuality on the part of the intended bride," but for intricate financial reasons having to do with the young Mr. Stevens's mother wishing to keep control of her son's trust. But the question of marrying anyone outside the Newport–New York–Boston circle was neither thinkable, nor thought of.

When Edith married Edward Robbins Wharton, a friend of one of her older brothers, it was certainly not for money. (After her father's death in 1882, she was herself in a solid financial position; and she would in time come into more money, so that by the turn of the century her regular income—apart from her literary earnings—was roughly $30,000 a year, a sum worth perhaps $200,000 in current dollars.) But was her marriage for love? Wellborn, handsome, gregarious, Teddy Wharton had his attractions. Describing her husband after his nervous breakdown, their divorce, and his death (in 1928), Edith laconically noted of him: "He was thirteen years older than myself, but the difference in age was lessened by his natural youthfulness, his good humor and gaiety, and the fact that he shared my love of animals and out-door life, and was soon to catch my travel-fever." But other things they did not share. R. W. B. Lewis, one of Edith Wharton's biographers, writes: "There is no question that the sexual side of the marriage was a disaster." The greatest barrier between them, however, was mental. Slow though the truth was in making itself evident, Edith Wharton—well read, widely curious, greatly energetic—had intellectual ambition and the talent to make good on it. Poor Teddy had neither much in the way of intellect nor any ambition whatsoever.

As for her intellectual—more specifically, literary—ambition, Edith Wharton had published a poem in *The Atlantic Monthly* and two more in the *New York World* at the age of sixteen. But then for a decade—she married at twenty-three—she published nothing. "I could not believe that a girl like myself," she wrote in a memoir, "could write anything worth reading, and my friends would certainly have agreed with me. . . . Indeed, being much less pretty than many of the girls, and less quick at the uptake than the young men, I might have suffered from an inferiority complex had such ailments been known." But they weren't, and she didn't.

Talent, especially literary talent, will show. Sometimes, to be sure, it arrives by circuitous paths. Having come into an inheritance from a deceased New York cousin, Edith bought a house in Newport. In her redoing the house with the aid of a society architect named Ogden Codman, it became clear that she, Edith, had strong ideas about interior design—ideas that Codman shared, for creating the effect of spaciousness and allowing more light into rooms. They decided to collaborate on a book setting forth these ideas. The book, entitled *The Decoration of Houses*, was rejected by one publishing firm but then accepted by Scribner's. Edith Wharton was on her way, slowly, to becoming a professional author.

A year before the publication of *The Decoration of Houses*, she had sent three poems off in the mail, one to each of the leading magazines of the day, *Scribner's, Harper's,* and the *Century.* Not knowing quite how to deal with editors, she enclosed her visiting card along with each of the poems. One day the mail brought her three letters of acceptance. "I can still see the narrow hall, the letter box out of which I fished the letters, and the flight of stairs up and down which I ran, senselessly and incessantly, in the attempt to give my excitement some muscular outlet." Soon she was sending stories off to magazines as well, and most of these, too, met with success. She was beginning to grope her way to her true vocation; storytelling was becoming her job.

While Edith Wharton had energy sufficient for several careers, increasingly the core of her life was in her writing. As her interest in writing grew and spread, absorbing more and more of her time and imagination, she herself seemed to grow stronger and stronger. She remarked in later years that she had only acquired a real personality of her own with the publication of her first book of short stories. Of her own household there was never any doubt that it was she who was the head, the person around whom all other activities were to be organized. Domestic and social duties took up some of her time, and travel remained one of her great passions, but now all days began, as she put it, "writing in bed in the early morning, as my reprehensible habit is." The daily stint in bed, her writing board propped up against her knees, became an act almost of mental hygiene; like brushing one's teeth, no day could begin without it. "I am born happy every morning," she once wrote.

In the early years of her career as a novelist—and her biographer, Lewis, notes that her sustained literary career began in earnest in the spring of 1898, when she was thirty-six —Edith suffered strains and hesitations, chiefly over the publication of her first volume of stories, and even submitted to a rest treatment at the Philadelphia hospital run by S. Weir Mitchell, famous at that time for treating nervous disorders in women. But all such disorders seemed to vanish once this book was published. Its title was *The Greater Inclination,* a proper title for Edith Wharton's own creative urgings. Over the next two and a half years she turned out stories, novels, translations, poems, travel sketches, plays, literary and dramatic criticism—and had become a woman of letters.

And yet "a woman of letters" has a slight ring of condescension. In her memoir, *A Backward Glance,* Edith Wharton writes that "the Land of Letters was henceforth to be my new country, and I gloried in my new citizenship." In the Land of Letters, at its higher reaches, gender matters not at all; one is either the real thing, an artist, or one is nothing. Edith Wharton, who operated at the highest reaches, soon proved herself the real thing: an artist to the bone. Many of her closest friends were men: among them Henry James, Paul Bourget, Howard Sturgis, Bernard Berenson, and Walter Berry (an American of her own social circle who was an early literary counselor and critic of her work). The women she was drawn to, at least until her later years, were those of independent spirit and artistic temperament, such as Violet Paget, the English writer who lived in Italy and wrote under the name Vernon Lee.

If Edith Wharton was a bluestocking, she was far from being that alone. Over her lifetime she purchased and furnished four houses, three of mansion size. She had a penchant for small dogs, Pekingese chief among them, and a dog was usually at the foot of her bed during her morning writing sessions. Gardening was an unceasing passion, and she once said that it and writing were the two pursuits that never palled. For her circle of friends she was a generous, perpetually elegant hostess. Because of her reserved manner—the straight back, the mouth clamped closed, the icy manner to strangers that was greatly owing to shyness—she was thought passionless. R. W. B. Lewis, in his biographical researches, discovered an affair she had had with an American journalist and adventurer named Morton Fullerton, which puts to rout finally all talk about Edith's coldness, indeed sexual frigidity. But the larger point is that there was nothing unfeminine about Edith Wharton; it was only that the writer predominated over the woman in her.

Literature was her religion and her sex and her family. Children, for example, seem never to have been a question in Edith Wharton's life. She had none. What Teddy Wharton's feelings on the subject might have been are not known; they cannot, in any event, have counted for much. Edith Wharton could scarcely have been said to have traveled light; on many of her various trips she brought along a secretary, two maids, a chauffeur, and at least one dog. Nicky Mariano, Bernard Berenson's friend and factotum, tells how Edith "looked after her servants with affectionate zeal and took a lively interest in their joys and sorrows." But looking after servants was one thing; looking after one's own children quite another. They were baggage heavier than she—even, one suspects, in a more loving marriage —wished to carry. Whatever else they may be, children are an impingement on freedom, and freedom was of the greatest importance to Edith Wharton.

Europe meant freedom, and she traveled there increasingly, eventually, in 1912, settling in permanently. Not only was the small circle of her dearest friends in Europe, but Europe meant extrication from American society, which, though her entrée to it was complete, she nonetheless found stultifying. In Paris, where she took up residence in an apartment at 53 rue de Varenne, she enjoyed a freedom even greater than that of the native-born French, who, as she put it, "were still enclosed in the old social pigeon holes, which they had begun to laugh at, but to which they still flew back." An additional advantage was that in even the most fashionable French society writers and literature were valued. "In Paris," Edith wrote, "no one could live without literature, and the fact that I was a professional writer, instead of frightening my fashionable friends, interested them."

Yet another symbol of Edith Wharton's love of freedom was her immediate love of the great innovation of the day, the motorcar, then still very much a toy of the rich. As soon as she drove in one, bumbling over the Campagna, clinging to her sailor hat, she determined that "as soon as I could make money enough I would buy a motor." The next year, 1904, the Whartons owned a Panhard-Levassor. A series of Mercedes, Packards, Daimlers would follow. For years to come she would show up at Lamb House, to drive Henry James about the English countryside. James would, habitually, complain about Edith Wharton's visits, her tendency to disorder his days. Yet he seems to have loved these outings. He called Edith his "Angel of Devastation."

James referred to Edith Wharton's "desolating, ravaging, burning, and destroying energy." This is hyperbolic, but could the energy that turned out nine books in eight years be truly exaggerated? These books, moreover, were not the scribblings of a rich woman amusing herself, but proved greatly successful not only critically but commercially. *The House of Mirth,* her novel of 1905, a masterful work since become an American classic, sold more than 125,000 copies during its first year of publication. Through the remainder of her life she would earn big money and spend most of it. In the midst of her maelstroms of activity, she did her work and kept her head about it. Praise seemed hardly to affect her; it was coming up to her own standards that she cared about.

Lord Kenneth Clark, in his memoirs, notes that Edith Wharton "had retained from her early days of loneliness in plutocratic New York an absolute horror of dinner-party society. On the other hand, she had also retained a dislike of bohemianism and disorder of all kinds." (In all her years in Paris she never paid a call at 27 rue des Fleurus, the home of Gertrude Stein and Alice B. Toklas.) Part of her problem socially was the very reverse of snobbery; that is, Edith Wharton tended to treat whomever she spoke with as her intellectual equal—which few people were. Her conversation, when she got going, could glitter. Henry Adams remarked that the most agreeably intelligent Americans were living in Paris, and that "Edith Wharton is almost the center of it." As for America, Edith's views about it were in perpetual flux. "The American landscape has no foreground," she wrote, "and the American mind no background." She could complain that Americans ate bananas for breakfast, or describe a hotel in Detroit as a "vile hole." Yet when Henry James, near his death in the middle of World War I, decided to become a British citizen, Edith Wharton was gravely disappointed in him. Bernard Berenson once declared that the four most American of all Americans were Henry Adams, Henry James, Edith Wharton, and himself.

In 1921 Edith Wharton would be awarded a Pulitzer Prize, but if a Nobel Prize were given for marriage, long-suffering division, perhaps it ought to have been awarded to Teddy Wharton. Being married to a serious literary artist is not often easy, and one has only to mention the names of Kate Dickens, Countess Tolstoy, and Leonard Woolf to underscore the point. Teddy Wharton belongs among them. When Edith was off with Henry James and her chauffeur on one of their motoring trips, he often traveled ahead, setting up hotel accommodations or scouting out restaurants. She let him run certain of her investments and their home in Lenox, Massachusetts. In a childlike way, Teddy Wharton admired his wife, an admiration, it appears, mingled with puzzlement. But he found himself bored, then stifled among the artists and intellectuals she mixed with. His financial dependence upon her was near complete. Life in Paris thoroughly depressed him. He began to acquire various ailments: insomnia, body pains, morbidity. One day he cashed in many of Edith's holdings and set up a mistress in an apartment in Boston. Adjudged to have flipped, he was later put in a sanatorium in Switzerland, where he was labeled manic-depressive. His comeback was never complete. In 1911 he and Edith separated; she put him on a monthly allowance of $500. In 1913, Edith Wharton divorced him, after twenty-eight years of a sad marriage. Poor Teddy had failed, but who, with a person of Edith's energy, independence, and artistic temperament, might have succeeded?

Fifty-one years old when finally divorced from her husband, Edith Wharton continued, as she would until her old age, to turn out books, buzz about galleries and country houses, acting the part of the perpetual-motion machine. Famous herself, she met on equal terms with the great artistic figures of her age: Yeats, Chaliapin, Thomas Hardy, George Meredith. She traveled through Germany with Bernard Berenson, whom she told she intended to eat the world "leaf by leaf." Not even at home in Paris did she seek repose, but was always off, dining under the trees in the Bois de Boulogne, or motoring out to Saint Cloud. But, invariably, at home or abroad, in the morning out would come the writing board.

Edith Wharton emerged from World War I as a Chevalier both of the French Legion of Honor and of the Belgian Order of Leopold. Both decorations came from her work during the war.

She saw after resettling refugees; she set up hospitals, convalescent homes, medical convoys in the field; she rescued children left homeless by the war; she raised funds to keep all these works afloat. She did all these things, moreover, not in the spirit of a rich woman giving her Tuesday afternoon to charity, but with sleeves rolled up, pitching in, full-time. She traveled to the front and wrote about it for American magazines, hoping thereby to arouse Americans, who had not yet entered the war, to its horrors and to the need for them to help bring it to an end.

When World War I was over, Edith Wharton rightly sensed that so, too, was the world she had grown up in, knew, and wrote about. Many of her friends had died in battle. Henry James had died, in his seventies, in 1916. Others of her old set—Howard Sturgis, Egerton Winthrop—died not long after the war. She was herself heading toward sixty. She began to feel that the war had so altered the world that she, as an artist, was no longer quite in touch with it in the way a novelist ought to be. She wrote to F. Scott Fitzgerald, who had earlier come to visit her: "I must represent the literary equivalent of tufted furniture and gas chandeliers." In 1920 she wrote *The Age of Innocence*, a novel set in the New York society of the 1870s in which she had come of age. Society in this book is treated quite differently from the way it is in her other fine society novel, *The House of Mirth:* it now seems somehow richer, less cruel, more layered with complexity. She had by no means let down her critical guard but at the same time there is now something wistful about old New York society in her view, a slight eulogistic note for something that, whatever its faults, also had virtues and is now passed away.

The Age of Innocence won the Pulitzer Prize for fiction in 1921. That prize marked the beginning of harvest time for Edith Wharton. Yale chipped in with an honorary degree, the first Doctor of Letters that it ever gave to a woman. She was awarded the gold medal, then membership in the National Institute of Arts and Letters, and after that in the American Academy of Arts and Letters. Her literary earnings were still high. Film rights to *The Age of Innocence* were sold. R. W. B. Lewis estimates that between 1920 and 1924 her writings brought in

nearly $250,000. She made many friends among the new genera-
tion of writers—Fitzgerald, Sinclair Lewis, Aldous Huxley, Cyril
Connolly—but felt herself distinctly a back number. In the thirties, with bolshevism in power, fascism ascendant, the Depression in full tilt, the edifice of the civilization she had known
seemed to be crumbling. "Bliss it is to be old," she wrote to a
friend. Her servants, who had long been with her, clearing the
way for her busy life for decades, had begun to grow ill. She
herself, at seventy-two, had a stroke. Yet, even with all this, she
was, as she once wrote to Bernard Berenson "an incorrigible
life-lover, life-wonderer, and adventurer." She remained an engine of art, writing till near the end of her life. She had another
stroke in the summer of 1937, and died, serenely at age seventy-
five, in the French countryside on August 11. She had been a
woman on whom nothing was lost, and she took from life all that
it had to give, leaving in return her elegant books and the lesson
that not even all the advantages in the world need crush a truly
exceptional person.

"Inequality," said William Dean Howells, "is as dear to the
American heart as liberty itself." Classless though American
society officially is, and without an established nobility of any
sort, the nation has had its social classes from the beginning, has
them now, and will doubtless have them always. In this the
United States is no different from any other society, except
perhaps in its pretensions, which have been, traditionally,
egalitarian. Joseph Schumpeter has made the point that social
class, unlike other institutions, cannot be studied from its incep-
tion—like, say, banking—for the utter absence of class has
never been discovered, neither historically nor ethnologically.

But if the United States, like every other society, has always
had a class system, it has been a class system with a pronounced
difference. Pitirim A. Sorokin has said that, "as a rule, other
conditions being equal, the longer the period of membership the
more class-minded [people] become." Other conditions are not
equal, at least in the United States, where the rule does not
apply, as Sorokin himself recognized. "For the same reason," he

writes, "in societies like that of the United States (especially in
the past), in which vertical mobility is strongly developed, the
class differentiation is bound to be less clear and effective than
in populations with weak vertical mobility." In sum, social class,
and class consciousness along with it, has played a less conspicuous role in America than in Europe, if only because in America,
such has been the fluidity of our class system, most people do
not stay in the same class long enough to develop firm class
attitudes.

Which is not to say that social class has not played an important part in American life, or that a rise in social class has not
been the target for the most various ambitions. Frequently it
has been through women, the wives of the newly arrived, that
this target has been most concentratedly set in focus; but men
have not been exempt from the ambition. Although this ambition
has had a very bad press—*social climber, parvenu, arriviste*
scarcely being terms of endearment—it need not of necessity be
an unseemly one. To start out a printer's apprentice, à la Benjamin Franklin, and end up at the court of France is not, after all,
an unpleasant journey.

The idea of Society, with a capital *S*, is necessarily a complicated one in America. Family, wealth, and talent have traditionally been the entering wedges into Society, in America as elsewhere, but in America this was complicated from the outset by
the fact that everyone was newly arrived. One cannot very well
attempt a climb if there is neither a ladder nor a window at its
end. Yet it did not take long for people in America to make claims
for their ancestors, for money to accumulate, for talent to show
itself. The rhythm of the social rise in the United States has been
for a progenitor to make his mark, through business acumen,
public service, or talent of various kinds, which allows him to
become, if he so desires or his conduct does not preclude, part
of Society. And if his children do not fall too far off the mark,
through unfortunate marriages, scandalous behavior, or simple
enervation, two or three generations later they can set out the
claim to being, in the loose American sense of the term, Aristocracy.

Much easier said than done, of course. Fame or fortune has

often enough been won by the individual, only to die with him, or to be largely spewed away by children and finished off by grandchildren. Fame and fortune fall within the compass of the individual, but Society, and thence Aristocracy, are a family affair. To ask a man and woman not only to achieve great things in their lifetimes but to be responsible as well for the achievements of their great-grandchildren is to ask a very good deal. "Many men can make a fortune," J. S. Bryan has written, "but very few can build a Family." And the dream of building a family of a kind fit for Society used once to be a fairly common dream of the ambitious. But as with other dreams of the ambitious, this one, too, seems to have dissolved.

The other side of building a family is having ancestors to look fondly back upon. Both Aristotle and Plato counseled against ancestor worship as a degraded form of living in the past, and neglecting the responsibilities of making the most of oneself in the present; but to little avail. Although the Japanese and the Chinese are most famous for ancestor worship, few societies, simple or complex, have been able to forgo it. A man as great as Cicero, because he was looked down upon as a *novus homo* by the optimates of Rome, is said never quite to have gotten over his feelings of inferiority. Chekhov, the son of a serf, spoke of the difficulty of wringing the slave out of his nature. If such quarto editions of mankind as these could feel so poignantly the absence of distinguished ancestors, lesser men can dependably be expected to fall back on ancestors, if any trace of distinction is to be found in their families. In twelfth-century Constantinople, aristocrats claimed as a badge of distinction that their ancestors had come over from Rome, in 330 A.D., with Constantine. The parallel here with America's Society of Mayflower Descendants is unmistakable. Le plus ça change . . .

To ancestor worship in the United States two new twists were added. The first is that hereditary distinction was not denoted by title; and the second was that, however remarkable some of the early settlers in this country may have been, there was little distinguished about them. Well documented is the fact that the passengers of the *Mayflower* were of generally humble origin. Of the forty-one men among them none was allowed to sign himself "Gent." Manual laborers for the greater part, these men and women had a high rate of illiteracy and precious little otherwise to recommend them in a social way. The settlers who came after, some of whom are now enshrined by descendants through such organizations as the First Families of Virginia, the Order of the Cincinnati, and the Daughters of the American Revolution, though socially of a higher order, were nonetheless, to use the derogating term, "in trade." They were the sons and grandsons of mercers and maltsters, drapers and skinners. Even the aristocracy of Charleston, oldest of the old in the United States, was, according to our best historian of Society, Dixon Wecter, "essentially mercantile, even as it is today [1937] when its Best Families sell real estate, liquor, and fertilizer." Anson Phelps Stokes reports a similar condition apropos of the early Best Families of New York: "The Bayards, Van Cortlands, Roosevelts, Livingstons, Schuylers, and Rhinelanders were the sugar-refining business. . . . Barclays, Rutgers, and Lispenards were brewers. . . . The Goelets and the Brevoorts were iron-mongers and the Schermerhorns were ship-chandlers." And so on. It is either chastising or inspiring, depending upon one's pretensions to aristocratic forebears or enthusiasm for democracy, to recall that the Reverend John Harvard, after whom the university is named, was the son of a butcher.

Pride in ancestry in the United States, then, has tended to come down to pride of place. Since everyone's family is, theoretically, equally old, precedence has tended to be accorded—or, most often, grabbed—by those with families who arrived in America first. Some few American families can point to real and continuous distinction among their families—the Adamses of Quincy, the Byrds of Virginia, the Biddles of Philadelphia, the Saltonstalls, Lowells, and Cabots of Boston. Some even fewer view the entire business with the candid good spirits that is perhaps the truest hallmark of aristocracy in America, such as Alice Roosevelt Longworth, who told the writer Cleveland Amory in 1960: "Hell's bells, the Roosevelts aren't Aristocrats at all in the sense of the word that I use it. As a matter of fact, I like the word 'patrician' better but the Roosevelt Family aren't that either. It's nonsense. The Roosevelts were Dutch peasants

who achieved burgherhood by making respectable marriages—
which few of them, I might add, have done since."

Apart from those few families who can trace true distinction in their ancestors, and aside from those who could scarcely
be less interested, the remainder who wish to claim distinguished American genealogy must, at least in part, manufacture
it. That it is largely manufactured does not make it any less
interesting. Society, as Dixon Wecter has it, "is the symbol of a
chiefly feminine achievement as impressive in its way as the
Brooklyn Bridge and the transcontinental railway." A highly
artificial construct, Society remains of interest because, for all
its artificiality, there is something quite natural about it.

Curiosity Shop □ In the men's room outside the office they
gathered. Messenger boys they were called, though "boys" was
altogether a misnomer, for none was younger than in his twenties and some looked to be in their fifties. They ran messages
around the city, from office to office, hand to hand: artwork from
an advertising agency over to a client in the business district,
uncorrected galley proof from a printer to the editorial offices of
a magazine, documents from an attorney to the trust officer of
a downtown bank.

Theirs is a rum job and they are a rum lot. Each among them
bears some patent evidence of having been dealt a bad hand in
life. One has a drooping eye and very little intelligence shining
from his good eye. Another drags a club foot upon which he
wears a vastly built-up shoe. Yet another has only part of his left
ear and on the left side of his head the hair grows in fitful
patches. Various in their defects, they are alike in their even
tenor of drabness and dispiritedness, in the sad vapors of hope-
lessness and failure they give off.

At the moment, though, they are jubilant. There in the
men's room they are jumping about and chanting: "Morris is a
dummy! Morris is a dummy! Morris is a dummy!" Morris, a
co-worker, has, it seems, delivered a package to the wrong address, and minutes before has been roundly bawled out by the
boss, who would not let him retrieve it, so angry was he, but sent

another boy in his stead. They dance around Morris, who, with his puffed-out cheeks, shapeless body, and opened mouth, has a mongoloid look. "Dummy! Dummy! Dummy!" Tears are in Morris's eyes. He says nothing and does not strike out. Instead he stares vacantly at his tormentors from under his vinyl cap, hoping it will soon be over. "Dummy! Dummy! Dummy!"

No matter how lowly the group, why is it that exclusion seems inevitably a stronger force than sympathy?

For Society the Goths are perennially at the gates—and the only question is, which select few among the many will be allowed in. In they will come, of this there can be no doubt. Some will buy their way in; some will marry their way in; some will win their way in by dint of their beauty, charm, or talent; and some will batter their way in by main force. The truth is, although the corporate entity composed of those already in might be the last to admit it, that Society needs regular replenishment by vigorous Goth blood if it is not to thin itself out too finely. Always has it been thus, and thus does it always figure to be. The story of Society is, in one of its major themes, the story of gate-crashing.

Cohesion and invasion are the thesis and antithesis of Society. A small group bound by common background, interests, and culture joins together in admirable unison. What makes it seem admirable—whether it actually is admirable is another question—is its ostensible superiority, the posture it adopts placing it implicitly above the ruck. This superiority can derive from its members' birth, or wealth, or culture. (According to an old story, the decisive question in Philadelphia was: Who was your grandfather? In Boston: How much do you know? And in New York: How much are you worth?) What the group does, the attitudes it embraces, what it comes to stand for—its artistic tastes, its sports, its addresses, the churches it attends, the schools it sends its children to—all these become emblematic of Society.

Because of Society's implicit position of superiority, whether it intends it or not, it arouses envy. Others, not yet in, want in. If cohesion be the positive principle of Society, its negative principle is exclusion. Exclusion, to those made to suffer it, stings. One way to alleviate the sting is to break past the excluding walls, and by whatever method comes to hand. Once inside one can go on to other things; or, as most who have come from outside have done when they have at last found themselves within, help shore up the walls against the next wave of invaders. And another wave will presently be at the gates—on this one can rely.

What, one might wonder, is the attraction? In the United States, Society has not been uniformly attractive to all who have been in a position to join it. John D. Rockefeller, Sr., and his wife were able to forgo it easily enough, and so, earlier, was the first John Jacob Astor, the son of a German butcher who himself originally made his money in the fur trade, and whose manners —Albert Gallatin noted that he "ate his ice cream and peas with a knife"—would in any event have made his entry difficult. Jay Gould, on the other hand, wanted in but was excluded, while the gates were opened for his children, their father's dirty money having been considered sufficiently laundered by the span of a generation, even though the Gould children, involved in multiple divorce, intrafamily litigation, and other high jinks, behaved more raucously than their father ever had. Most people, being invited in, cannot find it in themselves to turn down the invitation. Ralph Pulitzer, in a book entitled *New York Society on Parade*, has put the matter well: "While in Europe the pleasures of Society are among the prerogatives of rank, in New York [and, by extension, elsewhere] the pleasure of 'rank' is the inducement to Society."

Various definitions of Society have been offered, but perhaps the most useful is that Society is enviable people. For better or worse, it is the elite. Sometimes it, Society, truly is better: made up of the most interesting, public-minded, and cultivated people. And sometimes it is truly worse: made up nearly exclusively of bores, boors, and boobs. What makes things tricky is that, as often as not, Society is made up of both kinds of people at once; it is, simultaneously, both better and worse.

One speaks of Society, but it is more correct, in the United States, to speak of societies. With the aid of a social Geiger counter a National Society could perhaps be assembled—comparable to, say, Ward McAllister's New York Four Hundred—yet the more evident fact is that various societies have existed in the various American cities. Over its history the *Social Register*— a book founded in 1888 and always, it is worth noting, produced for profit—published nineteen separate volumes covering as many as twenty-five cities. The cities covered by a *Social Register* volume have included New York, Boston, Philadelphia, Baltimore, Chicago, Washington, D.C., St. Louis, Buffalo, Pittsburgh, San Francisco, Cleveland, Cincinnati-Dayton, Providence, Minneapolis-Saint Paul, Seattle-Portland, Pasadena-Los Angeles, Detroit, and Richmond-Charleston-Savannah-Atlanta. Gauging by *Social Register* figures, E. Digby Baltzell once estimated the numerical extent of the upper class in the United States at one-tenth of one percent of all American families. But the *Social Register*, to which one has to apply for admission, does not by any means include all that passes for Society in the United States. In a muted way, most middling-size cities have Society: their children may not go off to prep school or Ivy League colleges, their claims to distinguished descent may be less extravagant, their club memberships not so exclusive, but their fortunes may be as great, their pretensions within their own realm as high, and their exclusionary powers no less formidable than in New York, Boston, or Philadelphia.

Then there are all the different societies that have sprung up alongside mainstream Society. Catholic Society for one, since, except in Baltimore, St. Louis, New Orleans, and San Francisco, Catholics had been systematically excluded from Society. Jewish Society, for another—or, more precisely, German-Jewish Society —for Jews were similarly excluded, and even more stringently: no Jews or dogs being a commonly understood restriction at many Society resorts. Black Society, too, has long been in existence, with black cotillions and charity balls held in many of the larger American cities. Much of this discrimination has since broken down, and Society has become a more mixed affair, yet the tendency has been for those who have traditionally been excluded to form exclusive (and, in their turn, exclusionary) groups of their own. What Stephen Birmingham has called "the

Right People" turn up everywhere; and Society, in this regard, becomes largely a matter of perspective.

Curiosity Shop □ Public high school though it was, many private distinctions reigned among its students. Some were richer, some poorer; some brighter, some duller; some more beautiful, some plainer. Roughly half the students were Jews, the other half Christian; with only a small number of exceptions, all were white. In background, culture, point of view, as a group they were certainly more alike than different. Yet they had, among themselves, decided upon a number of distinctions much greater than either God or their social conditions conferred upon them. As they passed in the halls during a break between classes, these distinctions could be seen in the waves of rayon, cotton, and wool they wore, fabrics of the club and fraternity and sorority jackets into which they had, on their own, divided themselves.

These divisions were, foremost, into obvious and fairly coherent types. Some clubs and fraternities specialized in athletes among their members, others in the socially graceful, yet others in amiable jokers, and others still in tough kids, then known as hoods. Among the girls, clubs and sororities divided off into those having exclusively pretty girls, those having girls best noted for their personalities, those interested in school activities. Sometimes, though not often, a differing type strayed into an unlikely group. Of these various groupings, some were considered more desirable, of higher status, in a word "better" than others. Blackballing was the means of exclusion: kids voted on other kids, with no great scruples in the direction of mercy, to bring them in or cast them out. Undismayed, those who were blackballed from the better accepted membership in the lesser fraternities or sororities; and those who were blackballed from these lesser fraternities and sororities turned right around and formed new fraternities and sororities of their own, from which they blackballed other kids. Somehow or other there was always someone left over to be blackballed. The social ladder seemed to know no bottom rung.

Did it know a top rung? Imagine a boy or girl who had gone to this high school and who had been accepted into the best fraternity. Would he have been happy? Probably he would, at least until time to go off to college. There he would discover another ladder—or, might it be, an extension of the same ladder? —waiting. Competing in the climb with him now would be boys who had gone to private schools or prep schools of social power. If he went to a state university, there would be those who had gone to more exclusive private universities. If he went to a private university, he would have to contend with those who went to Ivy League schools. If he went to an Ivy League school, there would be those who go off to "Oxbridge" in England to consider. And so it goes—up, up, up. As the rungs get higher, they get smaller, the air grows more rarefied. The ladder of social distinction is rather like Jacob's ladder in the hymn in which Heaven is tantalizingly promised, but never, no not in this life, does one quite arrive where Jacob did.

Of the various entrées to Society in the United States, the surest passport has been the dollar. In America the distinction between plutocracy and aristocracy has always been a blurry one. While money has not been the sole criterion for entry to Society, people have been dropped, or have had to drop themselves, from Society for having too little money, while the record shows no one to have departed from it for having too much. "Boston and Philadelphia may look somewhat dubiously upon new money," Dixon Wecter reported, "yet they give short shrift to the old patrician who has gone bankrupt." The Astors, the Vanderbilts, the Whitneys, the great lions among Society families, it is well to remember, were all hugely rich. In *A Backward Glance,* Edith Wharton notes that one of her mother's inflexible rules was: "Never talk about money, and think about it as little as possible." To talk about money betrayed an absence of good breeding, but to think about it as little as possible presupposes the presence of it in plentitude.

"The mobility" is how Abigail Adams characterized the American people; and in their mobility the chief pass, with only few exceptions, has been money. It is the old story of nobs (old families) versus swells (newcomers), the gentleman versus the self-made man, antitrade versus trade. In America purses have generally been longer than pedigrees; and where pedigrees were embarrassingly short, purses could purchase them. Rise and fall has been the characteristic rhythm of Society families. The fathers struggle so that sons and grandsons may live in more elegant ease. Each new generation of the Vanderbilt family is said to have marked an advance in social quality and a slackened appetite for commerce, although its progenitor, Commodore Vanderbilt, a tobacco-chewer and a pincher of servant-girls' bottoms, left low enough standards in the former and high enough rewards from the latter to make both eminently possible. But for families of lesser fortune, the loss of interest in commerce held its perils. John Adams, progenitor of a family that did not soon lose its distinctive blend of intellect and character, wrote: "I must study politics and war that my sons may have the liberty to study mathematics and philosophy. My sons ought to study mathematics and philosophy . . . in order to give their children a right to study painting, poetry, music, architecture, statuary, tapestry and porcelain." But for the majority of American Society families Adams's passage would require rewriting so as to read: "I must engage in trade and study the stock market so that my sons may have the liberty to live in the spacious margins of leisure, breeding horses and dogs and living half the year in Europe . . . so that their sons may engage in multiple divorces, alcoholism, and other forms of self-destructive behavior."

In his chronicle *Who Killed Society?* Cleveland Amory harbors the theory that among Society families the third generation is crucial to the continuation of the family's standing. According to this theory, the family founder, the man who makes the first big money, is tough-minded, often coarse in manner as is perhaps necessary to a pioneer, and has a strong if not necessarily amiable character. Having things made easier for them by the money earned by the founding father, the second generation is generally made of less stern stuff. While the wife of the founding father is usually herself of the lower ranks, with her energies largely devoted to support of her husband and care of her family, the aspirations of the second-generation wives, themselves often women of some standing, are turned outward toward Society. Often their husbands live in dilettantish leisure; sometimes in active dissipation. Abilities and gifts corrode for having no target to fire themselves upon. (Edith Wharton and Henry James have written memorably about such men.) The third generation is thus of the utmost importance. Whether it will return to the strong character of its progenitor—reviving earlier family energy, perhaps applied now to public service or one of the learned professions rather than business—or plod farther down the path of social triviality to ultimate dissolution, with the family eventually falling into oblivion, is determined by this, the third in line of generations.

Yet the fall of some families has made possible the rise of others. Despite the precise figures sometimes bandied about, such as the social arbiter Ward McAllister's once famous Four Hundred (a figure said to derive from the number of people who could be comfortably fitted into Mrs. Astor's ballroom), Society has been fairly elastic about the numbers who can be admitted, always provided that it doesn't become so large as to lose its cachet of exclusiveness. Several are the ways in—as many as are the ways of social climbing—but chief among them has been through marriage. In *Democracy,* one of the two novels he wrote, Henry Adams remarked: "The capacity of women to make unsuitable marriages must be considered as the cornerstone of Society." More than anything else, hypergamy, or marriage to a person of superior rank, has traditionally permitted the pot of Society to keep on the boil.

Because the United States has no caste of nobility, upward mobility has tended to run from the sons of upstart families to the daughters of patrician families. In Europe, the trend had been in the other direction: social power came with the title, which only sons carried. But in the United States wealthy but socially obscure families, such as the early Vanderbilts, Astors, and Belmonts once were, got a social leg up by marrying their sons to the daughters of such older and socially prominent families as the Livingstons, Armstrongs, Schermerhorns, and Perrys. In some instances upstart families with wealth were able to buy for their daughters or granddaughters an impoverished European or English nobleman, often accompanying these nubile daughters and granddaughters abroad in what Cleveland Amory has called "the title search"; and for a time a family's rank, in New York Society, was partly measured by the eminence of its European in-laws. Whether through sons marrying patrician American women, or daughters marrying titled Europeans, purse and pedigree were in this manner wed.

As often as not the motive behind the wedding of purse and pedigree was mutual need. Purse aspires to pedigree, the one thing it cannot, flat out, buy; and pedigree, down on its funds, requires purse, if only to maintain itself after its commercial instincts have atrophied. Whatever else it is, Society is, in Dixon Wecter's phrase, "the most expensive hobby in the world." For those who have viewed their participation in Society as not a hobby but a profession, the expense is not less. Large houses, the best schools, automobiles and boats, the costliness of returning entertainment, servants, clubs, travel, keeping up with fashion (which, as someone once remarked, is generally so ugly that it needs to be changed every six months)—these things cost money, great wads of it. Although one need not have undertaken such activities on the Medici-like scale of the Astors or the Vanderbilts, even the quiet good taste of conservative society has always been immensely costly. To have climbed higher to the international set entailed shoots in Austria, the races at Ascot, leisurely weeks in Paris, winter journeys to Cannes, spacious visits to Monte Carlo—in short, high expenditure. Society, it used from time to time to be announced, was in need of new blood, but it was closer to the truth to say that what was needed were fresh injections of new money.

In at least three broad waves—in the 1780s and 1790s, in the 1840s, and in the 1880s—plutocracy, through supplying those fresh injections of money by way of marriage, made incursions upon aristocracy, the former blending with the latter, diluting it, and finally, in our time, radically altering whatever character it might once have had. There is as little point in deploring as in applauding this. The process is quite as natural—and as ineluctable—as the tides wearing down the rocks of the shore.

Curiosity Shop ▫ "Why the rich look different from you and me," the advertisement announces, twisting a line from F. Scott Fitzgerald. A slightly blurry photograph, in black and white, of an elegant woman with lush dark hair appears in the advertisement, which continues: "You cannot help but notice her. There is an aura of difference that goes beyond expensive clothing or being beautifully endowed by nature." The disappointing punch line turns out to be that the reason is our lady's skin, for the advertisement is pitching a cleansing cream. Too bad, for the question is a good one: Why do the rich look different from you and me?

Different though not always or necessarily better. Novelists write about the fine carriage of the rich; art critics and historians speak of an aristocratic face: good bones, clear eyes, a nose that does not disappoint. To be sure, there are wealthy women with bad skin; aristocratic men—Winston Churchill is a prime example—with lumpy features; and tyrants with pleasing lips. Yet, as a character in a John Marquand novel says of whomever he encounters, "I can tell whether he went to a really good boarding school or a second-rate one," so can one tell from the face of whomever one meets something of his life story up to the moment. In the faces of the wellborn and the wealthy there is frequently a lambency, a glow of something that is not light but akin to light. As grinding poverty will over the years make a face dimmer, so will sustained good fortune brighten one up. George Orwell said that at fifty a person gets the face he deserves, but he was wrong.

The handful of writers, novelists most of them, who have taken Society for their subject have tended to divide into two camps: those who viewed Society from within and those who viewed it from without. In France, Balzac, Stendhal, and Proust took Society for their subject, the latter nearly exclusively as his setting. In England, the charge used to be made against Dickens, in his novelistic ambitions the English counterpart of Balzac, that the one character he could not create in the entire range of human types was that of the gentleman. In the United States, the principal novelists concerned with Society as subject and setting were Henry James, Henry Adams, and Edith Wharton, all of whom wrote about it from within: James in its international aspect, Adams about its Washington phase during the late 1860s, Wharton chiefly reverting back to the old New York Society of her youth. In this century two Irish-Americans, F. Scott Fitzgerald and John O'Hara, wrote about Society from without, and John Marquand wrote about it from a standpoint midway between inside and outside. Contemporarily, Louis Auchincloss, in his novels and stories, has written about Society from within, while Richard Yates, in at least one of his novels, *Easter Parade*, has written about it from without. That Society appears to be disappearing as a subject for novelists is itself significant.

Different though these various writers are—in style, temperament, penetration, achievement—the stories they have to tell about Society are essentially one story. Although it has a multitude of varying strains and points of view, and may be come at from a multitude of different angles, the story is chiefly about life in a gilded cage. Sometimes the cage is built to keep the mob out; sometimes it imprisons those within. Sometimes the cage seems heaven itself; sometimes it seems nothing less than a monkey house. Rare are those spirits who can take Society for what at its best it might be: a means of enjoyment and occasional escape from work. More common are those for whom the cage of Society is an end in itself. "When it becomes the thing worked for," as a character in Wharton's *The House of Mirth* puts it, "it distorts all the relations of life."

Inside the gilded cage are the elect, outside the rabble gaping in. (Gaping but sometimes laughing, for few things are so delightful as the scandalous behavior of one's social betters—as the existence of every gossip columnist proves.) Inside life can become phantasmagorical; one can become lost in the glitter, the elegance, the forests of family trees. If order can be the reigning virtue of life in the cage, monotony can be its vice. Much there is in life that is not countenanced in the cage; many experiences are sealed off to its occupants in a style of life where decency is more highly esteemed than courage and scandal more greatly dreaded than cancer. If the cage protects from the harshness of life outside its gilded confines, the price of its protection to its inhabitants is often innocence: "The innocence," as Edith Wharton remarked in *The Age of Innocence,* "that seals the mind against imagination and the heart against experience."

In one of its fictional strains the story of Society is that of the figure poised on the edge of the cage, being pulled by opposing forces, one yanking him back to the comforts of the cage, the other yanking him forth to the larger world. In *The Age of Innocence* and in John Marquand's *H. M. Pulham, Esquire,* this is precisely the conflict; and in each instance the principal character—Newland Archer in the Wharton novel, Harry Pulham in the Marquand—is riven by the pull of family and tradition as against the pull of personal happiness with a woman who is, socially, beyond the pale. In both novels—as also in Marquand's *The Late George Apley*—the pull of tradition proves the stronger, and family ties (the bars of the cage) win out over emotional yearnings. The conflict is real, and it has to do with the question of whether one is entitled to purchase one's own happiness at the price of other people's misery. To answer the question negatively implies an acquiescence in stoicism, if not active sadness, for to put the interests of others before one's own is, in however small a way, always heroic.

Heroic, that is, if tradition has any serious meaning—if Society itself is worth protecting. It is a measure of how thin the idea of tradition in Society has worn that the selfsame decision of Wharton's Newland Archer and Marquand's Harry Pulham seems, in the former case, admirable, and, in the latter, rather pathetically empty. Edith Wharton was in every way a superior writer to John Marquand, yet, this apart, one of the chief differences between her novel and his is that in hers Society, as an entity, is more plausible as a subject. Society had quite as many frivolous and trivial and mean-spirited people in Edith Wharton's time as in John Marquand's (the publication dates of the two novels are, for Mrs. Wharton's, 1920 and, for Mr. Marquand's, 1941, although the chief action in *The Age of Innocence* is laid in the 1870s), but the idea of Society is more graspable in Edith Wharton's work because her mixture contains more interesting kinds of characters than his: more nonconformity, idiosyncrasy, differentiation within the conformity of Society generally. As a character in *H. M. Pulham, Esquire* says to Harry Pulham of another (rather cardboard) character in the novel: "He's just been taught a book of rules—nice people do this, the right people do that—and that's the trouble with polite society. They may have had brains once, but they're atrophied." Harry Pulham, at another point, remarks to himself of his own youth, and of an earlier stage in the life of Society: "Everything was simple then, and I often wish I were back in that time, because it was the time for which I was trained to live."

In the literature about Society, as in Society itself, the present is always postlapsarian. No matter what the date, it is always closing time in the gardens of Society. Newland Archer, in Wharton's *The Age of Innocence*, reflects upon a time that Harry Pulham yearns to return to: "If society chose to open its doors to vulgar women the harm was not great, though the gain was doubtful; but once it got in the way of tolerating men of obscure origin and tainted wealth the end was total disintegration—and at no distant date." In considerations of Society, it seems, yesterday was paradisiacal, today is filled with evil bodings, tomorrow brings the deluge. Writing in 1928 Edith Wharton noted: "In the Paris I knew, the Paris of twenty-five years ago, everybody would have told me that... *tout le monde* had long since come in, that all the social conventions were tottering or already demolished, and that the Faubourg [Saint-Germain] had become as promiscuous as the Fair of Neuilly. The same thing was no doubt said a hundred years earlier, and two hundred years, even, and probably something not unlike it was heard in the more exclusive *salons* of Babylon and Ur."

In Society, too, one man's meat is another's poison. Thus, what for others represented a time of grandeur for Society, the late 1860s, for Henry Adams, writing about Society in Washington, D.C., in his novel *Democracy*, was a time that presented a spectacle of laughable vulgarity. At a White House reception, the heroine of *Democracy*, Madeleine Lee, "felt a sudden conviction that this was to be the end of American society; its realization and dream at once. She groaned in spirit." In *Democracy* we have old Boston judging Washington and finding it more than

wanting. In *The House of Mirth* we have, in the person of Edith
Wharton, old New York judging new New York and finding it,
similarly, no improvement; quite the reverse. What about Society in Chicago, characterized by Dixon Wecter even at its height,
as "a paradise for parvenus"? Yet from the point of view of
social Cleveland, Chicago Society is the Faubourg Saint-Ger-
main. Then there is Los Angeles, about which Ethel Barrymore
once announced: "Los Angeles Society is anybody who went to
high school." (Notice Miss Barrymore does not say "graduated"
from high school.) So it goes, and so it was ever thus. In about
1320 Marsilius of Padua, writing about the prospect of electing
sovereigns, expressed his fear that they would have the arrogance of the *nouveaux riches*. *Nouveaux riches* in 1320—wonderful!

"They're a rotten crowd," Nick Carraway said to Jay
Gatsby. "You're worth the whole damn bunch put together." F.
Scott Fitzgerald's is the view of Society from without, as his
hero Jay Gatsby is in large part the story of the ultimate outsider. His, Fitzgerald's, verdict on Society, as represented by the
rich and aloof Tom and Daisy Buchanan and Jordan Baker, is
severe. First there is Jordan Baker, who cheats at golf and
drives a car thoughtlessly, letting other drivers watch out for
her. Then there are Tom and Daisy: "They were careless people
. . . they smashed up things and creatures and then retreated
back into their money or their vast carelessness, or whatever it
was that kept them together, and let other people clean up the
mess they had made."

Yet in Fitzgerald, as in John O'Hara and John Marquand,
a strong yearning accompanies all the criticisms they have to
make about Society. They were much taken up by the splendors
of the life of Society even as they were contemptuous of it. They
resent the rich and wellborn even as they are drawn to them. The
phenomenon is not uncommon. Even so great as writer as Proust
shared it. While satirizing the old society of the Faubourg Saint-
Germain, in his *A Remembrance of Things Past,* he is also
clearly dazzled by it. Perhaps it is of the nature of the satirist
to attack the very things he is drawn to, lest the force of the
attraction overpower his critical judgment. In a little piece in his

book *Pleasures and Days* entitled "A Dinner in Society," Proust, thoroughly and deftly, excoriates the inanities of a Parisian Society dinner. "And he had neglected," Proust writes about his narrator, who is obviously himself, "the one trait they had in common, or rather the same collective folly, the same prevalent epidemic with which they were all afflicted: snobbishness." Yet he, Proust, goes out onto the boulevard after the dinner filled with a sharp sense of well-being. People pass him by, and "he felt himself to be the glorious center of their attention; he opened his overcoat to let them admire his gleaming white shirt front, so very becoming to him, the dark red carnation in his buttonhole. Thus he offered himself to the admiration of the passers-by and to their affection which he so voluptuously shared." From what does this feeling of expansive well-being in Proust stem? Proust does not say but leaves his readers to conclude: from that most exquisite of social pleasures—a form of having one's pâté de foie gras and eating it, too—of enjoying the company of Society and criticizing it, too.

Yet the combination of attraction and revulsion that is part of Marcel Proust's magnificence as a novelist has not been generally available to American novelists. An American writer living at the same time as Proust was pretty much closed off from Society for the strong reason that Society in America closed itself off to writers and artists—even writers and artists among its own—in a way that was not true in Europe. Although Mrs. Stuyvesant Fish, in the latter part of the nineteenth century in New York, widened her Society circle to include talented and attractive and amusing people who had no social or financial standing, as late as the middle 1940s, Louis Auchincloss, as he reports in his autobiography, *A Writer's Capital*, allowed his parents to persuade him to bring out his first novel under a pseudonym. Their feeling was that those parts of the novel that had to do with the New York Society life into which Auchincloss was born would be greeted with derision by the family's social circle, and that, moreover, publishing a novel might hurt young Louis with the law firm of Sullivan and Cromwell, to which he had only recently attached himself.

Would there have been better novels about American Society, and would that Society have come to be viewed differently than it now is, if American writers had had freer access to it? Difficult to say. Yet Henry James, whose way to Society was not blocked in England or Europe, bore Society no grudges, and thus was able to see it plain as an artist ought: as yet another arena for the working out of moral codes and conflicts; more grist for the refining mill of his imagination. In the United States there has been Edith Wharton, to the manner (and manor) born; and then things fall off precipitately. The last writer to come out of Society and to take Society for his subject is Louis Auchincloss, and to him has fallen the doleful task of chronicling not its decline—Society is always, after all, declining—but its fall. Auchincloss has said that he has never been "disillusioned" by Society. "I was," he writes in his autobiography, "perfectly clear from the beginning that I was interested in the story of money: how it was made, inherited, lost, spent." True though that may be, it is not the truth entire. It is often the depredations of new money upon Society that most excites Louis Auchincloss's imagination. Here, in the following patch of dialogue from his novel *A World of Profit,* is the characteristic Auchinclossian note:

> That you, born a Shallcross and married to a millionaire, should feel obliged to adopt the tactics of the commonest social climber, while your brother, educated as a gentleman, should go into partnership with an unscrupulous contractor, seems to me the epitaph of an era. In Russia, it took a revolution to destroy the aristocracy. Here, just hand us the rope.

Who handed Society the rope? Did it die honorably? How have the attending physicians made out the death certificate?

Curiosity Shop ▫ It not being sufficient that he ride into town in the back of a Mercedes limousine of a tan whose richness matches his own, a beautiful woman of the creamiest hues seated by his side, he has also to lean back to read the morning paper with his feet up on the back of the front seat. Those shoes

on that leather upholstery: cordovan on calf, there for every
passerby on the freeway to view. Several phrases jump to mind:
Desecration! The arrogance of power! The filthy rich! Storm the
Bastille!

And yet, why? It is, after all, his property, to do with as he
likes. One does not get angry, or certainly in nothing like the
same way, when one sees a poor man treat his property with a
similar contempt. It is, moreover, only inanimate property; not
at all like a man beating his horse. Who is being harmed by those
feet over that seat? The liveried chauffeur does not seem to
mind. Is our sympathy here reserved for the Mercedes, the thing
made with such care and at such cost? Is it defilement of property in the abstract that outrages? Hardly likely, since the front
seat of the car will scarcely be the worse for wear.

No, it is that man who makes one angry. His behavior is
unseemly, flaunting. What he is flaunting—throwing in the faces
of those his car passes—is the world's injustice. Why have the
world's gifts fallen to him in such disproportion? His position,
those feet make clear, is sultanic; the rest of us, compared to
him, seem so many Turks sweating in the sun on the road to
Istanbul. We prefer our wealthy to be quiet and seemly. Money
carries a certain responsibility, not the least of which is to pretend that it makes no difference. "He's a millionaire many times
over," we say, "but you would never know it to look at him. Lives
in the neighborhood in which he grew up. Drives a four-year-old
Dodge. Married to the same woman for thirty-five years. Salt of
the earth." Our fellow in the Mercedes is salt, too—salt rubbed
in wounds one had not even realized one had suffered until his
car drove by.

Marcel Proust, who was himself both, said that Society was
finished the moment it admitted Jews and homosexuals. Yet one
could make a stronger argument that Society was finished the
moment when, so to say, it went public: when it came out of its
houses and exclusive resorts and began congregating in restaurants and the ballrooms of hotels—and when, above all, it began
to allow the press, with its insistent photographers, to record its

carryings-on for the public at large. In *The Age of Innocence*, a woman of old New York Society, the mother of a bride, deciding against showing her daughter's wedding presents at the reception, remarks: "I should as soon turn the reporters loose in my house." Not so very long afterward no Society wedding, or other event of any social magnitude, would be considered complete without the publicity given to it by reporters. Like caterers and florists and servants, the press became an auxiliary arm of Society. But an essential auxiliary, for in time the arm came to resemble something rather more like a vital organ. Without the press's confirmation—in the form of Society pages, gossip columns, and the rest—Society could not always recognize who was a part of it. "Society," as Hedda Hopper once said, "is people who would go to hell rather than not see their names in print."

What seems to have transmogrified Society in this century is that, where once family was at its foundation, in the latter half of the nineteenth century family was replaced by money, and has since been replaced by publicity. The Repeal of Reticence, as one writer called the hunger for publicity on the part of those with social standing, made the notion of social standing a very different thing than it once was. William Randolph Hearst, who knew something about both money and publicity, said, "Only the rich man is interesting," which at least partially explains the interest of the press in Society. Society was, in two words, "good copy." The Society page, once a regular feature of every metropolitan paper, even those of middling-size cities, vastly helped create social consciousness in the United States. In middling and smaller cities the arrival of great numbers of immigrants almost overnight turned into Society such figures as dentists, real estate men, car dealers, and, of course, their wives. Society, in large cities and small, was composed of those whose names were on the Society page. In view of this it is scarcely surprising that before long the press itself became Society; in our own time, certainly, this has been true of such press or, as we should say now, "media" families like the Luces, the Hearsts, and the Paleys.

While Society always had its social arbiters—its grandes dames or its men of the dancing-master type—Society columnists now did the arbitrating. Figures such as Cholly Knickerbocker (the late Maury Paul) in New York could interject almost anyone they pleased into Society; and in smaller towns than New York the rule of such men and women could be even more despotic. Not that the columnist arbiters were any less arbitrary than such nineteenth-century arbiters as Ward McAllister. But, for one thing, they could not be so easily dismissed. ("McAllister is a discharged servant," said Mr. Stuyvesant Fish, when McAllister was thought to have overstepped his bounds. "That is all.") For another, the Society press as often as not—and increasingly more often than not—wrote with cutting contempt about that upon which they earned their bread. *The Rich and Other Atrocities,* the title of a collection of journalistic pieces by Charlotte Curtis, who was the principal Society writer for *The New York Times,* neatly provides the characteristic tone of blithe contempt taken by the Society writer of our day.

When Truman Capote gave his party for Katharine Graham at the Plaza Hotel in 1966—the great social bash of the 1960s— Charlotte Curtis, who wrote about it and also published the guest list in *The New York Times,* was herself invited not as a reporter but as a guest: a figure of social standing in her own right. The Capote guest list is a splendid index to the new mixture that makes up contemporary Society. On it one finds showbusiness figures next to old families (Marlene Dietrich and Mr. and Mrs. C. Douglas Dillon), commercial families next to British nobility (Mr. and Mrs. Henry J. Heinz II—"the pickle king," in Miss Curtis's account—and Lord Hardwicke), New York-Washington linked up with Hollywood-Las Vegas (Mr. and Mrs. Clifton Daniel and Mr. and Mrs. Sammy Davis, Jr.), international Society and American politics (Prince and Princess Stanislaus Radziwill and Senator and Mrs. John Sherman Cooper), Detroit and Cambridge (Mr. and Mrs. Henry Ford II and John Kenneth Galbraith). Many of Mr. Capote's guests were people of the kind that Miss Curtis refers to as "disposable celebrities." But what emerges from such zany juxtapositions is a new social amalgam: to purse and pedigree has now been added the element of publicity, or at any rate the ability to attract it.

Although more egalitarian than formerly—actors and academics, writers and singers, Jews and blacks have now been allowed in—Society itself, the "enviable people," do not seem less trivial. Under the glare of publicity they seem even more so. And they seem even more disposable. If Truman Capote were redoing his guest list today, how many of the names on his 1966 list would need to be shorn away to make room for Halston and Calvin, Bianca and Mick, Ahmet and Egon, John and Barbra, Shirley and Cher—names which themselves may, in another few years, have to be shorn away to make room for still fresher ones.

Curiosity Shop □ A green BMW, current year's model, pulls up to the curb and from it emerge a lady reporter in a khaki pantsuit and a photographer in a safari jacket. The photographer speaks English with a foreign accent, the reporter in up-to-the-moment American idiom. They work for *People* magazine, and this is rather a conventional, even slightly boring, assignment for them—it will take up at most two pages somewhere near the back of the magazine. The man they have come to interview has written a book about a social problem, and the book has attracted a certain amount of interest. The reporter has skimmed the book and talked to the author, who is also a university professor, over the telephone. He has mixed feelings about publicity of this kind. He would like his book to be better known, and he is not opposed to his book making as much money as possible. He wants the publicity, but he wants it for—and on—the book. Over the telephone he has told the reporter that he will not allow his two daughters to be photographed; and his wife, who values her privacy, will submit to being neither photographed nor interviewed. The photographer shoots him from every angle; the reporter pumps him for quotable statements. He refuses to be photographed in front of one of his classes; he agrees to be photographed jogging in a warmup suit, even though he has already run earlier in the day. The reporter will be able to write 600, maybe 800 words tops. Her story, she decides, is that here is a university professor who is no dweller in an ivory tower. It isn't much, but the best she can do with it. As the photographer pulls the BMW away from the curb, she

says, "Well, that was certainly a drag." An hour later, the professor's wife returns home, and asks him how it went. "Hell,"
he says, "sheer hell. An entire day down the trough." "Well,"
she says, "it was probably worth it—in exchange for a lost day
of work, you will have gained, after the magazine with you in
it comes out, two days of fame."

Who killed Society?, Cleveland Amory asked in a book of that
title in the 1960s, and brought in, in answer, some interesting
indictments. From his chronicle, though, one cannot be sure of
the time of the murder. Several moments present themselves:
the day in 1870 when Archibald Gracie King decided to hold his
daughter's debut into Society in a public place, the largest room
in Delmonico's restaurant; the death, in 1908, of Mrs. Astor; the
sinking, in 1912, of the *Titanic* with its many passengers from
le gratin; the destruction of the old Cornelius Vanderbilt house
on Fifth Avenue in 1942; the death, in 1952, of Mrs. Hamilton
McKnown Twombly, the last granddaughter of Commodore
Vanderbilt, who for roughly seventy-five years (she died at age
ninety-eight) held court in Newport, New York City, and Flor-
ham, her estate in New Jersey; the death of Mr. Augustus Van
Horne Stuyvesant, Jr., the last Stuyvesant and a man who, as
Mr. Amory says, was of the generation who treated lawyers like
servants; the commercials done earlier for Pond's cold cream,
through the agency of J. Walter Thompson, by Mrs. Oliver Har-
riman, Mrs. August Belmont, and Mrs. Alice Roosevelt Longworth; the beginning of the difficulty in finding servants, of
sufficient quality and number, to maintain Society in its leisurely
daily habits; the hunger for celebrity which set in with the advent of café society (c. 1919); the spread of divorce; the loss of
interest in manners, with all this implied for standards of entertainment, deportment, and dress; and so on and on. What Cleveland Amory wrote about the Vanderbilt scions—"too much
money and publicity and too little character and stability"—has
application to Society at large in this century. Or, as Mrs. Gloria
Vanderbilt is quoted in Mr. Amory's pages as saying: "I guess
when all is said and done, the people who should have set the

standards, didn't." Mrs. Vanderbilt herself later made a heavy score in selling blue jeans with her name on them.

But when all is said and done, the question is less *who* than *what* killed Society? Forces—political, historical, economic—have certainly played as great a part as personality. One such force, it has been argued, is that of the growth of the power of the state; and power of a kind that needs to be distinguished from the taxing power of the state, which can, if not protected against, dismantle great fortunes. But it is power of a different order that is in question here. "Each class," Joseph Schumpeter wrote in *Imperialism and Social Classes*, "is always linked to a special function. That is the real core of all theories of the division of labor and occupation in the field of class phenomena." The traditional functions of the class that made up Society in the United States have been governing and entrepreneurial activity. But the latter, entrepreneurship, has been vastly altered with the advent of the modern corporation, which so frequently divides ownership (expressed in stock) from control (expressed in managerial positions). Robert Nisbet has put the point well: "When economic power derives no longer exclusively from the processes of capital accumulation, or even management, when it is a reflection of positions in the economy which arise from and are sustained by labor and government, the relationship between property and class becomes more and more tenuous."

The state, in Robert Nisbet's view, has increasingly usurped the functions of the traditional upper class—to the point where class of all kinds has become increasingly difficult to make out at all. Few are the remaining distinctions that can now be laid to class. Nisbet writes: "Whether with respect to consumption or production, then, class lines are exceedingly difficult to discover in modern society except in backwater areas. About the most that research comes up with is that wealthy persons spend their money more freely, choose, when possible, better schools for their children, buy clothes at Brooks or Magnin's, rather than at Penney's, avail themselves of better medical attention, and belong to more clubs. But while all this is interesting, it says little about anything as substantive as a social class is supposed to be."

Joseph Schumpeter was much impressed with the high degree of turnover in the upper classes over the centuries—the
rise and slide of families. The reasons for the slide did not
seem to him surprising: after generations of supremacy, a loss
of interest in self-discipline might occur in a family, or a loss of
innovative powers, or even a loss of something as fundamental
as physical energy. What was crucial to a family's maintaining
its place in the aristocratic or upper class, in Schumpeter's
view, was "the successful accomplishment of pertinent tasks."
Because the upper classes, Schumpeter felt, were traditionally
set up to engage in pertinent tasks, many among them, even
when these tasks changed radically (from, say, military to ad-
ministrative tasks), were able to hold on in Europe for generations numbering into the hundreds of years. "But," Schumpeter wrote, "it is precisely because a decline in the social
importance of a class function—the inadequate exercise and
surrender of that function—sets the members of the class free
that the decline in class position which might be expected oc-
curs only if the class is unable to adapt itself to some other
function that rates the same social importance as the old one."

The question is, Why haven't the upper classes in the
United States—the classes that have made up Society as it is
commonly understood in America—been able to adapt themselves to new functions of social importance? Writing in 1964,
E. Digby Baltzell, in the conclusion to his book *The Protestant
Establishment, Aristocracy and Caste in America,* noted
that although the White Anglo-Saxon Protestant upper class in
America might still be deferred to and envied because of its
privileged status, it was no longer thought honorable. Its standards of admission, Baltzell wrote, "have gradually come to
demand the dishonorable treatment of far too many distinguished Americans for it to continue, as a class, to fill its traditional function of moral leadership." Baltzell refers, of course,
to the anti-Semitism that has always been a strong strain in
the character of the American upper class, and a prominent
one in a man of such intellectual standing as Henry Adams.
Society and the upper class ought perhaps not to be used inter-
changeably, but Dixon Wecter's summing up of the contribu-

tion of Society applies nearly down the line to the upper class
in America. Wecter writes:

> In review, the self-justifications of society in America are
> none too impressive. It has bought Old Masters, but fed few
> living artists. Its tastes in music and opera have been both
> timid and grandiose, and its patronage of literature has
> been negligible. Unhappily it forsook politics more than a
> century ago [Wecter wrote in 1937] .... With generosity it
> has sometimes given to charity and education, though it has
> wasted other great sums in foolish ways. To the wisdom,
> goodness, and piety of mankind it has afforded at best an
> erratic and whimsical support.

Dixon Wecter is not pleased about this, and he ends *The
Saga of American Society* with a French quotation from
James Boswell *("Un gentilhomme est toujours gentilhomme"),* to which, somewhat wistfully, he appends in closing: "Lacking the simplicity, courage, generosity, and honor of
this ideal the life of mankind would indeed be poorer." E.
Digby Baltzell, too, ends his book of 1964 on a note of highly
restrained optimism, from which wistfulness is not altogether
absent: "In an age ... when so many talented Americans are
absorbed in success-striving and status-seeking, the institution-
alization of a minority community which relieves distinguished
men and their families from further status struggles is more
important than ever—but only when its membership requirements are based on talent and moral distinction rather than
ethnic or racial ancestry." But, returning to the subject in an
essay of 1976 entitled "The Protestant Establishment Revi-
sited," Baltzell withdrew whatever optimism he had shown earlier: "When I wrote *The Protestant Establishment* during the
administration of President Kennedy, I still had faith in the
ability of the WASP establishment to assimilate talented men
and women of other ethnic and religious origins into its ranks.
I have no such faith today."

The reason Professor Baltzell could have no such faith was
that, by the 1970s, the upper class was, as a class, in tatters—

psychological tatters, that is, roundly despised and not least by its own members. In *Mr. Sammler's Planet,* Saul Bellow remarks of his protagonist, the wise European observer, Artur Sammler: "In thought, Mr. Sammler was testy with White Protestant America for not keeping better order. Cowardly surrender. Not a strong ruling class. Eager in a secret humiliating way to come down and mingle with all the minority mobs, and scream against themselves." Baltzell's essay sets italics under Bellow's observation about the upper class, in pointing out how the fourth generation of the American upper class was often at the forefront of the student radical revolt in the late 1960s. And the journalist Tom Wolfe put the same point in capital letters in "Radical Chic," his sharp exposé of a class intent upon its own destruction.

What one thinks of as Society—although it carries on today in enfeebled form in some large cities—has now for the most part been replaced, certainly in the public interest, by café or international society. This is not a recent happening, but has been decades in the making. Margot Asquith, in her autobiography, puts the date more than sixty years ago: "The first world war destroyed Society. After the war café society took over. ... It spread from America to England. Since the second world war the social life of the rich has become even more incoherent and even less capable of classification. They no longer comprehend with their circle the educated, the civilized, or the significant."

Café society—as it existed in the 1920s, as it exists less charmingly now—is, in effect, aristocracy without any of the responsibility, good manners, or geographical roots that was once associated with the upper class in all countries. "Fashion," wrote William Hazlitt, "is gentility running away from vulgarity, and afraid of being overtaken." Today something akin to the reverse seems to have occurred. Hot for publicity, terrified lest they seem not of the very moment, the fashionable rush toward vulgarity and usually—whether in the form of an outrageously priced restaurant or a new discotheque—overtake it.

No one today claims other than that the flame of Society is

guttering, and the question is, what will be different about life should it be snuffed out? Much can be—and already has been—said against Society in America, and most of this truly said: its anti-Semitism; its multiform snobberies, more cruel than amusing; its ample appetite for private pleasure, which generally exceeded its appetite for public responsibility; its indolence, its opulence, its antipathies so much greater than its sympathies. All this has been documented, with the result that the very idea of Society, of an upper class, has fallen onto bad days. This is scarcely the first time this has happened, of course, and John Stuart Mill, in *On Liberty*, more than a century ago rightly warned of its accompanying possible effect: "When . . . ," Mill wrote, "a class, formerly ascendant, has lost its ascendancy, or where its ascendancy is unpopular, the prevailing moral sentiments frequently bear the impress of an impatient dislike of superiority."

If Society is gone, what goes with it? One thing that goes is a channel for a certain kind of ambition—family ambition. No small item, this, and it is well to remember, as Robert Nisbet points out, "that the historical evidence is very clear indeed that the efflorescence of the high periods of culture, the so-called Golden Ages of history—the Athens of Pericles, Augustan Rome, the Florence of the Medicis, Shakespeare's England—have been periods in which the spirit of aristocracy was powerful, preoccupation with inherited rank obsessing." The idea of class has always been rather suspect in the United States—most Americans, to avoid the issue, place themselves in the middle class—yet the hunger for status (in an address, an automobile, a clothing label, a university) runs as rampant as ever. The pole of status is more slippery than the old ladder of class, and does not, for knowing no top, bring any more happiness—perhaps less. Some say the sad contemporary preoccupation with status is the direct result of the absence of class.

To a man of ambition the absence of an upper class can mean no goal, apart from the ephemeral ones of money and power in his lifetime, for him to aspire to. It means the end of his ambition for his family, each of whose members, after his passing, will be on his or her own. It can mean also the end of a certain kind of responsibility—for implicit in social class, working as well as upper class, are certain values: of honesty, of reliability, of decency, of the duty to keep the game going. In the world of status, a world bereft of class, the world in which more and more of us now live, it is every man for himself. In such a world ambition becomes less public, more private; striving to secure position for one's children's children becomes rather preposterous. Ambition itself is thus deprived of much of its interest in the future.

Swiss Family Kennedy

Even now it isn't easy to find someone who has had a good word to say about Joseph P. Kennedy, father of, among others, John, Robert, and Edward. Here are some of the bad words that have been said of him: ruthless, selfish, vicious, inane, crude, tunnel-visioned, blatant, Jew-hater, pigeon-livered. From Harold Ickes to Harold Nicolson—and in the range of human types that is quite a stretch—nearly everyone agreed that Joe Kennedy was bad news. But those who thought the very worst of him allowed that Joe was a great family man. He put first things first. "The measure of a man's success in life is not the money he's made," said Joe, who measured up very well indeed by this standard. "It's the kind of family he has raised. In that I've been mighty lucky." Of course, were it not for his family—his sons, really—Joseph P. Kennedy would by now have become little more than a dimly remembered figure from the 1930s, a historical actor from the echelon below Cordell Hull and Father Coughlin.

While he was still alive, from the standpoint of his sons' ambitions in public life, the dimmer a figure Joseph P. Kennedy became the better. The night his son John Fitzgerald Kennedy was nominated as the Democratic party's candidate for President of the United States, in Los Angeles in 1960, Joe watched the proceedings over a television set at the Beverly Hills home of Marion Davies. Two days later, when John gave his acceptance speech, Joe had removed himself all the way to New York, where he listened to the speech at the Waldorf Towers apartment of Henry Luce. And so it would be during Jack's brief presidency and, again, with the careers of Bobby and Ted. Joe Kennedy had to stay in the background; more than a risk, he was a certain political liability. In their public life, their father's influence was a thing the Kennedy sons felt called upon to deny. Whether Joe Kennedy was disappointed about this is not known. Doubtless he was; but if he was, he never complained. Besides, the boys never repudiated *him*—only nearly everything that he had ever stood for.

What did Joseph P. Kennedy stand for? He was an earnest Catholic who sent his sons to Protestant schools, an Irish-American who felt himself pleased to be among the aristocratic Cliveden set in England, a capitalist who helped bring Franklin Delano Roosevelt's New Deal to power, a famous stock-market manipulator who was the first chairman of the Securities and Exchange Commission, a resentful victim more than once of the social blackball who himself lived in places from which others were restricted. Joe Kennedy insisted that money never be discussed at the dinner table. He was famous for his profanity. He loved serious music. An isolationist and appeaser in international relations, he was flat-out combative in personal and business relations. From stock-market speculation to boat racing, it was not how one played the game that counted with Joe, it was winning or losing that counted—and winning counted for more. He was a loving father and a mortal enemy. He had the thin-lipped look of the mortgage banker (which he once was) from without, while within raged the stomach ulcers of a man in a powerful hurry.

The old distinction between shanty and lace-curtain Irish held the former to be luckless and the latter on the move upward and outward. Until Joseph P. Kennedy's father, the clan Kennedy in America looked to be shanty. The grandfather, Patrick Kennedy, came to the United States in 1848 at the age of twenty-five, and died, of cholera, ten years later. His son, Patrick Joseph, Joe's father, had to drop out of grammar school to go to work as a stevedore on the East Boston waterfront. But it was Pat Kennedy who turned the family lace-ward. He worked hard, bought a saloon in Haymarket Square, became a political figure in East Boston, and eventually sat in the state legislature.

Joseph Patrick Kennedy was the first of Pat Kennedy's children. Born in 1888, Joe grew up in Irish East Boston but not in anything resembling poverty. In the life of East Boston his father was a small power. Although there was a sufficiency of money in the family, this did not cause young Joe Kennedy to ease up. Quite the reverse. Growing up among immigrants and the sons of immigrants, he learned readily enough the importance of money: the many things it could do, how it separated people, the measure of control it lent to one's life. Joe worked all the usual run of boys' jobs: hawking newspapers, running errands, taking theater tickets. He was a redhead, competitive and fierce-tempered, even pugnacious.

Joe went to the famous Boston Latin School, and thence to Harvard. The combination of street smarts and connections made in the best schools served him well. Certainly he was not most people's idea of the ideal Harvard graduate: cerebral, detached, cultivated. In fact, Joe Kennedy was a fire-eater. He was ready to do dull work or dirty work or whatever it took to get the job done. What, one might here ask, was the job? At this time a precise answer was not available, though amassing lots of money was a useful beginning. Joe worked as a bank examiner, learning the banking business; he worked as a realtor, learning the real estate business. By 1913, at the age of twenty-five, through care and cunning he became president of a small bank called the Columbia Trust Company. This made him the youngest bank president in the State of Massachusetts, perhaps in the nation. The Columbia Trust Company had less than a quarter million dollars in capital. Still, small though the bank was, to be the youngest bank president gave Joe Kennedy a claim on the attention of the City of Boston. It was to be the first of many such claims.

The second was when Joe Kennedy married Rose Fitzgerald, the eldest daughter of the mayor of Boston, John F. Fitzgerald, the fabled Honey Fitz, the very type of the backslapping and jig-dancing Irish politician in America. Convent educated though not at all retreating, Rose Fitzgerald was her father's female representative, often standing in for her mother, since Honey Fitz's wife was a shy woman with no taste for the clangor of political life. Rose felt no such distaste, but, on the contrary, troped toward the limelight, had an appetite for competition into the bargain, didn't in the least mind a good political scrap. Rose was a perfect wife for Joe, although Honey Fitz was far from Joseph Kennedy's notion of a perfect father-in-law. More often than not he was an embarrassment, this traditional Irish politico, with his singing and baby-kissing and hand-pumping and public carryings-on. The Fitzgeralds were heedless of Yankee Boston Society, with its sniffishness, and were quite content to live among their own. Not so Joe, whose aim, at least at the outset, was to infiltrate Yankee Society. Easier said than done, however. When Joe, after renting a summer home in Cohasset, applied for membership in the Cohasset Country Club, whose members included many old Boston families, he was turned down cold. Honey Fitz was a social encumbrance to Joe's aspirations, as Joe himself would one day be a political encumbrance to his own sons' aspirations.

By the time of Honey Fitz's last hurrah, in 1922, Joe Kennedy was well on his way to becoming a man of substantial wealth. He tooled around Boston in a limousine, chauffeur-driven. He had already tried his hand at banking, running a shipyard (under Charles M. Schwab during World War I), and, above all, in the stock market. As a young man, Joe's strategy was to attach his small wagon to engines more powerful than his own. Thus, in the market, he became a junior associate of Galen Stone, of the firm of Hayden, Stone and Company, running the stock department in their Boston office. Joe's reputation as a player was that of a man closemouthed and tightfisted; a man always extracting information but seldom coming across with any. "Player" is a misnomer applied to Joe Kennedy. He certainly saw no element of play in the stock market. "The desire to win, rather than the excitement involved," he once said, "seems to me to be the compelling force behind speculation."

Joe Kennedy was a bear for work; he had reserves of energy, great vitality; he could—often did—work a fourteen-hour day for long stretches. He neither drank nor smoked. He had sure financial instincts and a fine sense of timing. He stayed out of the Florida real estate bubble of the 1920s until it burst, then went in big. He went into the movie business just as it went on the upswing, first buying a chain of theaters, later becoming head of the Film Booking Office of America, Inc., Keith-Albee-Orpheum, and Pathé. In less than three years in the movie business he walked away $5 million richer. He pulled out of the stock market in time to avoid the devastations of the Crash of 1929 touching his personal wealth. Anticipating the end of Prohibition, and through his connection with James Roosevelt (FDR's son), Joe was able to swing the job of U.S. agent for Gordon's Gin, Dewar's Scotch, and Haig & Haig. Yet again, at the end of World War II he bought the Merchandise Mart in Chicago, from Marshall Field & Company, putting up a mere $1 million in out-of-pocket cash, for a purchase price of under $13 million—less than the building would soon bring in in annual rentals. By 1957 *Fortune* magazine set Joseph P. Kennedy's personal wealth at roughly $250 million.

But by the end of the 1920s Joseph P. Kennedy had acquired a most mixed reputation. He was the cold-eyed businessman under tight control—the control required for the fiery temper that could go off at any moment. A certain touchiness, an unexplained surliness, an unfocused fury burned in Joe Kennedy. He enjoyed the emoluments of his success—the big house in Hyannisport bought in 1928, with others in Palm Springs and Bronxville to come—but they didn't allow him to let up on himself. He smoldered with ambition. Yet to do what? He had by the early 1930s developed into a powerful engine of his own. But in what direction would he drive off?

"No interest of mine is as great an interest as my interest in them," said Joe Kennedy of his children. However pharisaical he might have been on other matters, no one ever doubted the intensity of Joseph Kennedy's feeling for his children—nor, it must be added, of theirs for him. Rose and Joe were at one about how to raise children. The way they did it was with a feeling of security within the family but at the same time developing in them a sense of a hostile environment outside the family. Anecdotes by the score have piled up about competition within the

Kennedy family and about the special Olympics that were part of daily life in their home. Typically, Eunice Kennedy Shriver reports: "I was twenty-four before I knew I didn't have to win something every day." "We don't want any losers around here," said Joe to the children. "In this family we want winners." As each of the Kennedy children came of age, he or she was given a trust fund that Joe had set up "so that," as he said, "any of my children, financially speaking, could look me in the eye and tell me to go to hell." Not that this, trust fund or not, was likely ever to happen.

Later it would be said—Joe Kennedy himself would say it often—that such status and financial security as he would be able to garner was for Rose and the nine children, for the family. That would be later. Always a family man, attentive to the needs of his children—striking off a letter to Jack to hit the books harder, or one to Bobby encouraging him to do his best—Joe's own career, far from done, was in a sense only truly underway in 1932. Joseph P. Kennedy was one of the first rich men to go over to Franklin Delano Roosevelt. "Go over to" more precisely means "give money to"—specifically, $25,000 to Roosevelt's campaign and a loan of $50,000 to the Democratic party. Joe was a Democrat less by personal point of view than by heritage. In contributing money, and later efforts of personal suasion, to FDR's campaign Joe was guided quite as much by personal ambition as by political conviction. Making money was never Joe Kennedy's problem, then or later. He was, in 1932, forty-four years old and already many times over a millionaire. If Joe had a problem, it was what to do with the remainder of his life.

It may have been a problem but, for Joe, it was not a question. He knew well enough what he wanted. He wanted to be Secretary of the Treasury under Roosevelt. He worked hard and efficiently to get FDR elected: fund-raising among his moneyed friends, helping to bring such people as William Randolph Hearst and Father Coughlin around to Roosevelt's side, offering ideas on the economy that were used in campaign speeches. Operating as a man behind the scenes, Joe was on the edge of Roosevelt's inner circle of advisers. But he was to be disappointed in his hopes for the Treasury job. Roosevelt, who had a taste for keeping people off balance when it came to making

appointments, instead chose a man named William H. Woodin.
Joe sulked in his tent. But he was soon called out, to take the job
of first chairman of the Securities and Exchange Commission. It
was a controversial appointment. As with so many other professional speculators, Joe Kennedy had himself played the stock
market every which way; it was because of men like him that
there was a need to regulate the stock market in the first place.
Appointing him chairman of the S.E.C. therefore seemed to
some rather like making John Dillinger warden of the state
prison of Indiana. As it turned out, he was very good indeed at
the job. His was neither a refined nor a well-stocked but an
exceedingly orderly mind. He was, Joe Kennedy, the sort of man
who rolled up his shirt sleeves and got the job done.

Joe was also a good man at details. "Little things are important," he once told a journalist. This applied to business, to
government, to family. Especially, perhaps, to family. If one of
the Kennedy children—and they were now nine, five girls and
four boys—was in a play at school or had an important game,
their father would arrange to be there, whatever the press of
business. His son Jack wrote from Choate to confess poor work
over the past term and to promise reform, to which Joe replied:
"After long experience in sizing up people I definitely know you
have the goods and you can go a long way. Now aren't you
foolish not to get all there is out of what God has given you."
There you have exactly Joe Kennedy's fatherly style: boosting
confidence, moralizing, striking the religious note. The children
were also told that, having been born with certain advantages,
they bore concomitant responsibilities. They must rise above the
ruck, distinguish themselves, win through. Sports, school, everything in the family was presented in competitive form.

As for Joe Kennedy's own competitive instincts, they were
briefly in enforced restraint. After a term with the S.E.C., he
returned to private life, where he worked as an occasional con-
sultant for RCA, Paramount Pictures, and other large corporations. He broadened and increased his own holdings. By the
mid-1930s he was paying in more than $600,000 in annual taxes.
He had become a prominent Catholic of the kind the Vatican
cultivated; Cardinal Pacelli (later to be Pope Pius XII) took tea
with the Kennedy family when he visited the United States. But

tea with Cardinal Pacelli did not translate into membership in the exclusively Protestant Cohasset Club in Palm Beach, from which the Kennedys were blackballed.

Another exclusive club Joe Kennedy could not seem to crack was the FDR Cabinet. When Secretary of the Treasury Woodin died in 1934, Roosevelt passed over Joe to appoint Henry Morgenthau, Jr., to the job. Joe had enemies among FDR's inner circle, most persistent among them perhaps being Harold Ickes, who in his diary noted of Joe that he was "a great publicity seeker who is apparently ambitious to be the first Catholic President of the United States." Ickes was off by a generation in this prediction, of course, although there were rumors that Joseph P. Kennedy was interested in the presidency in 1940. These rumors, as it turned out, were for the most part inspired by the press. Kennedys and the press—theirs was to be a long and symbiotic relationship, each feeding off the other, endlessly, and for years to come.

In 1938, FDR, paying off a long string of political debts at long last, offered Joe Kennedy one of the most succulent of political plums—the Court of Saint James's. Joe was the first Irishman to serve as American ambassador to England. The press, English and American, lapped it up. "The U.S.A.'s Nine-Child Envoy," one British paper called him. And such a photogenic family, too. The Kennedys were taken up in England by the Cliveden set. At the outset of a weekend at Windsor Castle the new American ambassador is said to have remarked to his wife, "Rose, this is a helluva way from East Boston." But, as Jimmy Durante used to say, they ain't seen nothin' yet.

The assignment to the Court of Saint James's was the apogee of Joseph P. Kennedy's public life—and also its nadir. Joe was assigned to the ambassadorship because it was felt that he would resist the blandishments of the British, but in the event he fell in completely with Neville Chamberlain, his government, and those who chose to meet the threat to civilization posed by the Nazis with a policy of appeasement. Why Joe Kennedy went over to the appeasers so readily—"This is not our fight," he continually reported back to the United States—has been the subject of much conjecture. Some have argued that, as an earnest capitalist, he viewed the war as destructive for capitalism.

Others have argued that he viewed fascism as a lesser evil than communism (a view he did not abandon even when Hitler's official policy of Jewish genocide was fairly clear, which gave him, Joe, everlastingly the reputation of an anti-Semite, something, years later, his sons, with their liberal constituencies, would have to fight against in their own careers). Still others have argued that Joe Kennedy was fearful of losing his own sons should America enter the war. "I have four sons," a colleague at the S.E.C. recalls him saying, "and I don't want them killed in a foreign war."

An ambassador, in Sir Henry Wotton's famous definition, is a man "sent to lie abroad for his country," but in Joseph Kennedy's case it soon began to seem that he was lying not for his country but for Neville Chamberlain's government. Things went from bad to worse. In time Joe gave speeches asking for coexistence with Hitler. Roosevelt, seeing what was up, no longer believed his own ambassador. Churchill was said to have despised Joe Kennedy; and when Churchill came into office, the Chamberlain government's policy now proven utterly foolish, the U.S. ambassador's usefulness was at an end. After FDR's election to a third term, in 1940, Joseph Kennedy resigned his ambassadorship, in tacit disgrace. He was all but finished in public life.

Above all political considerations, perhaps the most persuasive explanation for Joe Kennedy's isolationism is that of self-interest. Self-interest, in this connection, meant concern for his two older sons, Joseph, Jr., and John. Joe Kennedy had acted on self-interest his life long, and it had brought him very far down the road. The world confirmed—in millions of dollars, in high office, in status—the efficacy of self-interest. A man of thin culture and no idealism, Joe made no attempt to cover over the fact that he was for Joseph P. Kennedy, a clear proponent of the screw-you-buddy, me-first philosophy. Behavior of this kind is common enough, except that in Joe Kennedy's case the doctrine of sheer self-interest extended to include his family. "Family egotism," Tolstoy called this phenomenon. "It is a dreadful egotism, for it commits the greatest cruelties in the name of love; as if to say, let the whole world perish so that my Serge may be happy."

Another Russian writer, Maxim Gorky, said that no man could consider his life worthy unless his children surpassed him in ability and achievement. Here was another doctrine to which Joe Kennedy implicitly subscribed. He was in any case fully as intent upon his children's advancement as upon his own. To John, after the publication of his Harvard bachelor's thesis under the title *Why England Slept*, his father wrote: "You would be surprised how a book that really makes the grade with high-class people stands you in good stead for years to come." And so such advice would go with all the Kennedy children. But especially did Joe Kennedy hold out high hopes for his first-born son, Joseph Kennedy, Jr. Handsome, mentally quick, a good athlete, interested in a political career, "Joe," as his brother John recalled, "was the star of our family. He did everything better than the rest of us." But in July 1944, flying on a mission whose goal was to bomb Nazi submarine pens off the coast of Belgium, Joseph Kennedy, Jr., was killed when his plane exploded in mid-flight. His father was desolated. "It was," his daughter Eunice later said, "the first thing that he valued tremendously that he ever lost."

The saga of the Kennedy sons has been the most often told in modern journalism. The tendency in all the various accounts—of John, of Robert, of Edward—is to mute their father's role after the boys' adolescence. According to most of these accounts, Joe ignited the competitive spark, inflamed them with ambition, and then stepped quietly out of the way once they reached manhood. Very tidy. More, though, was entailed.

The Kennedy boys loved their father, but once in public life they knew him to be an embarrassment. Joe sensed this himself. Thus, when Jack first went into politics, running for Congress in 1946, Joe unloaded his interest in the liquor industry, and, insofar as possible, kept to the background. The two, Jack and his father, were not often photographed together when Jack was in the House of Representatives or in the Senate. Yet he, Jack, was to arrive at both places as a result of extraordinary outlays of campaign money—money efficiently but nonetheless lavishly spent. A similarly heavy outlay of money made possible the defeat of Hubert Humphrey in the West Virginia primary of

1960, paving the way to John Kennedy's nomination for the presidency. As one of Joe Kennedy's biographers said of him: "Few wealthy men ever approached [Joe] Kennedy's mastery of the techniques of using money to satisfy personal ambition."

What was Joseph Kennedy's personal ambition? What was John Kennedy's personal ambition? What was Bobby's? What Ted's? The three sons each in his time wanted to be President of the United States, and one (to date) achieved it. Ambition they all had in plenty, but what was at the center of it? Was there anything more than the thrust of it, the ardent desire to continue onward and upward? Great though his own success had been, Joe Kennedy had viewed it as incomplete. The boys would complete it for him. And so they seem to have done. From East Boston to the White House is a pretty good patch to travel in the span of only one generation.

Yet for all their success, there was something flawed in Joseph Kennedy's sons. Not tragically flawed, either, but rather more fundamentally, more mundanely, flawed. The middle brother, Bobby, had an idealist's fervor but lacked any clear ideals to which to apply that fervor: whether on behalf of Senator Joseph McCarthy, against Jimmy Hoffa, or in support of Cesar Chavez, Bobby Kennedy was equally perfervid. More important, these boys seemed never to come through under real pressure. When John F. Kennedy was in the Senate he wrote a book entitled *Profiles in Courage*—portraits of notable U.S. Senators, it won a Pulitzer Prize—which caused a Senate colleague to remark, of Jack Kennedy's own senatorial career, that he would have himself done better to have shown more courage and less profile. The quip can be applied to each of the three Kennedy brothers. Jack failed to distinguish himself in the House of Representatives, in the Senate, and in the White House; and in the last, apart from all his high-blown rhetoric, he was utterly cowed by Congress, achieving in his time in office nothing grander than a tax cut; paralyzed by the South in civil rights, where civil rights workers claimed that they could not depend on the help of the federal government; and driven slightly hysterical by the Soviet Union, coming to grief over the Bay of Pigs and then risking all facing down the Russians in Cuba. It is hard but true to say that only assassination saved him from going down into history as one of the great presidential mediocrities. Robert Kennedy, for all his fervor and supposed political ruthlessness, failed to take on Lyndon Johnson in 1968, waiting till Senator Eugene McCarthy had dislodged Johnson, and only then, the coast clear, jumping in himself. And, finally, Teddy, who always seemed so stumbling when the heat was on.

When John Kennedy was in the White House, and Robert Kennedy was his attorney-general, and Teddy Kennedy announced that he was going to run for the U.S. Senate from Massachusetts in 1962, a political-satire magazine of the day began something it called The Edward M. Kennedy Foundation, whose alleged purpose was to aid mediocre young men who want to go right to the top. It was a good joke—but not for long. With the death of John Kennedy, the family, once distrusted, became reverenced. With the death, five years later, of Robert Kennedy, the family very nearly became sacrosanct. Thus a writer in *The New York Times Magazine* could say of Teddy: "There is something politically provocative about the aloneness of this Kennedy, a feeling that if he wants the presidency, the American people almost somehow owe it to him because of what happened to his brothers."

Joseph Kennedy suffered a stroke in 1961 that left him partly paralyzed and unable to speak. He died eight years later, in 1969, after two of his sons had been assassinated. But the Kennedy name, once scandalized by Joe's appeasement in World War II and by his general aggressiveness, was now a golden one in American politics. That his sons seemed to have been all promise and no delivery, the only figures in American politics judged not by their deeds but by their intentions, might have amused Joe Kennedy, if in an ironic way. Not that he, Joe, was a man much given to ironic amusement, but this was blatant. Even he, who had been so aflame with ambition as a young man, would see how in the apotheosis of his sons—all three of them never really more than fledgling in their achievements—his countrymen had confused, almost beyond sorting out, the very idea of ambition itself.

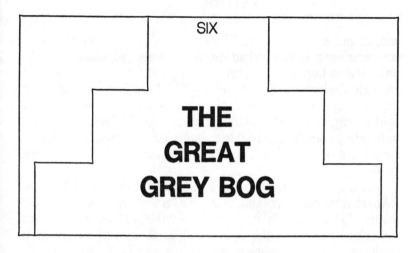

SIX

THE
GREAT
GREY BOG

F. Scott Fitzgerald

"I talk with the authority of failure," F. Scott Fitzgerald confided to his notebook, "Ernest [Hemingway] with the authority of success." He also noted: "There are no second acts in American lives." Characteristic utterances, each of these, striking the characteristic Fitzgeraldian pose. *Raplaplat* is the French word for it, meaning fagged out, washed out, nearly finished. From his middle thirties F. Scott Fitzgerald was *raplaplat*. In 1939, then forty-three years old, Fitzgerald, according to a young Budd Schulberg, "looked more like sixty." Having a mad wife and fighting a losing battle with alcoholism helped age him, to be sure, but Fitzgerald seemed to dress and act and generally to cotton to the part. Maxwell Perkins, his friend and editor, wrote to a third party that Scott's role of late was "the man burned out at forty"; and then, commenting on Fitzgerald's propensity for self-dramatization, Perkins remarked: "If he will only begin to dramatize himself as the man who came back now, everything will be all right."

But of course it was not to be all right. Fitzgerald struggled in his last years—he died at forty-four—to stay on the wagon. He worked as a screenwriter, turned out his Pat Hobby stories for *Esquire*, but his true energy, his heart's blood, went into *The Last Tycoon*, the novel about Irving Thalberg, the Hollywood mogul and another comet, like Fitzgerald, that lit up the skies and was early extinguished. (A word is needed, someone once said, somewhere between talent and genius; it could be applied to both Thalberg and Fitzgerald.) *The Last Tycoon* is a novel about a brilliant man who dies young by a brilliant writer who, still young, dies in the middle of composing it, leaving a heart-achingly incomplete, possible masterpiece—symmetry scarcely gets more fearful than this. It was the stuff of which myths are made.

A myth is precisely what F. Scott Fitzgerald had become. "Apart from his increasing stature as a writer," Cyril Connolly wrote, "Fitzgerald is now firmly established as a myth, an American version of the Dying God, an Adonis of letters born with the century, flowering in the twenties, the Jazz Age which he perfectly expressed and almost created, and then quietly wilting through the thirties to expire—as a deity of spring and summer should—on December 21, 1940, at the winter solstice and the end of an epoch." In literature, Fitzgerald's career was not the first to furnish fodder for such a myth; John Keats, who died at twenty-six, and Percy Bysshe Shelley, who died at twenty-nine, and Aleksander Sergeevich Pushkin, who died at thirty-eight, presented earlier versions of the selfsame myth. What sets the Scott Fitzgerald version apart is that it was home-grown; he, Fitzgerald, seems himself to have planted the seeds for it.

Fitzgerald was quite wrong about there being no second acts in American lives—as his own life proves. Fitzgerald's first act was that of the booming American success; his second act was that of the wilting American failure. What is notable is that the failed Fitzgerald has, over the long haul, become an even greater success than the successful Fitzgerald. Premature success, in his case, was followed by premature failure—and the latter, reported by Fitzgerald himself, has had even more allure. In his last years F. Scott Fitzgerald may have been out of print, out of funds, and out of luck, but he was not out of style—*le style raplaplat*—and style of a kind that was to prove so winning to future generations.

The first act, if one did not scrutinize it too closely, was not without its own allure. Fitzgerald later described it, his early success, as a time "when the fulfilled future and the wistful past were mingled in a single gorgeous moment—when life was literally a dream." His is one of the best-known stories in American literary history: the brash young man in a hurry writes the best-selling novel that enables him to win the hand of the beautiful southern belle—a girl so attractive that, during World War I, flyers at an air base near her home were issued specific instructions not to fly stunts over her house to impress her. *This Side of Paradise,* Fitzgerald's first novel, published when he was twenty-three, put money in his pocket, Zelda Sayre in his bed, and himself on a pedestal. "King of American youth," Glenway Wescott called him.

In this century the most potent American novelists have been brimful of desire; brimful and running over. Desire—sheer wanting—is what Theodore Dreiser and F. Scott Fitzgerald have in common, although Dreiser was as homely as Fitzgerald was handsome, as graceless as Fitzgerald was stylish. Desire is something one is born not with but into. Dreiser was sufficiently lowborn to want to claw out of the hole; Fitzgerald was born just high enough to want to climb to the top. As he was later to describe his family's social position to a friend, the Fitzgeralds generally lived in "a house below the average of a street above the average."

"I didn't have the two top things—great animal magnetism or money," Fitzgerald said. "I had the two second things, though, good looks and intelligence." He also had a third— mother love. Fitzgerald's mother was the oldest of four children of an Irish immigrant, McQuillan by name, who had made money in the wholesale grocery business in Saint Paul, Minnesota. But it was money without breeding: roughneck Irish money. Fitzgerald's mother was a tireless reader of bad books, a wildly disordered woman who gave in to her son's every wish, causing him later to remark, "I didn't know till I was fifteen that there was anyone in the world except me." Fitzgerald's father, descended from the Maryland Scotts and Keys who had been in this country since the seventeenth century, represented lineage without money to back it up. Edward Fitzgerald was a flop who, after a number of drab failures, retreated to Saint Paul to become a salesman for his in-laws' grocery business. Yet from his father, whom he loved, Fitzgerald learned something of the code of the gentleman. "In my younger and more vulnerable years my father gave me some advice that I've been turning over in my mind ever since," *The Great Gatsby* begins. " 'Whenever you feel like criticizing anyone,' he told me, 'just remember that all the people in this world haven't had the advantages that you've had.' "

So spoke Nick Carraway, the narrator of *The Great Gatsby;* yet it is likely that F. Scott Fitzgerald more often remembered all the people in the world who *had* advantages that he didn't have. Although not invariably an advantage, aspirations he did have. His biographers describe him as an imaginative young boy, always inventing games and plays in which he reserved for himself the central role. Somewhat pushy, a self-starter, he operated under the burden of a sense of inferiority, an early social embarrassment in the highly social-minded city of Saint Paul, where his mother's erratic behavior and parvenu origins and his father's failures were an encumbrance. Never a good student, he was sent, with the financial help of one of his aunts, to the Newman School, a Catholic boarding school, where his boastfulness soon made him one of the most unpopular boys and where his awareness that he was among the poorest boys in a rich boys' school drove him to greater flights of self-promotion still. He was later, of course, to be one of the chief chroniclers of the rich, but mixed with his admiration for the rich, as he would later concede, was "an abiding distrust, an animosity towards the leisure class—not the conviction of a revolutionist but the smoldering hatred of a peasant."

A true self-dramatizer, he found a natural interest in dramatics, and as an adolescent wrote and acted in local theater groups in Saint Paul. Word of Princeton's Triangle Club, famous for its play productions, made him want to go to Princeton. (In the years of his decline, he wrote about his love for the theater, and especially for musical comedy, to his daughter: "Sometimes I wish I had gone along with [Cole Porter and Rodgers and Hart and the rest] but I guess I am too much a moralist at heart, and really want to preach at people in some acceptable form, rather than to entertain.") His aunt objected to Princeton, preferring that he not go to a Protestant school, and at his first shot at it he failed the Princeton entrance examination, passing it the second time round and overriding his aunt's objections. Fitzgerald entered Princeton with the class of 1917. The two, F. Scott Fitzgerald and Princeton, have been wed in the popular imagination ever since.

Some thirty-five years later Edmund Wilson, Fitzgerald's classmate at Princeton, wrote to their teacher Christian Gauss that he thought Princeton had not served Fitzgerald well. In place of the strength to be derived from moral principle necessary to a writer, Wilson wrote, Princeton "gave you too much respect for money and country-house social prestige." Along with others of his classmates, Fitzgerald, Wilson felt, fell victim to it. Princeton taught less the vigor needed for success than the pleasures of its benefits.

"I think of Princeton," remarks Amory Blaine, the hero of *This Side of Paradise*, "as being lazy, and good-looking and aristocratic." Of the three, the young F. Scott Fitzgerald had only the good looks. Lazy he emphatically was not; if anything he may have been rather too energetic for Princeton. John Peale Bishop, the poet and another classmate, commented about the almost enforced casualness of the Princetonian style of his day: "Any extreme in habiliment, pleasures or opinions is apt to be characterized as 'running it out,' and to 'run it out' is to lose all chance of social distinction." Fitzgerald must have come very close to running it out. He tried out (at 138 pounds) for football as a freshman, wrote for *The Tiger*, was lighting man and helped to write lyrics for the Triangle Club's spring show. So heated was his campaign to become an important figure at Princeton that he came near flunking out, and would have done, but for an illness that gave him a respectable excuse for leaving school. He was allowed back to Princeton on probation, the terms of which banned him from extracurricular activities and hence from being elected president of the Triangle Club, on which his heart was set.

Desire denied was to become something of a fixed pattern

with the young F. Scott Fitzgerald. Athletic glory, which he was unequipped for, eluded him; theatrical glory, for which he yearned, eluded him as well. A love affair with a girl from Smith College and the cushy Chicago suburb of Lake Forest foundered on economic shoals. ("Poor boys," someone told him, "shouldn't think of marrying rich girls.") Commissioned a second lieutenant in World War I—uniforms custom-made from Brooks Brothers in New York—he never got overseas to see the war at firsthand; another desire denied. Instead he spent his army days stateside, working in his spare hours at the novel that was, after many reworkings, to be *This Side of Paradise*. The book's original title was "The Romantic Egotist," which would not have been an inappropriate title for the autobiography of the young Fitzgerald.

Where his desire was not thwarted was in his choice of a wife. Assigned to Camp Sheridan, near Montgomery, Alabama, at a country-club dance he met and immediately fell in love with the then eighteen-year-old Zelda Sayre. His love was returned, with one very long string attached: Zelda made it plain to him that, with her tastes and temperament, she could not possibly see her way to marrying a man without enough money to allow her to live as she wished. How she wished to live, as was later to be famously known, was as extravagantly as possible. Until such money was available to Fitzgerald he was held, in his own phrase, "firmly at bay." Out of the army, working at an advertising agency, he sold his first short story to H. L. Mencken's *Smart Set*. His payment was thirty dollars. "I spent the thirty dollars," he later noted, "on a magenta feather fan for a girl in Alabama."

With the publication of Fitzgerald's first novel, and its consequent commercial success (nearly 33,000 copies sold in the first six months), his ship had come in, although, as he could scarcely know, it was headed out again on stormy seas. Boy wins girl, and enters upon a life resembling nothing so much as a prettily done movie filmed by a camera with gossamer over the lens. Money rolls in in abundance—his earnings continue to double and redouble—but then rolls out again in even greater abundance. Cut and dissolve to Europe. Apartment in Paris. The atelier of

Gertrude Stein and Alice B. Toklas. Cap d'Antibes. The great expatriate party on the Riviera. Cut and dissolve to the United States. Manorial houses in Maryland. Holidays in California. A splash in the Pulitzer fountain outside the Plaza in New York. Money for movie rights; short stories turned out by the yard, some bringing in as much as $4,000 apiece; heavy publishers' advances. But somehow never enough to cover expenses. *The Great Gatsby* is published in 1925—letters of critical acclaim from T. S. Eliot and Edith Wharton—but disappoints financial expectations. Living expenses and the pressure of sheer living make taking time out to work exclusively on another novel impossible. Eight years and a major economic depression go by until his next novel, *Tender Is the Night* (1934), which wins him neither acclaim nor money. The gossamer before the camera's lens turns out not to be gossamer at all but an alcoholic haze.

After the fall, F. Scott Fitzgerald spent his best energies trying to pick up the pieces and as the Gibbon of his own decline. Summing up this decline, he writes to a friend: "A prejudiced enemy might say it was all drink, a fond mama might say it was not providing for the future in better days, a psychologist might say it was a nervous collapse—it was perhaps partly all these things. . . . My life looked like a hopeless mess there for a while and the point was I didn't want it to be better. I had completely ceased to give a good Goddamn." Zelda was certifiably mad, packed away in a costly sanatorium; their daughter was in costly private school. Busted out though he was, he refused to have Zelda put in a less expensive institution, or—a bit of a snob even when down at the heel—his daughter go to public school. He turned to Hollywood; and though he was never well regarded there, most of his work having been rejected, nevertheless he brought in a weekly salary, according to Budd Schulberg, of $1,500 a week, which he used to meet his towering expenses and to pay back his large debts.

In 1936, at the age of thirty-nine, F. Scott Fitzgerald publicly announced, in the pages of *Esquire,* his crack-up. Perhaps most men who had truly cracked up would not have the interest or the energy to describe it in detail in public; but then most men are not writers, nor even among writers so supremely the romantic egotist as was Fitzgerald. Years before, Edna St. Vincent Millay had said that to meet F. Scott Fitzgerald was to think of a stupid old woman who has been left an extremely valuable diamond. In this metaphor the diamond, of course, was Fitzgerald's splendid talent, the stupidity referred to his inability to husband it at all properly. The talent was indisputable. As a phrasemaker alone, F. Scott Fitzgerald could take a reader's breath away with his "bruised sunsets," "chinchilla clouds," "fresh, green breast of the new world." As the anatomist of his own crack-up, none of this power was depleted, but instead it merely seemed as if he had a new subject to lavish it upon, as when he describes himself, in the midst of his crack-up, as wishing "he were twenty and going to a beach club all dolled up like a Turner sunset or Guido Reni's dawn." Even his admitted prejudices—"I liked old men . . . Katharine Hepburn's face on the screen . . . and Miriam Hopkins's face, and old friends if I saw them once a year and could remember their ghosts"—were charmingly stylish. He claimed to have lost interest in life, to have lost vitality, to become a "cracked plate" ("not the dish that he had ordered for his forties"), but he made of his failure an elegant thing, next to which success seemed crude, coarse, blatant, gross.

In truth it was nowhere near so elegant. It was falling off and climbing back up on the wagon; vomiting and trembling and terror of death. His drunks of his last years could be furious, breaking out, as Edmund Wilson noted, "into frenzied aggression, of self-hatred that seeks for relief by directing its fury against someone else." The obverse side of Fitzgerald's charm was sometimes brutality. Sheilah Graham, who loved him and whose love placed her in the position of helping him pick up the pieces from decades of emotional messiness, recounted, along with his good qualities, his many little meannesses, his snobberies, his lashings-out. Rightly or wrongly, not much of this is remembered. What is remembered is the arc of his life: the beautiful young man, the wondrous early success, the elegant defeat more touching than any success.

The result has been that F. Scott Fitzgerald has had not merely a second but a third act to his life. After his death, his work was resuscitated and his reputation has grown well beyond any bounds it knew even at the height of his early success. Not only has this been so in academic circles—where everything he has ever written has been put back in print and examined in biographies, critical studies, and a regular *Hemingway-Fitzgerald Newsletter*—but among the public at large. High school girls adoringly worship at the Fitzgerald shrine. Young men go off to college hoping, in a muddleheaded way, to duplicate what they construe to be his joyous collegiate life. Novelists of more mature years attempt to live their lives along the lines of a Fitzgerald scenario: lives of celebrity-mongering, heavy drinking, full-time partying. The Gatsby look in clothes design has been prominent. Scott has become a favored name for boy children among middle-class parents. F. Scott Fitzgerald's failure, no question about it, has become an unprecedented success.

There are no how-to manuals on the subject of failure. Failure is something one learns easily enough on one's own. Moreover, the explanations for failure are more easily come by, more readily persuasive, than those usually attributed to success. Failure seems less a matter of luck, more a matter of character, than success. To say, as for so many years people have, that behind every successful man there is a woman is to say a cliché: a statement alike stale and unbelievable; or, if believable, then in need of elaborate qualification. But to reverse the cliché, to say that behind every failed man is a woman, is to say something not only immediately graspable but far more persuasive. How easily one can see that woman, who has either trodden down her man by driving him too hard, or thwarted his ambition by acting as a drag on his career, or demoralized him by desertion. As with most reasons for failure, as opposed to those put forth to explain success, these seem, somehow, more compelling.

Failure of a certain kind even has a dignity denied to success. The Trojan leader Hector, at least to the modern reader of the *Iliad*, is a much nobler character than the sulking Achilles. In the same vein, it has been said that, in the autobiographies of successful men, the story loses interest immediately after success has been achieved. Failure, on the other hand, has the flavor of tragedy about it. The potential for high success is not in everyone, but the potential for complete and utter failure is. Not everyone can compile a great fortune or steer the destiny of an empire, but anyone can end up on skid row or a suicide at the bottom of the sea or on the pavement beneath a skyscraper. Failure, in its potentialities, is far and away more democratic than success; it awaits us all.

Then, too, there are failures and failures. A noble failure is much admired, if not easily imitated. In such a failure one goes down, all right, but down for what one believes in: one fails with one's principles unscathed, one's integrity intact, even if one's principles are wrong principles and one's integrity perhaps otiose. Consider General Lee surrendering at Appomattox, and how it is he, the loser, and not the victorious General Grant, who has always held sway in the imagination. To achieve a noble failure it is perhaps best of all to die for one's cause, but even short of death a stylish defeat, a noble failure, can gain moral resonance of a kind that success rarely attains. Socrates and Jesus are the two most notable noble failures.

Below the level of noble failures—which require an ample historical stage on which to be enacted—are what might be termed necessary failures. Such failures are necessary because they take place in circumstances in which to succeed carries with it a price, in personal pain or ignominy, greater than success is deemed to be worth. There are things an honorable man will not, and a decent man cannot, do; and if the price of not doing them is failure, so be it. There are also true conflicts—between aspiration and family or personal health, between the pulls of the active and of the contemplative life—and these cannot always be resolved in favor of worldly ambition. In all such instances failure, if such it be, is chosen, and as such, as a conscious act, is judged less painful than failure that arrives unbidden.

But the greatest number of failures, the great grey bog of failure, consists of those who are quite willing to pay the price of succeeding (however high it might be), have no scruples of any kind about doing what is necessary, nor any conflicts dragging on their energies, but who are nonetheless denied success.

Desire is not wanting in them; some decisive element is. Does their reach exceed their grasp? Or are they simply short of abilities? Or do they suffer a defeating flaw? Or have they plain rotten luck? Misbegotten in their aspirations, deceived in their self-estimation, weighed down by a lack of judgment or maladroit timing or faulty instinct, whichever may be the case, fortune frowns upon them and the gates clang in their faces.

Would most persons rather succeed blatantly or fail stylishly? These are not, of course, the only alternatives, and even those who are not driven to succeed struggle if only to avert visible signs of too evident failure. If recent changes in institutions are any indication, fewer and fewer people work (or wish to work) without a net beneath them—which is to say that security, as expressed by seniority among unionists, tenure among academics, and plush pensions among executives, has become perhaps as great a goad today as ambition was in an earlier day. As the character Maggie in *Cat on a Hot Tin Roof* says: "You can be young without money, but you can't be old without it." But there are failures that cut deeper than financial failure.

While Napoleonic yearnings may be less, few people surely find their own prestige of negligible concern. Thus in recent decades there has been a proliferation—and concomitant inflation—of job titles. In academic life, for example, to reach the end of one's career without achieving the rank of full professor is, ipso facto, to be adjudged a failure. So now nearly everyone who sticks it out in academic life, no matter how undistinguished, becomes a full professor; and consequently the title "distinguished professor" has become more widespread. Similarly, in banks and corporations, vice-presidents have also proliferated; and in many large banks the title "junior vice-president" is common. Why have all these high-sounding though in fact rather empty titles been pressed into service? A cynical answer is that such titles are less costly than giving people more money. A sad answer is that people above all do not wish to *appear* failures, no matter what truth about themselves they harbor in their hearts.

"Tell me what you desire, and I will tell you what you are," wrote Henri Frédéric Amiel in his *Intimate Journal*. Not always an easy thing, though, to know what one desires. What is more, many people, if they were quite clear about their desires, might be ashamed to own up to them, even to themselves; and, one hastens to add, one is not talking here about dark Freudian desires. It has become less easy, for example, for a young man or woman to say, straight out, "I want to earn no less than $250,000 a year, for what that sum will bring me in goods and freedom," without being thought crass. Or: "I desire to mold the opinion of great numbers," without being thought cunning. Or: "I wish to control the destiny of nations," without being thought crazed. No, most of us, if pressed to tell what it is we desire, can probably come up with little more than an earnest desire not to fail, to end up somewhere well above the bottom, so that, whatever our true failings, they will be known only to ourselves. Ambition, increasingly, ends with the wish merely to avoid failure.

Curiosity Shop □ "It was a horrible, ugly life," the man says, "a horrible, ugly life." He has repeated the line a few times now, almost as if it were part of a litany. He is talking to other men at a long table, men who are, as he is, busted-out gamblers. They are part of a group called Gamblers Anonymous. If he, along with the other men in the room, had not failed at his gambling, one may be sure he would not be here now. He tells an anecdote about his own degraded gambling days, pauses, sums up: "It was a horrible, ugly life, a horrible, ugly life." He would find himself sitting in bars until the early morning hours waiting to contract loans at insanely high interest rates. One morning when his wife took their children to the doctor, he called in a used-furniture dealer and told him he was planning to refurnish the apartment and wanted a flat price for everything in the place. Every bit of furniture was removed and paid for, just in time for him to make the first race at a suburban track. "The funny thing is," he says, recounting it now, "I really believed it myself. I mean, I really intended to refurnish the place on my winnings at the track that afternoon. Of course, when I got back, I was broke, totally crapped out." He went on to tell stories of a wife crying herself to sleep, of children who grew up not knowing their father, of a flow of bad checks, of juice-racket loans, of running off to relatives to borrow money to stave off being beaten or possibly killed by heavies in the employ of Syndicate men. "It was a horrible, ugly life," he says, "a horrible, ugly life."

He is a man in his late forties or early fifties. It is difficult to determine his exact age with any precision, mainly because of his eyes, which seem so very old. The lids are heavy, their skin crinkly, crêped as plastic surgeons say, giving his eyes a puffy look. He is dapper in a striped sweater and cream-colored trousers. He has a fine smile, knowing and warm. Also good hands, with long, tapering fingers, a coat of polish on the nails. He is a loser, but rather a stylish one.

Seated around the table listening to him are other losers. They are a mixed lot. On a check of hands around the table one notices manicures and nails blackened by rough labor, pinky rings and swollen knuckles—hands, in sum, that belie a wide range of social class and styles of living. Some of the men are what once used to be known as snappy dressers: got up in turtlenecks and blazers, or in dark shirts and wide silk print ties, clothes that would go down well in Las Vegas or Lake Tahoe or the Bahamas. Others dress more plainly, no hint of the sporting life in their attire. Still others are in outfits that clearly show their working-class origins. They are Jewish and Italian, Polish and German, Irish and Anglo-Saxon. Their ages range from early twenties to late fifties.

What they have in common is that they are—or at least were—all players: some high rollers, some not so very high though high enough to ruin their marriages, or to cost them their jobs, or to land them in jail for stealing to get enough money to keep them in action. For now, at least while seated around this table in the basement of a church, they are full of atonement. Their gambling, they hold, is an addiction, like that to alcohol or drugs. But what more truly unites them is loss. They are losers, one and all. Recidivism is apparently fairly high among reformed gamblers, and many of these men, despite their confessions and the clarity of their current perspective, will return to the fray. What they have in common above all, it turns out, is a sharp distaste for reality, an impatience with the day-to-day building up of achievement toward their aspirations. They wanted it, and wanted it without delay. They are men who have heard seductive voices, whispering to them, "Let 'er rip! Bet it all! Do it!" They did, and lost, and lost again and yet again. And so they meet here tonight, struggling to help one another, telling one another what a horrible, ugly life it was. And it is heartrending, this spectacle of misery needing company.

Is it better to have been a has-been than a never-was? A never-was is, of course, a neologism, a spin-off (another neologism) from the original and better known phrase "has-been." No difficulty, certainly, about the definition of a has-been, which the *Oxford English Dictionary* defines, simply enough, thus: "One that *has been* but is no longer: a person or thing whose career or efficiency belongs to the past, or whose best days are over." The *O.E.D.* records its first use in print in English in 1606. Has-beens had been around long before, always having proved bothersome to others—has-beens in politics, men who formerly held power, Machiavelli instructed his Prince, were to be done away with—and doubtless even more bothersome to themselves. See *King Lear.*

The condition of has-been, of one who has known success and prominence and then slid back amid the ruck, is a condition of failure of a particularly poignant kind. Having once climbed to the peak, and then having slipped all the way down, many have not the courage to begin the climb again—or the appetite to recommence living in the lowlands, as witness the defenestrations and other suicides following the stock market crash of 1929. Has-beens come in all ages. One's best days can be over quite early; and to live out the remainder as second or third-best can be a grey, even wretched prospect.

Contained within the notion of the has-been are certain unspoken assumptions about the shape a human life ought to take. Two such assumptions predominate. The first is a view of life as a record of unimpeded progress, in which each year finds one getting better and better, earning more money, gaining greater mastery over one's work, acquiring more recognition and higher rewards. The picture here is one of a line graph, with the line of a life going unbrokenly up, up, up. The second assumption about the shape a life ought, ideally, to take might be pictured as a gently sloping arc, delineating a life that gradually rises to reach its apex in a person's middle years and then just as gradually begins a graceful descent toward the close of life. No bumps, no shocks, no true reversals of fortune. Pleasant to be able to believe in either of these depictions of progress through life; and not only do many people. believe in them, but some indeed achieve them.

The has-been does great violence to such cozy assumptions. The has-been is even something of a walking insult to the idea of progress in life. He is a dropout, but not by volition. More accurately, he has been bounced out, sometimes by forces external to himself, sometimes by his own unintended doing. The danger of becoming a has-been is built into some kinds of work. The athlete, for an obvious example, figures to live out the better part of his life with his best days behind him. The classic (if also clichéd) instance is of the boxer, used up and tossed out onto the street, his face scarred and his brains scrambled. But even athletes who have ended their careers happily (Stan Musial, say, or John Havlicek, or Eddie Arcaro), their pockets filled with money, the walls of their dens lined with trophies, the graciousness of retirement gently following the glory of playing days—even about such men as these, there is something wistful and finally a little sad. Dancers, opera singers, courtesans, gigolos, anyone whose career is bounded by physical performance, can expect a similarly long dusk in which to recall the now-faded sun of better days, when life was more stirring.

If physiology creates one sort of has-been, psychology creates another sort. Chief among this latter category are those who seem to have no trouble gaining success, but for whom the great problem is holding on to it. Even the most solid achievement makes them edgy. They must push on, and sometimes quite irrationally so. Overreaching is the common name for this common enough phenomenon. What is uncommon is the variety of ways in which it is done. Examples abound. The man who makes hundreds of thousands of dollars a year but finds it necessary to cheat in a blatant way on his income tax for only a few thousands, and risks losing it all. The man who, having a small gold mine of a business, feels the need to throw his money into another business, about which he knows nothing—and with predictable results. A taste for the wrong women, for plunging, for high-stakes gambling, things that often crop up after success and are themselves certain antidotes against success, stand as proof that some people simply cannot endure succeeding. Is the problem a lack of character? Or is it that such people are interested only in the journey that ambition sets them upon, while the arrival, success, soon palls and they find a way, consciously or unconsciously, to be off on the journey again?

Into this same pyschological category fall those for whom the fear of becoming a has-been is so great that the fear itself stultifies them and thus guarantees that such they will become. This is a fear most deeply held by those who do creative work; composers and painters and writers are especially plagued by it —by the fear, specifically, that their talent, whose origin is itself somewhat mysterious, will dry up and their purpose in life be at an end. John Leggett's interesting book *Ross & Tom* (1974) documents two such cases: the careers of two early, indeed spectacular, literary successes, those of the novelists Ross Lockridge (author of *Raintree County*) and Thomas Heggen (author of *Mister Roberts*). Very different in style and in temperament —Lockridge was a tireless self-promoter, Heggen a habitual self-denigrator—in their early twenties both men were accorded the world's glittering prizes: money in the hundreds of thousands and fame beyond either man's expectations. Yet each lived in dread of being unable to match his early éclat. And so— Lockridge through asphyxiating himself by leaving his car engine running in a locked garage, Heggen by overdosing himself with barbiturates and submerging in a bathtub—each avoided the fear of becoming an early has-been by choosing oblivion.

But perhaps the ultimate has-been is the gangster, at least as we have come to know him through the movies. He is a specialist in failure, and as such a warning to us all. Robert Warshow, in his essay "The Gangster as Tragic Hero," has put the point neatly:

> At bottom the gangster is doomed because he is under the obligation to succeed, not because the means he employs are unlawful. In the deeper layers of the modern consciousness, *all* means are unlawful, every attempt to succeed is an act of aggression, leaving one alone and guilty and defenseless among enemies: one is *punished* for success. This is our intolerable dilemma: that failure is a kind of death and success is evil and dangerous, is—ultimately—impossible. The effect of the gangster film is to embody this dilemma in the person of the gangster and resolve it by his death. The dilemma is resolved because it is *his* death, not ours. We are safe; for the moment, we can acquiesce in our failure, we can choose to fail.

Curiosity Shop □ "Well," said the man, recently retired after selling his eight dry-cleaning shops for something in excess of half a million dollars, "my day starts off pretty much as it always has. I'm an early riser. So I wake at six, shower and shave. I put on a suit and tie, as I used to do. Some habits you don't change. I don't wake Evelyn. Now that the kids are grown and out on their own, she likes to sleep a little later. I get in the Lincoln and drive to the deli, where I have my breakfast. Now I eat more leisurely than I used to: juice, coffee, dry cereal, a couple of eggs scrambled hard, sometimes an English muffin, sometimes maybe a Danish. I read both the morning papers—see how my stock is doing, check the ball scores, look into the international situation. Sometimes I schmooze a little with Feldman, the owner, whom I've known for years. By now it's about eight-thirty, maybe eight-forty-five. I get back in the Lincoln, pull out of the lot, turn on an all-day news show on the car radio. Then I say to myself, "Sid, it's not even nine o'clock.

How in the hell are you going to get through this goddamn day?"

A character in "The Butterfly," a story by Chekhov, remarks: "Surely it must be dull to be a simple, undistinguished, unknown person, with a face so worn and furrowed, and bad manners." Leaving aside the bad manners, no one would dispute, even in a democratic age, that the world is full of simple, undistinguished persons. Yet how many think themselves so? Unknown might be conceded, but those ready to grant that they are simple or undistinguished (at least, undistinguished from their fellow men and women) are precious few. All but the truly dull-witted carry about with them a self-drama, fueled by varying degrees of self-deception no doubt, but in this drama they are not simple but highly complicated and not undistinguished but fascinatingly distinctive. That man or woman who says he or she is simple and undistinguished is probably most to be distrusted as vain and devious.

Yet some people do think themselves decided failures, and doubtless one of the largest categories of such people comprises those who think themselves failures even in the face of the world's disagreement. Included in this category are all the men and women who feel that they have misspent not alone their youths but their lives. Although they may have succeeded grandly in business or journalism or administration, they nonetheless believe that they have denied their true natures, violated themselves in some essential way. No one close to them may possess the candor to say it aloud, but they themselves know the truth about themselves—and the truth, as they construe it, is that they are sellouts.

The phrase "to sell out" has its origin in American politics, where it originally meant to betray one's party or cause or associates. The phrase was given an especially heavy workout during the years of intense radical sectarian politics in the United States in the 1930s. But it has lived on well beyond these years, and become absorbed not only in the language but in the psychology of the college-educated. At various stages of one's

career one must now ask—or at any rate many people do ask—
Am I being true to myself? Or am I selling out? But to whom
does one sell out? Who is it, more precisely, who is buying? And
what exactly is being sold?

To answer the last question first: What is being sold out is
putatively one's soul, although in an age as secular as ours soul
might go by the synonyms "talent" or "authentic self" or "integrity." As for the buyer, the agency to whom one sells out, it is
the devil—though again, in our secular age, the devil goes by the
labels "capitalist system" or "the money boys" or "the power
brokers." To sell out, whatever language one chooses to adapt
to describe both the bought and the sold, is to strike a Faustian
bargain with the Devil, an exchange of one's soul or essential
self for the world's prizes.

Selling out, in this view, is rather a dramatic thing to do. To
those with a penchant for self-dramatizing, it has always held
out a special allure. Among artists manqués it has had more than
allure. Not all, but great numbers of journalists, screenwriters,
commercial artists, composers of popular music, used to indulge
the self-drama of thinking themselves sellouts. A journalist or
screenwriter ought instead to be writing great novels; a commercial artist ought to be advancing yet further forward the
avant-garde; a composer of popular music ought to be working
in the great traditions of serious music. But no, they have sold
out, to Henry Luce, or Hollywood, or advertising agencies, or
record companies; they have gone "commercial," fallen into the
fleshpots. They have betrayed their talent, and hence themselves
—and, oh, what a crushing sadness it all is!

Or would be, if it were true. But is it? The first thing to be
noted about the drama of selling out is that it is a highly self-
serving one. It assumes, right off, that one truly does have
something important to sell—that one is a sufficiently significant
person for the Devil to want to do a deal with. Another, less
dramatic reading is nowhere near so self-exalting. "I work at
what I work at because it [journalism, commercial art, advertis-
ing] is what I do best. Granted, I might have aimed a bit higher
—and once did—but in calculating the risks, I did not like the
odds; and so I have chosen to do what I do now. I think I know

what my true quality is. I am not ashamed." In occupations allied with the arts few people would make such a declaration. Why should they, after all, when the drama of the sellout is so ready at hand? "I could have created something serious and enduring. And perhaps I would have done. But I married young; children came along. It is one thing to sacrifice amenities on one's own account; quite another to ask one's family to do so. Besides, society does not really value art. So I sold out. I am ashamed."

Yet such a declaration as this last really implies that it is society that ought to be ashamed. Why, after all, should a man or woman have to make the decision to earn his bread rather than be allowed to work unimpeded at his art? Something is clearly amiss here; or would be, if many artists found their sole choice that between starving and selling out; or if great works were going undone because of financial pressure squeezing potentially great artists out of their true calling. But it is closer to the truth to say that the large number of people who think themselves sellouts in this sense probably have vastly inflated views of their talent. They work, the very great majority of them, in television or on newsmagazines because that is, quite precisely, what they are best fit for. One of the fringe benefits of such jobs is to think oneself a sellout.

But it is not among would-be artists, or artists manqué, alone that the notion of selling out can hold sway. Many men and women in business feel its pull too, although they tend to speak less of selling out than of joining the rat race (as it was once called). Implicit in the notion of the rat race—as in, earlier, the notion of the man in the grey-flannel suit—is the loss of one's identity. One is a rat, like many another rat, in the race with all the rest of the rats. Still, one lays claim to awareness. Writing about a man in the advertising business, Tom Wolfe notes, "Madison Avenue crash helmet is another of Parker's terms. It refers to the kind of felt hat that is worn with a crease down the center and no dents in the sides, a sort of homburg without a flanged brim. He calls it a Madison Avenue crash helmet and then wears one." Thus one is a rat but a superior—because aware—rat.

Now that zoological metaphors have been replaced by mechanistic ones, people speak less of a rat race and more of what they are pleased to call the System. One is, in business, a cog in the machinery of the System, or so a certain kind of conventional wisdom holds. Best, again according to the conventional wisdom, to extricate oneself, to drop out—as, say, Brooks Firestone dropped out. "Brooks Firestone," an advertisement for *People* magazine ran, "went to work at granddad's rubber company like a good Firestone should. But he soon tired of it. Now he's in California building a respectable winery. 'I am a classic executive dropout.'"

For a certain kind of businessman, building "a respectable winery" is roughly equivalent to writing a great novel, or painting important pictures—it is devoting one's life to art. It reminds one of Lionel Trilling's remark that "the life of competition for spiritual status is not without its own peculiar sordidness and absurdity." It is also a fantasy. To make such a fantasy real one may have to be no less well endowed than a Firestone. Meanwhile, one can only nourish soothing thoughts of oneself as a sellout or enmeshed in the System—thoughts which, soothing though they might at first be, in time become exacerbating.

"What a pity, Manvers, the fashion has gone out for selling oneself to the devil," says the hero of Disraeli's novel *Vivian Grey*.

"Good gracious, Mr. Grey!"

"On my honour, I am quite serious. It does appear to me to be a very great pity. What a capital plan for younger brothers! It's a kind of thing I've been trying to do all my life, and never could succeed."

Curiosity Shop □ Every city of any ample size has at least one, and large cities have scores of them: old office buildings, where aspiration and dreams once resided, but from which the action has moved elsewhere, leaving a name on the door but, most decidedly, nothing like a Bigelow on the floor. The directories of such buildings have a curious likeness; they list the names of theatrical agents, inventors, sales representatives, jobbers, many another business that never got off the ground. Behind the isinglass windows of their outer doors, who knows what dramas are played out? But they are nowhere near so grand as the occupants of these offices—most of them older men now—had planned. Some of the firms have grand names: Midwest Continental, Acme Manufacturing, Tri-State Construction. The founder of Acme Manufacturing, picking so impersonal a name, must have had large dreams when he set out in business: plants on both coasts, a chauffeur to drive him to work mornings while he studied the stock market, perhaps a private airplane, a business of the kind sons would go into and sons of sons. The result, more likely, is that Acme Manufacturing has made a living for its owner, but not much more than that: a one-man operation with its owner's wife coming in one day a week to do the books and handle the typing for the firm's trickle of correspondence. There may be a few sleepers in these old buildings—businesses quietly bringing in high profits on low expenses—but for the most part their offices are filled with the heartbreak of men who never quite made it, and are not going to in this life.

A special kind of failure is that of the person who fails at success. Of necessity the number of such failures is smaller than any other category of the failed, and for an obvious reason. To fail at success one has first of all to succeed; and to fail dramatically at success one must succeed big—to have, as Balzac once put it, "mad success, success of the kind that crushes people who lack the physical and moral strength to bear it." Perhaps it is not altogether surprising that many people do not have the requisite success. In the rush of a mad success it is not easy to maintain the necessary balance: to calibrate one's true value on the one hand, and never to forget one's ultimate insignificance on the other.

Many people who fail at success—who, in effect, blow it— seem almost pleased at having done so. Success, their behavior implies, is not something that people like themselves can take in stride; rather as if failure were the salt of the earth. Their own success strikes them, somehow, as evidence of a blatant kind that they must be doing something wrong. As largehearted people are inclined to find virtue in misfortune, so they look upon their own good fortune as a sure sign of inner vice. That they cannot take their success with self-assurance or calm dignity is for them a badge of their humanity.

The actor Richard Dreyfuss and the socialist writer Michael Harrington are two men who in recent years have had mad successes—quick, unexpected, stunning—and who have offered themselves up, in interviews and in autobiographical writings, as case studies in the art of failing at success. A Beverly Hills Jewish boy living on the periphery of Hollywood show business, a Saint Louis Catholic working in the socialist movement in New York, two more different types than Richard Dreyfuss and Michael Harrington are not easily imagined. Both, true, share left-wing politics. But what they above all have in common is that neither could take it when the chips were up.

Yet another difference between Richard Dreyfuss and Michael Harrington is that Dreyfuss, the actor, set out to succeed, whereas success never even seems to have occurred to Harrington as a possibility. Want it and plan for it though he did, his success nevertheless caught Dreyfuss unawares. "It really took me by surprise, this success," he told a journalist for *Esquire* magazine. "It is something I fought for and wanted and held out to myself as *the* goal. I had thought more, and thought more completely, about being a star than anyone else I knew. I thought I knew what it was going to be. Here I was, this guy who knew he wanted to be a star his whole life, and suddenly I found myself acting like a twelve-year-old. I didn't anticipate the guilt and the fear of success. I didn't anticipate the downside of success at all."

Not only did Dreyfuss want success, he was a young man with a game plan: the plan called for his winning through by the age of thirty-two. First he would hone his acting skills, perhaps in a repertory company; next work at increasing his strength in those dramaturgical areas in which he felt himself weakest, for example the classics. Confident of his talent, he felt time was on his side. "I was never in a hurry," he has said in retrospect, "[never] knew any angst about not being a star at twenty-two. . . . I wasn't concerned because it was all going to come." Come of course it did, though rather sooner than Dreyfuss had expected. The tide swept in, and Richard Dreyfuss, still in his twenties, was taken at the flood.

The tide, in this instance, came with an offer Dreyfuss accepted to play in a movie entitled *American Graffiti,* which became a hit beyond anyone's expectations. Certainly Dreyfuss had no such expectations for it, and he said afterward that he took the part offered him because he wished to be out of Los Angeles for the aftermath of a breakup with a girl friend. Further—and unrefusable—offers followed the success of *American Graffiti: The Apprenticeship of Duddy Kravitz, Jaws, Close Encounters of the Third Kind,* and *The Goodbye Girl,* for which Dreyfuss won an Oscar, leaving him, at thirty (two years ahead of schedule), at the top of his profession as a screen actor and with no place to go but down.

Until the arrival of this early success, Richard Dreyfuss contends, he was a hustling, knockabout, happy-go-lucky actor, pleased enough to be scouting up work; like so many unarrived actors, he was the perennial supplicant. But now with his success others began supplicating to Richard Dreyfuss. Strangers recognized him on the street. He learned a producer had bribed his answering service to get his private telephone number. His own hotly competitive family began deferring to him. Money poured in. His response was bad behavior. "I had enormous guilt feelings about how easily things had come to me," he reports, "and I started to resist the position I was in by drinking a lot, doing drugs, eating too much, being childish, denigrating my talent, and generally doing a lot of things that were getting in my way."

But Richard Dreyfuss, in the language of the soap operas, is battling back. According to the account in *Esquire,* "he's giving success one hell of a fight." Therapy has played a large part; for a stretch, he, Dreyfuss, was a five-day-a-week psychoanalysand. Since he is now able to command something on the order of $1.5 million for a film, he was allowed to assert his independence by walking off a film he had contracted to do—and detested—at a penalty to himself of $350,000. He has all the toys of the movie star (Beverly Hills mansion, New York apartment, big Mercedes) and the politics that, despite what would seem an open contradiction, so often go with them: "My politics are still the same. Look, Eugene Debs never said we shouldn't be comfortable. He just said we shall *all* be comfortable." But too comfortable, psychologically, is more than he, Dreyfuss, can apparently stand. Los Angeles, for example, has become too much for him, for in that city he finds that his celebrity carries too much weight. New York is more to his taste. "In New York," he told the reporter from *Esquire*, "I'm dog shit." The *Esquire* article does not report that Richard Dreyfuss smiled when he said this, but one imagines that he did. Prosperity and fame offer an embarrassment of choices, yet to be able to be treated as Richard Dreyfuss prefers to be treated in New York is not a choice one would have thought, before now, appealing.

Although Michael Harrington's was nowhere near so grand a success as Richard Dreyfuss's—neither so much money nor such widespread fame was attached—it was, in its way, even more unexpected and certainly more drastic in its effect. A single book brought Harrington, a lifelong socialist, success; more precisely, a single review in *The New Yorker* of *The Other America*, a book he wrote on the subject of poverty in the United States, made him, in political circles, something of an instant celebrity: suddenly invited everywhere to lecture, working with Sargent Shriver to set up the War on Poverty, aloft aboard jets flying to this conference or that workshop. Greater triumphs have been registered, but it helps to know that, until the success of his book brought him renown as the great expert on poverty, Michael Harrington prided himself on never having earned more than $5,000 a year. Now, suddenly, he was getting $1,500 for a single lecture. "If it's bourgy [bourgeois], it can't be good," Harrington's socialist comrades used to say. Now here he was, almost in spite of himself, earning a bourgeois income and become, given his privileged position with Sargent Shriver and the Lyndon Johnson administration, a bit of an establishment figure into the bargain.

Michael Harrington's bout with success, as he later wrote about in an autobiographical volume entitled *Fragments of the*

Century, left him puzzled and resentful. This puzzlement and resentment ended in a nervous breakdown. One Sunday evening in San Diego, giving yet another of his lectures on poverty in America, Harrington felt the room nearly go out from under on him, so that he had to complete his lecture sitting in a chair. At first he thought this attack of vertigo a mere matter of overwork —the result of too crowded a schedule. But it happened again and yet again; his anxiety spread, for these were full-blown anxiety attacks, assailing him on the street, even at home.

What had happened? In retrospect Harrington concluded that his view of himself as essentially an outsider, the out-at-the-elbow political bohemian, scraped too sharply against his new position as an insider, the discussant at White House conferences, and rubbed him psychically raw. Everything he had hitherto done was, as he put it, "based on a rejection of bourgeois norms of aspiration." Quite without intending it, Harrington walked blindly into success. "Like the Zen archer," he noted, "I hit the target because I did not aim at it."

This certainly seems true enough. Harrington did not write his book intending it to become a best seller, or even a celebrated cause. *The Other America* is not even a highly readable book; Michael Harrington, if the truth be known, is not a very gifted writer. His was a success of timing. John F. Kennedy had recently been assassinated, Lyndon Johnson had taken over the presidency; talk of Great Societies was in the air. Michael Harrington's book provided news that, from a political point of view, a great many people wanted to hear. His interest in the poor had long preceded this book; but suddenly his preoccupation of long standing had become of national interest. He was the "poverty guy."

In *Fragments of the Century,* Michael Harrington leaves his struggle with success oddly unresolved. He notes that he put in, as a result of this success, four years with a Freudian psychoanalyst. Like a good socialist soldier, he quotes Marx to elucidate aspects of his own mental crisis. He complains, as he puts it, of "the profoundly bourgeois character of the nuclear family" —by which he means that he and his wife wanted children, and that costs money. "I had been caught up," he remarks, "against my will, in the surge of upward mobility that followed World War II, and that is a difficult fate for a man who originally wanted to be a poet." Toward the close of his account of his success and the breakdown it caused, Michael Harrington, by then nearly fifty years old, wrote: "I still feel ambiguous about money and power and success."

With Michael Harrington as with Richard Dreyfuss, the question is not so much about the reality of their suffering with their successes, but about what the suffering itself means. The difficult question is: Is their determination—as well as that of others determined to fail at success—anything more than a grim determination not to grow up?

Curiosity Shop □ Considerable attention has been paid to various of the human psychological states and conditions, but no one, apart from a few American novelists, has written about the special psychological burden of being unemployed—or, more precisely, unemployed when one wishes very much to be employed. As with all other extreme psychological states—certain crippling phobias come to mind—when one is unemployed the tone, the shape, the feel of one's days are different beyond compare; it is as if the world were not quite the same place as one once knew it. Life seems so finely organized, when you are unemployed, and what it seems finely organized for is to exclude yourself. While you live under an enforced idleness, everyone else seems so fully occupied; and watching them go about their days you are sharply reminded of the obvious point that the word *occupied* is at the root of the word *occupation*. Unemployed, unoccupied, you know not what to do but consider one of two things: the world's injustice or your own unworthiness.

Part of the psychological burden of being unemployed is carried in the coin of self-pity. You see others going about their business. Why have you no business of your own to attend to? Why does the world not more readily appreciate your ability? Why are friends and family not more understanding? For them to qualify as sufficiently understanding they would have to share your own rage at the world's indifference, a thing they seem, in their own preoccupations, unwilling to do. Of course you cannot expect anyone else, even those you care most about, to understand. You are, when unemployed, alone, isolated, desolated, a man who is an island: an island where time hangs heavy, activity is nil, and the only strong emotion is feeling dolorously sorry for yourself.

When one is unemployed for long, self-pity can be counted upon to twist itself into self-scorn—and, in the case of some, into self-deprecation. Without work you feel yourself without value; or at a minimum uncertain of your value. Jobs that might once have been thought well beyond the pale of possibility suddenly acquire an allure. To be a clerk in a department store, after all, comes to seem not such a bad deal. One works in a bright place; one's duties are clearly defined; one may not be well paid, but one is blessedly free of responsibility. Or consider a postman: works out of doors, no boss peering over his shoulder, good benefits, and fine pension. Forget that before being out of work you never gave such jobs a first let alone a second thought.

The longer your stretch of unemployment, the more attractive such jobs seem, the less attractive, correspondingly, you yourself seem. At interviews for new jobs you feel yourself pushing. Is your tone wrong? In attempting to speak about your strengths did you lapse into bragging? Did you ask for too much money? For too little? Did you come across as too conservative? Not conservative enough? What is the significance of the fact that the interview for this job was briefer than the interview for the previous job, for which you were turned down? Trying to gauge your own performance as well as the reaction to it becomes more and more difficult. In a curious way, being unemployed is a full-time job: that is, you can scarcely ever think about anything else. Yet how could it be otherwise in a country where you are defined by your answer to the question, "What do you do?" To do nothing undermines confidence, saps energy, and cuts into self-respect like no other work on earth.

In a book entitled *The Four Seasons of Success*, Budd Schulberg, who is also the author of *What Makes Sammy Run?*, wrote: "Is there any other culture in which the words *winner* and *loser* carry such apocalyptic force?" The words *winner* and *loser* are still very much around—still very potent—but it has become less easy to tell the one from the other. Once conventional wisdom had it that winners were those men and women who piled up the most money or fame or power. A less conventional view—put forth, for example, by Nathaniel Hawthorne in his story "The Great Stone Face"—had it that the only true winner was the man of true goodness. Conventional and unconventional, neither of these views has the cogency it once did. Motives behind the quest for money or fame or power are now thought suspect; goodness itself no longer compels credence. Winners, therefore, are not so easy to make out.

Losers, correspondingly, are no more easily discerned. Consider bankruptcy. In fiscal 1978, *The Wall Street Journal* reports, bankruptcy was declared by 196,967 persons; this was 4 percent more than in the previous year, yet below the record 224,354 persons set in fiscal 1975, after a recession year. Surely once bankruptcy was the indisputable badge of the loser. A bankrupt was a despised figure. "A bankrupt," remarks Balzac's character the miser Monsieur Grandet in the novel *Eugénie Grandet,* "is a thief that the law unfortunately takes under its protection." And in another of his novels, *Lost Illusions,* Balzac has his young hero Lucien Chardon speculate, "Has not a man who comes to defeat done to death all those middle-class virtues on which society is built?" Bankruptcy was, in Balzac's day and before and for better than a century afterward, tantamount to instant and perpetual ignominy. Bankruptcy brought disgrace to a man and his family and indeed his children's children; it meant he had let down the side; it could be—and very often was—sufficient cause for suicide.

Suicide certainly seems the last possible thought in courtrooms hearing bankruptcy cases nowadays, when bankruptcy proceedings have come close to becoming rote proceedings. Walk into a courtroom where bankruptcies are being heard and one finds a room dominated by lawyers. If anything the reigning atmosphere is one of high boredom. Much traffic files in and out of the courtroom. Lawyers and their clients go off into rooms to negotiate debts; some to see if the bankrupt party will not "reaffirm" some part of his debt. For most of the people undergoing bankruptcy—and they are preponderantly men—these proceedings come as something of a relief. When the court session is over they will be unshackled from their debts; they will have a chance to begin their financial lives afresh. As some people now send out divorce announcements, so nowadays some people are said to throw bankruptcy parties.

"The feeling at the end of it all is liberating," according to Raymond Mungo, a man who has gone through a bankruptcy and later wrote up his reflections on it for the magazine *Mother Jones*. Raymond Mungo is a former student activist, a writer whose background includes a stint in the commune movement in the United States. His bankruptcy came about as a result of his injudicious use of credit cards. With charging airplane tickets for himself and friends, renting cars, getting bank loans, and generally mismanaging his financial life, Mungo racked up debts of roughly $100,000. "In my life," he writes, "$100,000 is more than I can hope to put together in one place no matter how hard I try." How hard Mungo did try he does not say. His qualms about the situation he landed himself in are not excessive. "So I'm a bankrupt, and it's wonderful in its way. It's not so horrible to write off debts to huge banks and corporations that helped induce me to use their money. These corporations have neither faces nor feelings."

Raymond Mungo makes bankruptcy—apart from the tenacity of some bill collectors—out to be rather a romp. Bankruptcy, in his view, "is a humane and libertarian concept for the 'small' person, an actual legal light intended to rescue ordinary citizens who, through unwise management of credit and funds or just plain ignorance of what they're doing, arrive at a condition of owing their souls to the company store." At times Mungo seeks to indict the system, as he is pleased to call it, for his own injudiciousness. He really didn't hurt anyone, he insists. Banks and credit companies allow for financial deadbeats like himself; it is figured into the wide profit margin they wring out of the rest of us, he argues. Besides, both kinds of financial institutions made substantial profits off him before he went under. Sounding rather the good Republican, the former communard Raymond Mungo asks: Was his own economic behavior any different from that of the United States, which goes deeper and deeper in debt? "Our cities and, finally, our nation, head squarely for bankruptcy, a vicious cycle that could poetically conclude with the banks themselves going bankrupt." Thus Mr. Mungo, in piling up his $100,000 debt, was in effect only, so to say, going with the flow—behaving not only like his countrymen but like his country's government. "I do view the whole experience as *lacking wisdom,*" he concludes; but aside from the pain that followed his finding himself in such heavy debt, "I had a hell of a good time at the expense of my good name, and I can't say that I regret it."

Raymond Mungo makes a case for bankruptcy of the kind one used to hear for divorce. It is, in other words, on the order of a positive right. Far from being something one need feel dismay or shame about, bankruptcy is—and here Raymond Mungo's politics come into play—"the people's weapon against the banks—one of the best we've got." Mungo's point seems to be that bankruptcy is chiefly a no-fault matter. The system is too much; the will of men and women too little. On every hand one is enticed to buy and borrow, to flash one's plastic, to take (as an English bank advertisement once put it) "the waiting out of wanting," so it is only natural that one respond to these enticements. But Raymond Mungo's larger point, buried under his self-justifications, is that bankruptcy, losing of an unambiguous kind, is not so bad; in a society as corrupt as ours, the real losers, he implies, are those still struggling to be, in a conventional way, winners.

Many in Raymond Mungo's generation and the generations that have followed his would at least agree that society sets a race in which it is simply better not to run. They have dropped out of the race, not so dramatically as in the 1960s through drugs or the commune movement but by deliberately deciding upon a course of what the sociologists term downward mobility. Downward mobility means nothing more than that one has stepped down in life from the position occupied by one's parents: socially, financially, occupationally. Social history in America presents great numbers of families who have gone from shirt sleeves to shirt sleeves in three generations; or families who have been wiped out by a single cataclysmic event, such as a major depression; and herds upon herds of individual black sheep. But this deliberate strategy on the part of young adults for moving downward is a phenomenon of a radically different order.

The son of a lawyer becomes a welder; the daughter of a distinguished academic takes a job at the post office; a thirty-five-year-old son of a surgeon runs (but does not own) a record store. These are not jobs taken up lightly, part-time or transitional jobs till something better comes along; they are what earnest-minded job counselors call "career choices." There is no way of knowing how many people make such choices, of course. But thirty or forty years ago these might have been jobs taken only by people on their way up, or seeking protection from economic turmoil (as many men and women took civil service jobs during the Depression of the 1930s); or then again, they might have been taken up by family black sheep, young men and women whose family ties were cut because their behavior was considered scandalous, or who lacked the gifts or the will to carry on family traditions, or who for special reasons of their own fell away. People nowadays do not disown or even disdain those of their children who choose downard mobility, which is an improvement; but neither do they quite know what to make of them, which shows how unsettling a phenomenon it still is.

Many of the young who have chosen downward mobility have a great deal to support their decision in the culture in which they have grown up. If they no longer wish to struggle for wealth, distinction, achievement, it is because they have been given to believe that both the struggle and the rewards are at bottom fraudulent. They have read that they are fraudulent; they have been told that they are fraudulent; and having been thus instructed, they go out into the world and find—fraudulence. At fraud they will not play. What they choose instead is the simpler life: working at the job, taking up the quotidian tasks, enjoying the uncomplicated pleasures. These are, it nearly goes without saying, the children of the middle and upper-middle classes. They have not failed life's tests; they have instead chosen not to take them.

The parents of such young people are not so much disapproving as frankly mystified. They often have not enough confidence in their own values to permit themselves anger or outrage at the prospect of waste in the lives of their children. Instead they hope that their sons and daughters will, as they say, "find themselves." As long as they are not on drugs, they say. Or, they are at least earning their own way, they say. Or, they seem happy enough, they say. They don't seem to be hurting anyone else, they say. It is their life to live, they say. But despite all they say, they are puzzled. After all, if their children want nothing to do with what they have won, does not what they have won seem as a result diminished? They cannot speak of, or even think about, their children as losers, even as these children reach their thirties and forties; they themselves once were but no longer are confident about what a winner is.

One cannot speak about winners and losers unless there is some rough agreement on fundamentals. But agreement on fundamentals is far from being had at this time in the United States of America. How important is work in one's life? Is achievement more important than happiness? Are the two separable? Does one truly have an obligation to make the best use of one's gifts? What is the just reward for a life of effort, and is it commensurate with the effort? When such questions are even asked—as they are, repeatedly, nowadays—fundamentals are in dispute, and no scorecard exists to tell the winners from the losers.

Curiosity Shop □ "I was making big bucks in those days, the middle 1950s, usually between sixty and seventy-five grand a year—and this was at a time, remember, when the dollar was still worth about sixty-five cents. Selling space for the magazine I worked for was no big problem then. I would go into an ad agency media-buying meeting, go through my paces—point to charts, spell out the demographics, the whole bit—but in fact the whole package was already wrapped up long before I walked into the room. My style in those days was high wining (not to be confused with highbinding or sidewinding, please). I'd find out who the main man was, the chief space buyer, the man who could say Yes—and I'd cultivate him like mad. Tickets to pro football games, theater tickets, French dinners with wives along or girl friends provided—whatever it took, I delivered it. Other guys tried the same thing. Nothing new about it. I think I worked it with a bit more charm than most.

"I blew it, I suppose, because it all came so easy—and seemed so unlikely to end. Only in my late thirties and already making such heavy bread, I guess I felt I could do no wrong. Including my drinking. I have always been a drinking man, from college days on, and still am. But in those days I suddenly found myself ducking into my favorite haunts at around ten-thirty in the morning. Then I started missing an occasional presentation at an ad agency. It wasn't, I told myself, as if these damn presentations had any real meaning. Well, word got back to the publisher, who told me to shape up or ship out. I told him that, if it was all the same to him, I thought I would ship out and that he could stick the job in his ear. Wasn't I, after all, the boy with the golden touch? I thought I'd step across the street and get another job. I got another job, all right, paying roughly a third of what I had been making and only after two and a half of the most miserable years—make that *the* most miserable years—of my life.

"We're not talking here about your everyday unemployment. We're talking about upper-middle-class unemployment. And we're talking about thirty-odd months of it. During my five or six glory years, before I walked out on my job, I bought a large house in a right suburb. There were four houses on our block, and because it is half country out there, the damn mailboxes are placed out near the road. Well, when you're unemployed and on the hunt for a new job, the mail becomes the big event of the day, and the mailman one of the leading characters in your life. He's carrying—you hope—answers to feeler letters you've sent out, job offers, responses to your own letters to creditors, checks, who knows what else. My problem was that I couldn't go out after the mail. I didn't want any of our neighbors to know I was out of a job, so I couldn't be bird-doggin' the mailman. If my wife was home, I'd send her out to the mailbox; if not, I'd have to wait till dark. It was as if I was in one of those gangster movies from the thirties, holed up in a hideout till the heat was off. Only the hideout was my own home, and my crime was having no job.

"Bills ran up early. I had some savings, but they didn't last a full year, not with a family of four and kids in private school. We bought almost nothing new—except of course food and school clothes for the kids. Going into my second year without a job, I saw there was no hope for it. I sat down and wrote out careful letters to all our creditors, telling them, hey, look, you can force me under, drive me into a personal bankruptcy, but if you do you're not going to get much more than a dime on every dollar I owe you. Work with me on this, I pleaded, and you'll get every penny back. Surprisingly, every one of my creditors, including the utility companies, went along with me. The only exception was a men's clothing store, where I had a bill for a big $32.

"The second year I borrowed money from an older brother, who is a dentist in Cleveland, but only enough to buy food and essentials and to pay the kids' school fees. You may laugh at this, but it was only in my second year of being out of work that it occurred to me to collect an unemployment check. If I ever knew about collecting unemployment, I must have forgotten about it. Then, when I remembered it, I felt embarrassed about going in to collect it. I've heard the usual stories about out-of-work actors driving up in Rolls-Royces in Hollywood to pick up their unemployment checks. I also know there is a sense in which I had the checks coming to me, having paid in on unemployment all the years of my working life. Still, though I joked about it with my wife, I was ashamed. What's more, the damned check didn't go very far in a high-nut household like ours; in winter the checks just about covered our heating bills and my cigarettes.

"In my kind of work most business is done over lunch, and that includes the business of getting jobs. If I'd hear about an opening somewhere, I'd call to check into it, but often the call might involve me in coming into the city for lunch. And if lunch was involved, I had to be ready to pick up the check. If I went with two or three other guys, with a couple rounds of drinks, the tab could pretty easily get up to sixty bucks. I'd sit there twitching inside through the meal, wondering if I was going to get stuck with the check. This was a hard thing for a man who has picked up more than his share of checks over the years.

"When I finally did get a job, it was through the mail. I sent off a résumé in answer to a small ad in *Advertising Age*. During the interview I found myself lying about how much money I made on my last job—and lying downward, claiming I was making a lot less money than I really was, lest I scare them off. My guess is that I'll probably never again make as much money as I did when I lost my job. In taking the job I did—the job I still have, by the way—I took two or three giant steps backwards. But that's all right. Believe it or not, I'm still in shell shock. Nearly three years without a job scared hell out of me. I'll take less money, I'll even accept the idea that I've already peaked in my professional life, to escape going through that again."

People who fail at success, or children of the prosperous middle classes who choose not to compete for success, are failures of a luxurious kind—privileged failures, one might term them—compared to the dismal failures of those men and women who work without a net under them. The latter are not life's intentional dropouts nor near-misses. These are people who risk a deal more than being merely ordinary. These are people for whom the great question in life is not "What shall I make of my life?" but "How shall I survive?" These are people who do not think of some Kafka-like literary abstraction called the abyss but who live in smelly clothes and on foul food and in fear of the cold.

"How fascinating our failures are!" wrote Oscar Wilde in connection with a visit, in 1882, to Jefferson Davis, the defeated president of the Confederacy, at his Texas plantation. But this was before Wilde's own failure, after his release from Reading Gaol following his imprisonment resulting from litigation with the father of Lord Alfred Douglas, when Wilde was himself failure incarnate: shabby and swollen and scandalized. Fascinating is the last thing failure is. True failure is a destroyer of self-respect. To fail decisively is almost certainly to lose one's perspective: to be filled with self-scorn that turns outward into envy, to review endlessly the accumulation of disappointed hopes, frustrated talents, wounded pretensions. It is regularly to anticipate misfortune and not be often mistaken; it is to live with full-time tedium; it is to look into the mirror and see waste staring back.

A toothless woman wearing galoshes in summer picks for scraps and findings in a street-corner trash basket; a man walks slowly along a downtown street, so he won't dislodge the newspapers lining his canvas shoes or knock too loose the buzz from last night's wine; a man in his late thirties who looks to be in his late sixties pulls his buttonless coat across his chest, stamping his feet, waiting for the blood-donor office to open; a shapeless woman of unknowable years, hair hanging lank with oiliness, got up in unmatched Goodwill clothes, walks about sucking on cigarettes, drugged to the eyeballs by the attendants at the halfway house for the insane where she lives. In spite of talk of affluence, in spite of the spread of welfare arrangements, people, large numbers of them, are swept under by failure. Some become deranged, some dipsomaniacal; some so blasted by life that it is a moot question whether they are drunk or crazy; some shuffle and fade away.

"The road downward has but few landings and level places," wrote Theodore Dreiser in *Sister Carrie,* a novel that, in its portrait of the character George Hurstwood, provides one of literature's most vivid laboratory-slide specimens of failure. Having himself started out low in life, having climbed a good way up, thence only to tumble back down, Dreiser knew all the bumps on the chute toward failure, all the splinters and rough places. He knew about the petty pride that resists commonsense action in reversing one's misfortune, the lassitude that drags a man further down, the mounting feelings of impotence that work against him. He knew about these things in large and in fine: about the meaning of an unemployed man's suddenly not shaving daily; about compulsive newspaper reading and seeking out warm places that take one away from looking for work; about how failure in effect desexes a man, slowly twisting him into a repulsively pitiable creature before the woman who once loved him. Dreiser knew about failure, and he knew it was no grand thing, but mean and narrow—and nothing more than misery.

Perhaps the only other novelist to know the subject so intimately was the Englishman George Gissing. For him poverty and failure were indivisible. In his best-known novel, *New Grub Street,* set in the world of literary journalism in London in the 1880s, Gissing, with artful dolor, writes relentlessly about what he calls "the demon of failure, of humiliation." "It seemed to him," he writes of Edwin Reardon, the failed hero in *New Grub Street,* "that the greatest happiness attainable would be to creep into some dark, warm corner, out of sight and memory of men, and lie there torpid, with a blessed half-consciousness that death was slowly overcoming him. Of all the sufferings collected into each four-and-twenty hours this of rising to a new day was the worst." How reminiscent this passage is to the suicide of Dreiser's Hurstwood, who turns off the gas in his flophouse room: " 'What's the use?' he said, weakly, as he stretched himself to rest."

Failure brings with it a yearning for death. Defeat in life is almost always a curse. Sometimes this defeat is merited, the result of flaws in character; sometimes it is unmerited, which makes it even more difficult to bear. Failure can in many instances be honorable, but it is seldom to be glorified. It is mostly grey, allowing for little in the way of large thoughts or compassionate feelings; it embitters most people made to undergo it, rendering them worse than they might naturally have been.

Yet despite its greyness, there is a tendency to look almost fondly upon failure, which is really the obverse side of the distrust of success. Thus a cult is made of poets who die young or artists who commit suicide: the chief implication of such cults is that the world and its harsh realities were not good enough for such sensitive souls—and neither, really, by extension are they quite good enough for us. But the harshest of the world's realities is that each of us is here for only a brief while—too briefly to dally in admiration of failure in the abstract or to feel anything other than sympathy for those who are put through its tortures.

Sadly for Adlai

MADLY FOR ADLAI read a campaign button from the two Eisen-hower-Stevenson presidential campaigns, and those who wore it truly meant it. People might like Ike but those who were for Stevenson were for Adlai no less than madly. Not since William Jennings Bryan had a presidential candidate so devoted a follow-ing; not since Theodore Roosevelt or Woodrow Wilson had a figure in national political life so thoroughly captured the fancy of the educated classes in America. Alongside the warmth and determined elegance with which his friends and admirers wrote about Adlai Stevenson after his death, the eulogies for John Fitzgerald Kennedy read as though spoken by a clergyman who had not known the deceased while he lived. From those who were attracted to him, Stevenson managed to evoke an astonishing degree of adoration. Listening to talk about Adlai Stevenson from those who adored him, it was quite easy to forget that he was a loser and a loser on a large scale: twice defeated for the presidency—neither time coming even close—and once awaiting a nomination from his party that never arrived. What was the attraction to Adlai Stevenson?

In the grandiloquently sentimental view, as put forth by the political writer Hans Morgenthau, Stevenson's "promise was ours, and so was his failure, and the tears we shed for him we shed for ourselves." Good graveside prose this, carefully ca-denced, hinting at the profound, sufficiently vague. But what was the promise being spoken of? What is the failure? And who is *we*?

About who Adlai Stevenson himself was, in his own mind, there could be little doubt. He was Adlai Stevenson II, and his paternal grandfather, Adlai Ewing Stevenson, had been vice-president of the United States under Grover Cleveland in 1893 and, in 1900, had been defeated for the same office when running with William Jennings Bryan. More important to Stevenson, or so his biographers tell us, his maternal great-grandfather was Jesse Weldon Fell. Fell proposed the idea for the Lincoln–Dou-glas debates and was later Lincoln's floor manager at the 1860 Republican convention. Fell was also Lincoln's personal lawyer

—the executor of his will—and served as associate justice of the U.S. Supreme Court. Adlai Stevenson's regard for these ancestors was very nearly Confucian in its reverence.

The family Adlai Stevenson was born into was not greatly rich but neither did it appear to want for much. Born in 1900 and raised in Bloomington, Illinois, Stevenson had a generally tranquil small-town boyhood. His family owned a large interest in the newspaper the *Bloomington Pantagraph*. Adlai's father was active in Democratic politics—for a time he was secretary of state in Illinois—and when national political figures passed through Bloomington they were likely to stop at the Stevenson house. In 1912 Woodrow Wilson, to whom the twelve-year-old Adlai was introduced, paid such a visit. (Decades afterward, with characteristic resignation, Stevenson would say that he was "doomed" to a life in politics.) The family spent its summers in Charlevoix, Michigan, then the Midwestern version of Newport, Rhode Island. There was money enough for Adlai's sister to study under Carl Jung in Switzerland. In Adlai's own life a single cataclysm ruffled the calm. When he was twelve a gun he was playing with at a party went off and killed a young female cousin—an incident that might have unstrung a boy less finely balanced.

Although Adlai Stevenson was to acquire the reputation for being an intellectual—an "egghead" was the then disparagingly intended term—in fact he seems never to have been interested in bookish things. As a boy he was altogether without intellectual distinction. He was a student who clearly favored the extra over the merely curricular, and his grades seldom rose above a gentleman's C. After a quite mediocre record in the public schools of Bloomington and Springfield, Illinois, Stevenson failed the entrance examinations for Princeton. In preparation for a second attempt at admission to Princeton, he was entered in Choate, the preparatory school where "habits of efficiency and industry" were instilled along with an "understanding of the enduring values and of the spirit of public service."

Once finally admitted to Princeton, Adlai Stevenson proceeded to achieve there the kind of undergraduate success that F. Scott Fitzgerald had earlier dreamed about. What is more,

Stevenson achieved it in the approved Princeton manner: quietly, casually, without seeming to strain for it. Adlai became an officer of Quadrangle, one of the school's most desirable eating clubs, managing editor of the *Daily Princetonian,* and a member of the prestigious Senior Council (class of '22).

Princeton marked Adlai Stevenson. As with F. Scott Fitzgerald, so with Adlai Stevenson, he doubtless acquired, to quote Edmund Wilson again, "too much respect for money and country-house social prestige." (Stevenson later lived in the horsy suburb of Libertyville, outside Chicago, on what he called his "farm"; a copy of the *Social Register* was always at his bedside. But rather better than Fitzgerald, Stevenson learned Princetonian notions of good form. He would never be one to come forth to make his desire plain—and this was eventually to cause him grief. Yet on the credit side his years at Princeton enabled Stevenson to set out his first lines to the cultivated and politically potent East Coast. When he went into politics his Eastern connections, like a letter of credit, were there for him to draw upon. It was through these connections that he was able to get jobs in government during the New Deal, and after that a prominent place with the American delegation to the United Nations Preparatory Commission in London.

After Princeton, Stevenson attended the Harvard Law School, which he found to be not much to his taste. "Everything is concentrated," he wrote home, "work, play, exercise." Toward the end of his second year at Harvard, he returned home, upon the death of a relative, to work as an editor of, and simultaneously to look after his family's interest in, the *Bloomington Pantagraph.* Two years later, however, he returned to law school, this time at Northwestern University, where he completed work on his degree and passed the Illinois bar. Before settling down to the practice of law, Adlai, along with two friends, went off on one final fling; carrying the credentials of a correspondent of the *Chicago Herald-American,* he set sail for the Soviet Union, where he hoped (although he did not succeed in this) to interview the inaccessible Soviet foreign minister, Grigori Vasilievich Chicherin.

Upon returning from this larky adventure, Stevenson became, through a Princeton connection, a law clerk in the old and solid Chicago law firm of Cutting, Moore, and Sidley. He moved into a bachelor apartment along the city's fashionable Gold Coast, and from there conducted a life commensurate with his social position and by now well-developed gregariousness. Although he was said to be putting in a fifty-hour week at his law firm, there was time in the summer to play tennis, shoot, and ride in the suburb of Lake Forest; during the winter, there was the Harvard-Yale-Princeton Club, squash, and the regular round of dances and parties. In 1928 Stevenson married Ellen Borden, the daughter of a wealthy Chicago real estate man, and the couple had their honeymoon in North Africa. His marriage was to be one of the central sorrows of Adlai Stevenson's life: causing him pain and humiliation when he was in it, and plaguing his political life after (through divorce) he got out of it.

When the Depression hit, it did not hit him personally very hard. He retained his interest in the Bloomington newspaper, and after his mother's death he came into real estate holdings. His wife's family, too, was still well off. But the Depression did turn his interests somewhat to civic responsibilities, if in a rather patrician way. He became interested, for example, in Jane Addams's Hull House, of which he later was to become a member of the board of trustees, and he joined the Chicago Council on Foreign Relations, of which he was later to become president. Blue ribbon stuff, most of it, and also slightly blue blood.

With the election of Franklin Delano Roosevelt, Stevenson, along with a number of other young lawyers, found himself caught up in the excitement of the New Deal. A few months later he was off to Washington to work as a special assistant to the general counsel of the Agricultural Adjustment Administration. For a brief time he also worked with the Federal Alcohol Administration. Returning to Chicago in the fall of 1934, he was appointed a government member of the code authorities of the wine and flour industries. In 1935 he was made a full partner in his law firm. Branching out now, he became president of the Legislative Voters League in Illinois, finance director of the Democratic National Committee during the 1936 presidential election campaign, and Illinois chairman of the National Council of Roosevelt Electors. These were the preliminary moves of a young man very much interested in a political career but not one who makes the vulgar error of starting anywhere near the bottom.

During World War II Stevenson served as personal assistant to Secretary of the Navy Frank Knox. There was some talk of Adlai's running for the United States Senate in 1942, but instead he continued to work with Secretary Knox, who died in 1944. Stevenson also put in a brief stint as head of an emergency mission to Sicily and Italy for the Foreign Economic Administration. After the war, he worked with Archibald MacLeish, then the assistant secretary of state with responsibility for postwar international organizations. By now having acquired something of a reputation as an expert on international affairs, Stevenson took over the American delegation to the United Nations Preparatory Commission in London, when Secretary of State Edward R. Stettinius, Jr., became ill. This was really the first government job he had had that allowed him to shed his anonymity, and everyone who witnessed his performance in London agreed that he handled things adroitly.

So adroitly, in fact, that, as a result of his London performance, Stevenson was offered ambassadorships in South America, the chairmanship of the Securities and Exchange Commission, and an assistant secretaryship of state—all of which he turned down. He was now forty-seven years old; his three sons were coming of age; and it was an open secret that his marriage was going very badly indeed. But rumors persisted that what he was truly interested in was a seat in the U.S. Senate. He certainly made what sounded like senatorial noises when he made his numerous speeches to the Council on Foreign Relations, at the University of Chicago, and elsewhere in Chicago. Asked about his ambitions for the Senate, he replied tc a Chicago reporter: "There is no sense being disingenuous about these things. My mind is open. Naturally, I'm interested." This may be the closest he ever came to being candid about his interest in political office.

As it turned out, he was placed that year, 1948, on the Democratic slate as the party's candidate for governor of Illi-

nois, while the party's senatorial candidate was a great expert
in state finances named Paul Douglas. That Stevenson's one
abiding interest was foreign affairs and that he had never served
on any but a federal level in government was of no moment next
to the fact that the party needed a war veteran to run against
the Republican senatorial incumbent, one Wayland Brooks.
Douglas, who had enlisted in the marines at the age of fifty,
filled the bill. Such are the vagaries (and calculations) of party
politics. The smart money had spoken, and Adlai Stevenson,
after agonizing over the decision to run for the governorship in
a manner that was to become habitual and greatly intensified in
later years, finally chose to listen.

Adlai Stevenson won the governorship, and by the largest
plurality in the history of the state. He proved a notably good
governor: reducing scandal, increasing state aid to education,
building better roads, bringing a higher caliber of men into
state government. Perhaps his real distinction lay in what he
refused to do. He vetoed a great many appropriations bills; he
refused (to the extent he could) to go along with the state's
patronage system; he turned back a bill that would have de-
manded a loyalty oath of all government employees, including
teachers. The major casualty of Stevenson's years as governor
was his marriage: late in 1949 Ellen Borden Stevenson sued
her husband for divorce on the grounds of incompatibility.
"Mrs. Stevenson," a Chicago paper noted, "never made any secret of the fact that she considered a political campaign dis-
rupting of home life and that she found political banquets boring." The failure of his marriage made Stevenson seem
something of a tragic figure, for it now appeared that he had
paid for his devotion to public life with the shattering of his
private life. The conflict between the private and the public
now clung to his career, investing it with an added dimension
of poignancy.

In his *Memoirs*, President Harry S Truman notes that he
only considered Adlai Stevenson for the presidential nominee of
the Democratic party after Fred M. Vinson, then chief justice of
the Supreme Court, turned him down. Truman was looking for
a man who would carry on the work of Truman: "It seems to me

that the Governor of Illinois has the background and what it takes. Think I'll talk to him." In Truman's account, Stevenson was "flabbergasted" by his, Truman's, offer of the nomination. But the story of the offer was leaked to the press; suddenly Stevenson was the subject of a *Time* cover story; and not long afterward an independent group was organized known as "Illinois Committee, Stevenson for President," whose hope, in the words of Walter Johnson, one of its co-chairmen, was "to set fire to the Stevenson talk around the country."

For a long while the problem seemed to be to set fire to Adlai Stevenson, who again and again demurred at the prospect of becoming a presidential candidate. Stevenson's 1952 candidacy was one of those rare occasions—it had happened only twice before, with James Garfield in 1880 and Charles Evans Hughes in 1916—when a presidential candidate was truly drafted by his party. In a sense, it was all out of Stevenson's hands, but only in a rather restricted sense. In later years he claimed that both the Democratic nomination and the office of the presidency were "unwanted" by him and he felt "no sense of adequacy." In fact, however, he could have stopped the draft movement on his behalf any time he chose to do so. General Sherman had set a precedent here by saying, flat out, he would not run even if nominated. Despite his protestations, his announced feelings of inadequacy, his proclaimed desire to have another term as governor of Illinois, Adlai Stevenson refused to make a strong disclaiming statement. Right up to the point of his actual nomination he insisted—again and again and yet again—that he *could* not run for the presidency, but he never said that he *would* not run for the presidency.

It was Bismarck, that least hesitant of politicians, who, sent with relatively little training to serve as Prussia's delegate to the German Federal Diet in 1848, said: "I shall do my duty. It is God's affair to give me understanding." In accepting the Democratic nomination, Stevenson invoked the Lord in very different terms:

I have asked the Merciful Father—the Father of us all—to let this cup pass from me. But from such dread responsibility one does not shrink in fear, in self-interest, or in false humility.

So, "If this cup not pass from me, except I drink it, Thy will be done."

Among those who heard Stevenson's acceptance speech was General Dwight D. Eisenhower, who listened to it while on a fishing trip with friends. Eisenhower's initial regard for Stevenson was said to be such that he declared that if he had known that Stevenson would be the Democratic nominee he, Eisenhower, would never have gone into politics. "Then it *happened,*" Eisenhower later recalled his own feelings listening to Stevenson's acceptance speech. "He got to that part . . . about having debated with himself about the nomination—and 'wishing that this cup might pass' from him. Right there I snapped off the TV set and said: 'After hearing that, fellows, I think he's a bigger fake than all the rest of them.' "

In the election itself Stevenson was of course soundly drubbed. "Both times I ran it was obviously hopeless," he told a reporter years afterward. "To run as a Democrat in 1952 was hopeless, let alone run against the No. 1 War Hero." Retrospective though such a statement was, it is nevertheless true. Stevenson could not have won the election; Eisenhower could only, through a piece of the most egregious stupidity, have lost it. Yet, as the historian Richard Hofstadter was later to write, "Stevenson's hopeless position might more readily have been accepted as such if the Republican campaign, in which Nixon and McCarthy seemed more conspicuous than Eisenhower, had not struck such a low note as to stir the will to believe that such men must be rejected by the public." Thus, hopeless though his position was, Adlai Stevenson came to seem the best of men in the worst of times.

Stevenson's conduct of the presidential campaign made him seem all the more admirable. As a Democrat, he was a patrician aligned with a plebeian tradition. His appeal was to a fundamental decency and reasonableness. He displayed wit and coolness in the face of coarse attack from the Republicans and the then

Republican press. He seemed simultaneously *in* politics and yet somehow *above* politics. But as with his governorship, his presidential campaign was distinguished less by any originality than by what he refused to do—and what he chiefly refused to do was sling mud, be cowed by roughhouse attacks, or lower the high tone he had set out to establish, as he put it, "to educate and elevate the people." He was known for writing as many of his own speeches as time allowed and for heavily rewriting those written for him by the speechwriters on his staff.

None of this prevented his going under in defeat. Yet it was a defeat that seemed only further to ennoble him. When Stevenson hinted at retreating from the fray of active politics, the novelist John Steinbeck wrote, in a letter printed in *The New Republic*, "You have given us a look at truth as a weapon, at reason as a tool, at humor as a method, and at democracy as a practical way of life. We would be crazy if we let you go.... Your greatness is the property of the nation, but to you it is a prison." In this letter Steinbeck filled out the legend that Adlai Stevenson would henceforth appear to be living. "We offer to cut your heart out and serve it up for the good of the nation." There it is: the great man who is called to power, wants no part of it, knows indeed all too well that it will cause him to suppress all that is more dear in his life (family, the contemplative life, friendship) but must nonetheless serve for the good of the nation.

When the subject of the 1956 presidential campaign arose Stevenson, predictably, demonstrated every kind of hesitation. Yet later, after he had agreed to run, when he found himself opposed for the nomination by Estes Kefauver, and thereby forced to run in primary elections, Stevenson was openly resentful, telling friends that he felt the Democratic party in effect owed him the nomination. Once in the race, though, Stevenson expressed a serious determination to win: "I'm not going to run again for the exercise," he said. "I've had all that kind of exercise I need. Another race like the last one and I will *really* have had it." Well, it turned out to be a worse race than the last one. Stevenson's indecisiveness, once reserved for grand decisions, now intruded upon petty matters. A not uncommon scene during the campaign had crowds of supporters and politicians waiting at airports while Stevenson's campaign plane circled aloft, the candidate within endlessly touching up his speech. So out of hand had things gotten that in the end Stevenson, on the election eve, descended to low tactics by making an issue of Eisenhower's health. "I must say bluntly," he announced, "that every piece of scientific evidence we have, every lesson of history and experience, indicates that a Republican victory tomorrow would mean that Richard M. Nixon would probably be President of this country within the next four years." On election day, Stevenson was utterly trounced, winning only seventy-four electoral votes to Eisenhower's 457.

Many people even now look upon Adlai Stevenson's two presidential defeats as symbolic of America's rejection of the intellectual in public life. Stevenson was not truly an intellectual, nor was John F. Kennedy, whose staff worked so hard to make him seem an intellectual. Yet there is a sense in which Stevenson made possible the emergence of John F. Kennedy as a presidential candidate. In quite another, more literal sense, he, Stevenson, did nothing to further Kennedy's ambition for the presidency, although Kennedy sought him out time and again. Stevenson found Kennedy, in their meetings as the 1960 election drew near, "tougher and blunter than I remember him in the past." Toughness and bluntness were not complimentary terms in the Stevensonian vocabulary. But a more important reason for Stevenson's not coming to Kennedy's aid in the younger man's drive to get the presidential nomination in 1960 was that Adlai Stevenson, despite all his statesmanlike sounds and ambiguous nondeclarations, really wanted that nomination for himself.

But Adlai Stevenson's inability to get his tongue around the simple phrase "I want it" finally made a third nomination for the presidency unavailable to him. At the Democratic convention Stevenson hedged and squirmed and quoted Robert Frost and made sad little jokes—and must have felt something go dead inside him as he began to realize that there was no stopping John Kennedy. Stevenson nonetheless attempted to do just that by telephoning Richard J. Daley, whom he had helped elect as mayor of Chicago, and who now headed the Illinois delegation.

Daley at first avoided answering Stevenson's call. When he finally did answer, Stevenson said that he hoped that the Illinois delegation wouldn't take the fact that he had not actively sought the nomination to mean that he didn't want it, or that he wouldn't campaign against Nixon with everything he had. According to Theodore H. White, Stevenson then asked "whether he had no support, period, or whether he had no support because it was the delegates' impression he was not a candidate. Daley replied that Stevenson had no support, period."

It is easy enough to be noble in defeat, at the great moment of actual failure, but it is afterward that things become awkward. Adlai Stevenson was sixty years old in 1960; he had to do something. He had hoped that Kennedy would appoint him secretary of state, but this was a hope destined to be denied. Instead he was offered the job of ambassador to the United Nations, with the job raised to Cabinet rank. "I have satisfactory assurances from the President-elect and the new Secretary that I shall have an adequate voice in the making of foreign policy," Stevenson said. Far from an adequate voice, Stevenson turned out to be an unwitting puppet. Information was kept from him, he was lied to, and led unbeknownst to himself to lie on the floor of the UN about the Bay of Pigs. Gossip brought him the report that Kennedy had referred to him as "my official liar." Adlai Stevenson's humiliation was complete.

More than once he spoke about retiring, about sitting on the sidelines with a glass of wine in his hand and watching the people dance. Yet he could not bring himself to do so. After the assassination of John F. Kennedy, Stevenson succumbed to the flattering cajolery of Lyndon Johnson and stayed on in his UN job. Perhaps he could not stand to be away from the action, from the power centers and the limelight life; perhaps he simply had nothing else to do. His last years leave a record of almost self-destructive vitality. He had always been extraordinarily active, but now, according to friends, he was overeating, his drinking had increased, and he played tennis with a ferocity that was madness in a man in his middle sixties. His death in London in the summer of 1965 came as a shock; but that he had died of a heart attack surprised none of his friends.

If death left Adlai Stevenson well short of accomplishing his desires, it at least put an end to his equivocations and ambiguities. Alas, it has been for the latter qualities that he has become best noted. Stevenson was better than this, of course. But he was riven by wanting power—doubtless to do good with, at least as he construed it—and by his inability to own up to it and, what is more, to do what is required to get it. This Stevenson would not, could not, do. In the end one has to be for Adlai—but sadly.

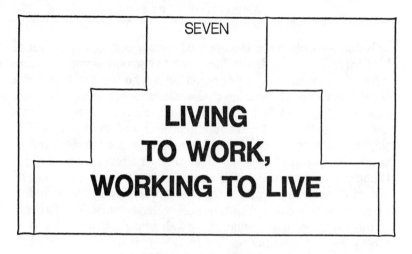

SEVEN

LIVING TO WORK, WORKING TO LIVE

The Babbitt of Modernism

If you saw him boarding one of the New Haven Railroad cars in New York for the trip back to Hartford, his arms filled with packages—a box of Turkish figs, two Spanish melons, ten persimmons, books wrapped in brown paper—a heavyset man, balding, in conventional business dress, it is most unlikely that you would have made him out for who he was. Who he was was Wallace Stevens, vice-president of the Hartford Accident and Indemnity Company and the winner of two National Book Awards, a Pulitzer Prize, the first great American poet to write in Technicolor. That you would not have recognized him would have been fine with him; he would have been perfectly pleased to pass for yet another businessman. "I try to draw a definite line between poetry and business," he wrote in a letter to a friend in the Far East, "and I am sure that most people here in Hartford know nothing about the poetry and I am equally sure that I don't want them to know because once they know they don't seem to get over it. I mean that once they know they never think of you as anything but a poet and, after all, one is inevitably much more complicated than that."

Wallace Stevens was a lawyer by training and a poet by birth. As a lawyer he handled claims against the Hartford Accident and Indemnity Company. Yet he managed to do so, rising to become an officer in the firm, without ignoring the claims of his own imagination. Invited to speak to a group of young executives at the University of Pennsylvania who were enrolled in a course supposed to broaden their cultural perspectives, Stevens demurred, saying: "I have never believed that it took a great deal to be both a poet and something else, and to lend myself to the opposite belief, as if to illustrate it and even expound it, would be difficult." No big deal though Stevens might have thought it, yet to bring off a career at business and another as a poet of the very front rank, one of the perhaps four or five great poets to write in America, still seems remarkable. To bring it off required determination, good sense about one's own strengths and weaknesses, equipoise—in a word, character.

In character, as in gifts of the mind, Wallace Stevens appears to have been somewhat precocious. He was born in 1879 in Reading, Pennsylvania. Dutch was in his background. His mother was a schoolteacher, early orphaned and out on her own; his father also taught school as a young man, then read law, becoming a moderately successful lawyer. Wallace was the second of five surviving Stevens children, three boys and two girls. His childhood seems to have been unrumpled, save for the aloofness of his father, of whom years later he would write: "I think that he loved to be at the house with us, but he was incapable of lifting a hand to attract any of us, so that, while we loved him as it was natural to do, we were also afraid of him, at least to the extent of holding off." (Wallace Stevens's daughter, Holly, editor of his letters and journals, would later note that "like his own father before him, mine did not entertain business associates at home; he needed a quiet place to 'create a life of his own.' ") But Stevens's father's distance closed with the increase of actual distance of his children, to whom, when they went off to college, he wrote warm and helpful letters. These letters were not free of the advice that is a father's right to give his children: "For life," his father wrote to Wallace, "is either a pastoral dream—the ideal of the tramp, or superannuated village farmer — Or it is the wild hurly-burly activity of the fellows who make the world richer and better by their being in it: the fellows whose services make the rest furnish them subsistence and yield them honor, whose services are *always* needed." Stevens, Sr., was a generous man but fair—he deducted his three sons' college fees from his will—and not about to delude his children about the ways of the world. His father wrote to Wallace while he was at Harvard that he, Wallace, must ready himself for life, for he will have " 'to paddle your own canoe' without help from home of any substantial character."

When Wallace Stevens entered Harvard, a three-year student and member of the class of 1900, many of the great figures were still there. William James and Josiah Royce were active in philosophy. Charles Eliot Norton taught his course in Dante. Stevens took the Rhetoric and English Composition course from Charles Townsend Copeland. He met George Santayana, who befriended him. He sat in on a course taught by Barrett Wendell. He took courses in French prose and in German, and in medieval and modern European history, although he, cosmopolitan in so many respects, would never his life long get to visit Europe. He became a member of the staff of the *Harvard Advocate*, for which he wrote sketches and poems. Robert Frost was a student at Harvard during this time; yet, while there, he and Wallace Stevens never met. Of another young poet at the university, a fellow named Livingood, Stevens wrote in his journal, "He needs stability of desire."

Stability of desire was not wanting in Wallace Stevens. One of many extraordinary things about him was that, very early in life, he knew what he wanted and knew, too, the general shape he wanted his life to take. Here is a journal entry he wrote before he was twenty years old: "The only practical life of the world, as a man of the world, not as a University Professor, a Retired Farmer or Citizen, a Philanthropist, a Preacher, a Poet, or the like, but as a bustling merchant, a money-making lawyer, a soldier, a politician is to be if unavoidable a pseudo-villain in the drama, a decent person in private life." By which Stevens meant, "We *must* come down, we *must* use tooth and nail, it is the law of nature: 'the survival of the fittest'; providing we maintain at the same time self-respect, integrity and fairness. I believe, as unhesitatingly as I believe in anything, in the efficacy and necessity of fact meeting fact—with a background of the ideal."

At graduation, Stevens was presented with that perennial but never boring question: What to do with his life? It could have taken any number of turns. On the literary side, he had had sufficient encouragement at Harvard to consider a full-time life in literature: working on magazines, publishing his poems, perhaps turning out translations. But, as he wrote in his journal, "I do not want to have to make a petty struggle for existence—physical or literary." He thought of himself as being directed by his own hopes and desires and those of his parents, but these hopes and desires were still inchoate. Thus far along his ambition was to make use of himself to the full, not dissipating his energy and talent. "I must try not to be a dilettante—half dream, half deed," he wrote. "I must be all dream or all deed."

Directly after graduation he moved to New York, and set out to become a journalist. New York, that eclectic and electric city, a European city, as the novelist Saul Bellow has called it, adding but of no known country, New York, where every young man or woman with ambition in America must at one time or another go to try out—this New York, at the turn of the century, Wallace Stevens found cold yet exciting, "a field of tireless and antagonistic interests—undoubtedly fascinating but horribly unreal." A great walker as a young man, he toured the city and its environs, sometimes on hikes of forty miles. He attended the funeral of Stephen Crane. He wondered whether literature was really a profession, while continuing to look for a job on a newspaper.

With letters of introduction from his Harvard teachers, he made the rounds of the New York newspapers of the day, the *Commercial Advertiser*, the *Evening Post, World, Journal, Herald, Munsey's* magazine, eventually landing work on the *New York Tribune*, at space rates. While scaring up stories, he worked with his own sonnets ringing in his head. Most evenings he was alone. Weekends he would often traipse out for long walks. His salary dictated careful living. Wishing for a wife, scarcely possible on his weekly wage of fifteen dollars at the paper, he noted in his journal: "I am certainly a domestic creature par excellence. It is brutal to myself to live alone." He seemed to be getting nowhere, and wrote to his father suggesting that he should quit his job and devote himself full time to his writing. But his father argued persuasively against that idea— "he seems always to have reason on his side, confound him"— and in the following autumn, that of 1901, he took his father's advice and entered the New York Law School. In later years Stevens would recall, respectfully, a line of Santayana's: "I have always bowed, however sadly, to expediency or fate."

Wallace Stevens passed the bar in 1904, and that same year met Elsie Viola Moll, the woman he would marry five years later. In between times he was employed by a number of law firms; entered into a law practice with a partner that was to fail; and finally settled in, in 1908, as a lawyer in the New York office of the American Bonding Company of Baltimore. He was to be associated with the insurance business for the remainder of his life. Stevens's life in business was far from all onward and upward. It was, for a substantial stretch, a grind. New Year's Eve 1905, at age twenty-five, he confessed in his journal that he was "frightened at the way things are going, so slowly, so unprofitably, so unambitiously." Doubts never permanently departed: "Practicing law," he noted, "is only lending people the use of your bald head." Still, in his thirtieth year, not yet married, he writes to his wife-to-be: "I am still decidedly young—not nearly so competent as I have an idea of being some day to be superior to circumstances."

In order to be superior to circumstances one must measure circumstances with real care. This Wallace Stevens never failed to do. His taste and capacity for a life of leisure and study was not less than that of others—if anything it may have been rather greater—but he always acknowledged, as he once put it in quotation marks, "the fell clutch of circumstances." Taking life as he found it, he commented on a boring volume of essays by a socialist writer that the writer argues about "irremediable things as if someone were to blame." To his wife-to-be, he wrote: "Whatever life may be, and whatever we may be—*here we are* and *il faut être aimable:* we must be amiable, as the French say." The nobility of men and women he felt lies "in what they endure and in the manner in which they endure it." Oscar Wilde once described a cynic as someone who knew the price of everything and the value of nothing. Careful, composed, stoical, Wallace Stevens knew the price of everything and also its value.

This was damned unpoetical of him. There is a script, almost a well-worn track, that poets are supposed to follow; or so their public and a great many poets themselves appear to believe. The script calls for living passionately and dying young and leaving a tragic aura. Or, alternately, living passionately and dying seedily—of alcoholism, suicide, madness—and leaving an aura of waste of the kind that comes from being misunderstood. "Diligence is not enough," said Delmore Schwartz, one of our many wasted American poets, of his own career. But for Wallace Stevens—who once remarked, sadly, of Dylan Thomas, that "he was an utterly improvident man"—diligence was a start. He defied the script for poets. He lived responsibly, he died gracefully and in the fullness of his years, and he left behind ample evidence in the form of his poetry that he had gotten the most out of his talent.

None of this might be exceptional if Stevens were a blustery poet in the manner of Kipling or even a gloomy poet in the manner of Edwin Arlington Robinson. But he was instead a thoroughly modern romantic, whose verse shimmered with sensuality and sophisticated intellection, and a man with as keenly developed an aesthetic sense as perhaps any American writer in this century. His vocation as a poet, although he usually spoke modestly of it, could not have been more securely anchored. "To practice an art, to need it and to love it, is the quickest way of learning that all happiness lies in oneself," he wrote to his wife. He worked at his poetry and he worked at his job. "I am far from being a genius—and must rely on hard and faithful work." Neither in poetry nor in the insurance business did he ascend by express elevator. His first publication, since an undergraduate at Harvard, came in 1915, when *Poetry* magazine accepted sections of his splendid long poem "Sunday Morning." Asked by Harriet Monroe for a biographical note of the kind that literary magazines often supply about their contributors, Stevens wrote, laconically: "I was born in Reading, Pennsylvania, am thirty-five years old, a lawyer, resident in New York, and have published no books." He was fully forty-four before he published his first book—to not very enthusiastic reviews—and fifty-five before he was made a vice-president of the Hartford Accident and Indemnity Company.

It would be an error to assume that Wallace Stevens's enthusiasm for insurance business was equal to his passion for poetry. In his early years at the Hartford he traveled extensively, sometimes being away three and four weeks at a stretch. "I have not had a poem in my head for a month, poor Yorick," he wrote home in the middle of one such trip. In Hartford, especially later, when he and his wife had bought their first and only home, he composed poems in his head while walking from his house to the Rock, as the Hartford's imposing five-column granite building was called by its employees. His day at the office could—often did—enervate. "It takes me so long to get the day out of my mind and to focus myself on what I am eager to do." Yet work at the insurance company gave him certain advantages in perspective not generally available to someone who had put all his energies into the fragile art of constructing poems. Among other things, Stevens was less likely to be influenced by literary opinion or stung by criticism. He claimed he had no desire to write a great deal, even though, as a poet, one tended to be judged by volume. "However," he wrote to Harriet Monroe, "having elected to regard poetry as a form of retreat, the judgment of people is neither here nor there."

Poetry was only one of his retreats; domestic life was another. He read widely, in French as well as in English; had a large collection of classical recordings; became an avid gardener. "I see a vast amount of nature, my source of supply," he wrote to Louis Untermeyer. Holly, the Stevens's only child, was born in 1924, when Wallace Stevens was forty-five. He had published his first book of poems, *Harmonium,* the year before. The book made no great critical stir; and commercially it was a joke, of the heartbreaking kind, for Stevens's first royalty check from his publishers for the first half of 1924 was for $6.70. Of this check he said· "I shall have to charter a boat and take my friends around the world."

A poet always cheats his boss, a proverb has it, meaning that a poet's mind is never for long on his work but on his poetry.

But Wallace Stevens appears to have been an exception. Between 1923 and 1929, for example, he wrote scarcely any poetry, and the preponderance of his energy went into his professional life. Becoming a vice-president at the Hartford was significant to him, and of more than money and status, although these considerations entered in. As his daughter Holly noted about her father's promotion: "Now at last he felt safe in devoting some of his time and energy to poetry without fear of being 'passed over' as an oddity, although he concealed his creative work from most of his insurance colleagues as well as he could for many years to come."

How important was money to Wallace Stevens? Less important, it appears, than it has been to many full-time poets. He never played the stock market. Comfortable though his salary must have been when he rose to a vice-presidency at the Hartford, it was apparently never enough to save money, as he put it, "in anything like real hunks." There was not the least hypocrisy about his own attitude toward money. Asked about why he had stopped writing poetry from 1923 to nearly 1930, he answered, "I didn't like the idea of being bedevilled all the time about money and I didn't for a moment like the idea of poverty, so I went to work like anybody else and kept at it for a good many years."

Stevens said he believed in "up-to-date capitalism," yet when he had a book printed in a small edition by a publisher who specialized in turning out elegant books he refused any royalties. When the poet Kenneth Patchen asked him to underwrite his, Patchen's, own book of poems, paying the printer's bill of $1,000, Stevens told Patchen that if he could come up with nineteen people to put up fifty dollars each, he would be the twentieth, but otherwise Patchen was on his own. He didn't believe poets deserved special treatment. Of Ezra Pound's conduct during World War II, he said: "While he may have many excuses I must say that I don't consider the fact that he is a man of genius as an excuse. Surely, such men are subject to the common disciplines." On the other hand, when people accused William Carlos Williams of being a Communist, Stevens came to his defense, saying that Williams "is the least subversive man in the world." Past seventy years old, and hence past retirement age, Stevens nonetheless continued to come to the office regularly, "because I like to do so and have use for the money, and never had any other reasons for doing so."

As for his uses for the money, Wallace Stevens always had a taste for small pleasures, simple and complex: "coffee and oranges in a sunny chair, and the green freedom of a cockatoo upon a rug." Thanking a friend for sending him some especially lush persimmons, he referred to himself as "a spiritual epicure." He was that, all right, and an orderly and restrained hedonist in the bargain. A friend in Ceylon sent him packages with oriental delicacies—"pickled apricots, candied gold fish and sugared canaries' knees," as he joked. He broke off an elaborate discussion about the theoretical underpinnings of his own poetry by remarking, "After all, I like Rhine wine, blue grapes, good cheese, endive and lots of books etc., etc., etc. as much as supreme fiction." He loved good tea and elegant fruit and handsomely printed books. He had a French agent from whom he bought, by mail, not very expensive paintings.

Wallace Stevens esteemed order, and order seems to have been the reigning note of his domestic life. "For my part," he wrote to a friend, "I never really lived until I had a home, and my own room, say, with a package of books from Paris or London." After the Depression the Stevenses never had servants or any regular help, and Wallace Stevens, poet and executive, used to pitch in by doing the dishes and scrubbing the kitchen floors. Formal and formidable, to other people he never referred to his wife by any other name than Mrs. Stevens. One of the reasons he gave for not traveling more, and notably not to Europe, was his wife's garden. The current combination at home, he noted, was "Berlioz and roses." Late in life he came to feel that "the habitual, the customary," had come to be as great a pleasure as any life had to offer. "The bread of life," he said, "is better than any soufflé."

About publicity Wallace Stevens cared not at all. When a journalist attempted to interest him in becoming the subject of an article in *Harper's Bazaar*, Stevens replied thank you but no thanks: "I just don't like personal publicity." Only once did he grant an interview. He seldom gave a poetry reading, even when the invitations to do so were many and lucrative: "It is merely that I don't care to do it and therefore am not able to do it." To an early friendly critic of his poetry, he wrote: "After all I write poetry because it is part of my piety; because, for me, it is the good life, and I don't intend to lift a finger to advance my interest, because I don't want to think of poetry that way."

All the grander, then, must he have felt when, without trumpery of any kind, recognition finally came to him. From 1930 on he had published slowly and steadily the poems he had worked on walking to and from work and on the weekends. He had acquired the esteem of the important American poets of the age among his contemporaries—Marianne Moore, Robert Frost, William Carlos Williams. In 1945 he was elected a member of the National Institute of Arts and Letters. Around 1950, though, his reputation widened and seemed to become more public, bursting the bounds of the somewhat self-enclosed world of poets. He began to be regarded as a major literary figure. "He had achieved," as his daughter put it, "the acceptance he desired." Making no compromises with his art, Wallace Stevens had achieved all one could ask as a poet. Literary prizes came to him and so did honorary degrees, from Wesleyan and Bard, from Columbia and Mount Holyoke, from Harvard and Yale. Yet even these distinctions did not throw him. Accepting the National Book Award for his *Collected Poems* in 1955, he made "a point of saying in my acceptance that awards and honors were not the real satisfactions of poetry and that the real satisfaction is poetry itself, which I believe to be true."

Would Wallace Stevens's artistic achievement have been even greater had he not had to spend so much time at the Hartford Accident and Indemnity Company? "To be cheerful about it," he wrote late in life, "I am now in the happy position of being able to say I don't know what would have happened if I had had more time. This is very much better than to have had all the time in the world and have found oneself inadequate." Apropos of people who seem to fall into good fortune, Stevens once remarked, "God is gracious to some very peculiar people." Something gratifying there is, though, about a life like Stevens's, in which seeds planted in youth, patiently tended and diligently cultivated, yield a full and fine harvest late in life. It is the way life is supposed to be and only too rarely is. In 1945, ten years before his death, on August 2, 1955, of cancer, Stevens wrote: "What is terribly lacking from life today is the well-developed individual, the master of life, or the man who by his mere appearance convinces you that a master of life is possible." Could Wallace Stevens have known that, in his own understated and distinguished way, he was himself such a master of life?

What is the worst that can be said—that has been said—about ambition? Here is a (surely) partial list:

To begin with, it, ambition, is often antisocial, and indeed is now outmoded, belonging to an age when individualism was more valued and useful than it is today. The person strongly imbued with ambition ignores the collectivity; socially detached, he is on his own and out for his own. Individuality and ambition are firmly linked. The ambitious individual, far from identifying himself and his fortunes with the group, wishes to rise above it. The ambitious man or woman sees the world as a battle; rival-rousness is his or her principal emotion: the world has limited prizes to offer, and he or she is determined to get his or hers. Ambition is, moreover, jesuitical; it can argue those possessed by it into believing that what they want for themselves is good for everyone—that the satisfaction of their own desires is best for the commonweal. At bottom the truly ambitious believe that it is a dog-eat-dog world, and they are distinguished by wanting to be the dogs who do the eating.

But the ambitious pay a steep price, it is felt, for harboring their antisocial and outmoded view of the world. To be ambitious is, by definition, to be driven. Balzac, in his novel *Lost Illusions*, speaks of a character who, having ambition roused in him, has been "imprudently doomed . . . to great suffering." In the same novel he speaks about another character, "a saintly creature," who "little knew that when ambition comes it puts an end to natural feeling." To be ambitious is not thus only to be driven but to be a bit inhuman into the bargain. The great men and women in history have always been able to flout the small but crucially important human emotions. Great figures may even despise mankind a little.

Ambition, it has been further if not argued at least implied, is inherently tragic in its consequences. If the ambitious, in their varying ways, strive after human grandeur, such striving does not come cheaply. In *Antigone*, Sophocles wrote: "That greatness never/Shall touch the life of man without destruction." What is, or can be, inherently tragic about ambition is that it is often insatiable. Ambition, deep-down ambition, can finally know no satisfaction. Ambition works on a person, eats away at him, grinds him down. So, at any rate, it is said.

Ambition is also, in the ordinary way of the world, it is argued, likely to corrupt those touched by it. Antisocial in its impulse, gnawing in its emotional effects, ambition let loose works its way into, and figures ultimately to rot, character. Macbeth, Lear's two disloyal daughters, Marc Antony, Coriolanus—it sometimes seems as if Shakespeare's plays are scarcely about anything other than corruption by way of ambition. Once a man is roused by ambition, the standard argument has it, his conscience goes into retreat. To be ambitious is to be, if not outside the bounds of morality, then to feel less constrained by those bounds. Absolute power corrupts absolutely, said Lord Acton in a famous *mot*, but merely a touch of ambition can achieve the same end.

From here it is but a short hop to believe that those who have achieved the common goals of ambition—money, fame, power—have achieved them through corruption of a greater or lesser degree, mostly a greater. Thus all politicians in high places, thought to be ambitious, are understood to be without moral scruples. How could they have such scruples—a weighty burden in a high climb—and still have risen as they have?

Behind ambition—and none too far behind—are commonly understood to lie vanity, greed, the will to power. Ambition, when given free rein, is certain to bring out the worst in people. The greatest victims of ambition, however, are those who achieve their goals. (Whom the gods would make mad, they first allow their dreams to come true . . . and so forth.) But of course those who do achieve the goals of their ambition are not the only victims of ambition. The field is liberally strewn with other casualties. Those, to name one category, whose lives have been poisoned by feverish but ill-defined ambition; those, to name another, who have felt the endless discouragement of living without the distinction they crave; and those, to name a third, paralyzed by fear of entering the battle to begin with.

What is the worst that can be said about ambition? In sum, that it is antisocial; that it is insatiable; that it is corrupting; that it leaves only victims, rendering men mad (like Macbeth) or insensately vulgar (like Sammy Glick) or pathetically broken (like Arthur Miller's Willy Loman). Of great men of ambition, Hegel, in his *Lectures on the Philosophy of History*, said: "Their whole life is labor and trouble. . . . They die early, like Alexander; they are murdered, like Caesar; transported to Saint Helena, like Napoleon." Theodore Dreiser spoke about "the virus of success," but the virus starts earlier—it enters the bloodstream with ambition. The ambitious view of life is forbidding and unforgiving. Its price is too high. It is inhuman in its demands; it is inhumane in its toll. If life is to be lived differently, if life is to be more spiritual, more tender-minded and large-hearted, ambition, clearly, must go. Or so it is said.

Curiosity Shop □ Some fifteen years ago a small circle of distinguished English and American scholars and intellectuals decided, for no other reason than their amusement, to attempt to name the great men still walking the earth. By "great" they did not necessarily mean someone of whom they necessarily approved. The figures chosen could be good or evil; what counted for them was, in a rough sense, amplitude, or largeness of character. They were looking for men and women still alive who counted in history—counted in the sense that, had they not lived, the world would seem a different place.

In their search for great men, they readily enough agreed that there was no one at the time in America who qualified. Nor did England have any great figures, although, were he still alive,

Winston Churchill would have qualified. Charles de Gaulle was alive, and they agreed that he did indeed qualify. So did Mao Tse-tung. In the arts, Picasso qualified; Igor Stravinsky was allowed in, though not so readily as Picasso. One man, André Malraux, because of interesting careers in both literature and the life of action, was considered a borderline case on which agreement could not be reached. And that was it.

Fifteen years later, all these men are dead. If the same circle met today, what names might they put forth? Perhaps one: Alexander Solzhenitsyn. But one has to strain to think of another. No statesman qualifies. No one from the so-called Third World, although maybe President Anwar Sadat is worth discussing. No composer, no artist, no poet. Along with Solzhenitsyn, the Russian dissidents as a group are most impressive. But there appear to be no men or women of world historical stature about. Why? Do we happen to be going through an arid time for human personality—an empty stretch in the history of human character —of a kind that has cropped up from time to time? Or is something else involved?

The worst that *can* be said about ambition is what frequently *is* said about ambition. How did this come about? How did "the tradition of ambition," once so firm and strong, become so wobbly and weak? Ambition itself is an ideal, something passed on from generation to generation, a quality that, like love or truthfulness or courage, it was once felt ought to be inculcated in the young. Ambition is an ideal to which one must aspire. But if ambition is to endure as an ideal, it must command wide respect. Ample is the evidence that this respect has begun to wear away. Luigi Barzini, in his memoir *O America!*, a book in the long tradition of foreign commentators on the American scene, wrote about the United States he found when he first visited this country in the 1920s:

Opportunity in America went hand in hand with a crippling personal burden—"the individual moral duty not to waste one hour [of life, to] achieve success and make money, build and produce more and more, and at the same time, persistently improve the world, untiringly trying to teach all men how to live, work, produce, consume and rule themselves the American way!" The irony is that I still believe the world would be a better place if some of the American ideals of my youth had prevailed everywhere, and first of all, in the United States itself.

If ambition is to be well regarded, the rewards of ambition—wealth, distinction, control over one's own destiny—must be deemed worthy of the sacrifices made on ambition's behalf. If the tradition of ambition is to have vitality, it must be widely shared; and it must especially be esteemed by people who are themselves admired, the educated not least among them. The educated not least because, nowadays more than ever before, it is they who have usurped the platforms of public discussion and wield the power of the spoken and written word in newspapers, in magazines, on television. In an odd way, it is the educated who have claimed to have given up on ambition as an ideal. What is odd is that it is they who have perhaps most benefited from ambition—if not always their own then from that of their parents and grandparents. There is a heavy note of hypocrisy in this; a case of closing the barn door after the horses have escaped—with the educated themselves astride them.

Take, as an example, *The Culture of Narcissism*, by Christopher Lasch, the work of a professor of history about, in his phrase, "the dotage of bourgeois society." Professor Lasch's book has a strongly anticapitalist bias. His is a book of the kind that tells Americans what swine they are, how corrupt their society is, how empty their lives are—and which becomes, despite this or perhaps because of it, a best seller. The commercial fate of *The Culture of Narcissism* is not the fault of the author; still, as a social scientist might say, it is an interesting datum. Capitalism, like the gods, apparently enjoys a good joke, and one of its recurring recent jokes is that of richly rewarding its most furious detractors.

One of Professor Lasch's chapters is entitled "Changing Modes of Making It: From Horatio Alger to the Happy Hooker." Professor Lasch means that Happy Hooker quite literally. The only way one achieves success in America today, in his estimation, is by prostituting oneself. "In the seventies . . . ," he wrote toward the decade's end, "it appears that the prostitute, not the salesman, best exemplifies the qualities indispensable to success in American society." Achievement, according to him, is finished. Instead publicity is the great desideratum. "Today men seek the kind of approval that applauds not their actions but their personal attributes. They wish to be not so much esteemed as admired. They crave not fame but the glamour and excitement of celebrity. They want to be envied rather than respected. Pride and acquisitiveness, the sins of an ascendant capitalism, have given way to vanity."

The world Professor Lasch describes is one of automatons—zombies, really—scrambling for empty prizes, scheming to get ahead, falsifying friendliness to hide "a murderous competition for goods and position." It is us of whom he speaks. How does Professor Lasch come to these views? By quoting from like-minded authors—sociologists and novelists (Joseph Heller among the latter) whose works have the same animus toward their subject as his does in the writing of history, and thus does this literature feed off itself—and by applying social clichés— "the shifting emphasis from capitalist production to consumption"—to arrive at preordained conclusions. What Professor Lasch concludes is that "the dotage of bourgeois society," the twilight of capitalism, is a nightmare prophesied in the writings of the Marquis de Sade. He writes: "In the resulting state of organized anarchy [such as we now live in], as Sade was the first to realize, pleasure becomes life's only business—pleasure, however, that is indistinguishable from rape, murder, unbridled aggression. In a society that has reduced reason to mere calculation, reason can impose no limits on the pursuit of pleasure—on the immediate gratification of every desire no matter how perverse, insane, criminal, or merely immoral."

What is of interest in a book like *The Culture of Narcissism* is not its exaggerated formulations, its twisted evidence, its overheated conclusions, but how readily it is accepted by large segments of the very people it so crudely caricatures. "American Life in an Age of Diminishing Expectations" is Professor Lasch's subtitle, and his own book—which, if taken seriously, will aid in further diminishing expectations—is part of a growing literature that feeds the malaise of exhaustion, helplessness, and self-hatred.

Some writers come at things in even larger spurts of despair than Professor Lasch, sounding the full high note of Spenglerian gloom. Here it is, played in a 1979 version, by I. Robert Sinai, another professor:

> The continued pursuit of economic growth by the "advanced" nations is producing a whole series of crises which threaten to tear them apart. Impelled by the boundless ambitions of the technocrats, driven forward by the apparently irresistible momentum which the existing institutions—political, economic, and technological—set up toward further economic and technological development, intoxicated by the ideals of economic growth and consumerism, caught in a frenzy of self-seeking and greed, the new industrial revolution is beginning to fissure the physical environment and to produce complex changes of ecological disruption. Industrial pollutants are spreading over the land, sea, and air. Clamor, dust, fumes, congestion, and visual destruction are the predominant features in all our built-up areas. The population explosion is making our overgrown cities uninhabitable, and the mounting frustrations of urban life manifest themselves in such symptoms as a seemingly chronic restlessness and discontent, the break-up of families, the growth of drug addition, obscenity, freak cults and violent forms of protest, self-assertion, and defiance. The palpable mass of uniform life, the insect-immensity of the city or beach crowd, induces destructive spasms, a blind need to lunge out and make room. Man becomes a bewildered spectator to what goes on about him, the consumer an uprooted, free-floating, volatile, and manipulated creature, the psyche is choked and smothered, and the civilization produced by

this galloping economy becomes unstable and filled with the most explosive tensions.

Professors Lasch and Sinai disagree on the causes of our downfall. Insofar as they believe in unitary causes, Lasch holds capitalism to be the villain, while Sinai blames a misfit democracy out of which has arisen a technocratic elite "infected with the values of the mass." Although nearly diametrically opposed in their politics, Lasch and Sinai are agreed in their general conclusions—and what they conclude, generally, is that the game is nearly up.

Curiosity Shop □ Among an important segment of the up-and-coming young in West Germany, *The New York Times* reported in the summer of 1979, Mercedes-Benz automobiles were considered "tacky, a statement of self-satisfaction and complacency that young professionals consider repugnant." A Mercedes in this set is a sign of high vulgarity, a car of the kind owned by Beverly Hills dentists or African cabinet ministers. In West Germany many among the very rich and powerful who do own high-line Mercedes automobiles—they are, after all, highly efficient pieces of machinery—remove the chrome numbers (the 380s, the 450SLs) from the left corner on the trunk, so that no one will know how expensive the automobiles are. Reversals of this kind, fundamental shifts in valuation, are not uncommon in the status life. Quite the contrary. The same *New York Times* article mentions other West Germans who, wishing to avoid the crowds at resorts along the sunny Mediterranean, seek out damp and grey places for their holidays. There goes another herd of independent minds.

Belittling the status life is an activity of long standing, and very easy to do. Most of what passes for status—from Dunhill lighters through designer clothes through memberships in clubs to the successes of one's children—is either sad or comical, often both, and scarcely ever calculated to remind one of the dignity of mankind. (To make fun of the status life with sufficient style can even, in some quarters, confer a status of its own.) Yet, when all that is said, it remains difficult to imagine life devoid of status, even of the hollowest kind. And, more important, it is by no means certain that life without status would be better.

Without the interjection of status, which makes possible so many subtle gradations in society, only three God-given qualities would count appreciably in social organization: intelligence, beauty, physical prowess. People who hadn't any of these qualities would fall by the way. Life would become more strictly meritocratic, and greater unhappiness would doubtless result for greater numbers. As things stand now, status often functions as a cushion of sorts, taking some of the bumps out of life. If one comes into the world without great intelligence, beauty, or physical prowess, status offers compensations. A man or woman can exult in things, in what he or she can do for his or her family. Interesting travel, good clothes, elegant cars, fine food, owning works of art, these may not be what life is supposed to be most essentially about, yet for some people they stand in reasonably well as a substitute. ("They say that food is a substitute for love," says a character in a story by Cyril Connolly. "Well it's certainly a bloody good one.") If one isn't able to accrue any of these status items—and there is status even in tennis shoes and children's toys—then one can at least enjoy mocking those who have, laughing at their robust vulgarity, despising their coarseness, deploring the silly waste of their lives. In the status life, even not having status has its pleasures.

The-world-is-rapidly-coming-to-an-end passages, like that of Professor Sinai, reveals nothing so much as a collective pessimism and draining of confidence.

How did the confidence of former days drain away? One can find reasons aplenty. A diminution of what were once thought endless natural resources. A loss of belief in national destiny—and along with it in foreign and military adventure. An almost systematic disqualification of types of the man of action—soldiers, businessmen, politicians—leaving the young free to admire only such relatively trivial types as entertainers and athletes, and an occasional artist. An attack on the ambitious person as a hollow type, everywhere depicted as a man or woman whose every step was thought to be regulated by considerations of personal advantage. An attack, coming from a somewhat different angle, on excellence itself, as exemplified by the contemporary standing of a word such as *elitism*—which has become something of a buzz word, a pejorative meant to equate, for those who use it pejoratively, the desire for excellence with social snobbery and political malevolence. A thinning out of the traditions that once made a life of action, fired by ambition, reaching for success, a perfectly honorable life. Nietzsche says somewhere that there is no action without illusion, which may or may not be true. But currently great numbers, confronted by the possibility of action, see only the prospect of illusion—and refrain.

Is ours, quite simply, not an age of ambition? Is the drama, the dream, of ambition played out, so that it can no longer animate souls, driving the best to their greatest exertions, the middling to do well, even the dull to rouse themselves? The dream of ambition seems most evidently played out when one finds fourth- and fifth-rate people—gossip columnists, false aristocrats, show-business figures, corporation dopes—who have everywhere risen to the top. Not that this phenomenon of the dull in the ascendant is altogether a new one, either. Henry James, in an essay on Turgenev, wrote: "Evil is insolent and strong; beauty enchanting but rare; goodness very apt to be weak; folly very apt to be defiant; wickedness to carry the day; imbeciles to be in great places, people of sense in small, and mankind generally, unhappy." Very well said, of course, but when Henry James wrote this, in England, to mention but one country, Gladstone and Disraeli were still alive, so were Darwin and John Stuart Mill, George Eliot and Matthew Arnold.

Isolated great figures can arise in any era and under almost any conditions. But some eras, certain conditions, are more conducive to the development of strong character than others. If it has any logic, human destiny, at its simplest level, is a compound of the qualities of an individual and of the spirit of the community in which that individual lives. "The community stagnates without the impulse of the individual. The impulse dies away without the sympathy of the community." So William James wrote in his essay "Great Men and Their Environment," making the point that "social evolution is a resultant of the interaction of two wholly distinct factors—the individual, deriving his peculiar gifts from the play of physiological and infra-social forces, but bearing all the power of initiative and origination in his hands; and, second, the social environment, with its power of adopting or rejecting both him and his gifts." Possibly genius can flourish without the sympathy of the community, but men and women who are not geniuses yet aspire to do their utmost can grow dispirited, depressed, demoralized without "the sympathy of the community."

Justice Holmes, a man of wider and deeper culture than any figure prominent in the national public life today, the least neurotic and most clear-minded of men, once wrote: "Life is action and passion; therefore it is required of a man that he should share the action and passion of his time at the peril of being judged not to have lived." What makes the judgment Holmes refers to devastating is that in the final analysis it is a self-judgment. Implicit in it is a question every person must ask of himself: Have I used all my faculties to the limit, have I lived to the fullest of my capacities? The contemporary problem is to decipher what, truly, is the action and passion of a time when both action and passion have been so often discredited.

Curiosity Shop □ Is there, in the extensive scale of human emotions, one that might be called disinterested envy? A contradiction in terms? How after all can envy, among the most intensely personal emotions, be disinterested? An example: One reads, in a newsmagazine, about an executive five years younger than oneself, who has just been named president of a large corporation. Or one sees an actress on a television talk show, who has three different films about to be released. Or, again, one learns about a high school classmate, never a particularly close friend, who is cleaning up in real estate in the northwest part of the country. Upon reading or watching or hearing each of these items one feels a pang, a slight stab, if one is to be honest about it, of hatred. Yet it is far from pure hatred. One doesn't wish any of these people—executive, actress, real estate man—ill. Nor does one wish to change places with them. One doesn't want anything these people have (with the possible exception of their money, but not even necessarily that). No, what one envies about them is something more general, more self-reflexive. Specifically, what one envies is that they seem to be living their lives to their full potential. There are perhaps more important things to do in the world than they do, but that isn't to the point here, that isn't what caused the pang in one's heart. What caused it is a sharp feeling of one's own shortcomings, one's own unused potential, one's own unmistakable sense that one ought to get more out of oneself. At bottom, disinterested envy is self-disappointment.

Has ambition come to take on the character of the situation that in current psychology is termed "the double bind"? The classic example of the double bind is, "I command you to disobey me." Obey and one is not following the command; disobey and one is in fact following the command—and hence obeying, and thus not disobeying, and so forth. Can the double bind of thinking about ambition be formulated as "Succeed at all costs but refrain from being ambitious"? Or is there no bind on the subject at all, either single or double, but merely expressed opinion belying behavior, another word for which is hypocrisy?

Certainly people do not seem less interested in success and its accoutrements now than formerly. Summer homes, European travel, BMWs—the locations, place names, and brand names may change but such items do not seem less in demand today than a decade or two ago. What has happened is that people cannot own up to their interest in success, cannot reveal their dreams, as easily and openly as once they could, lest they be thought pushing, acquisitive, vulgar. Instead we are treated to fine pharisaical spectacles, which now more than ever seem in ample supply: the revolutionary lawyer quartered in the $250,000 Manhattan condominium, the critic of American materialism with a Southampton summer home, the publisher of radical books who takes his meals in three-star restaurants, the journalist advocating participatory democracy in all phases of life, whose own children are enrolled in private schools. For such people and many more perhaps not so egregious, the proper formulation is, "Succeed at all costs but refrain from *appearing* ambitious."

But many people do truly feel a bind of sorts. They want to succeed, desire what success brings, are hungry for achievement, but do not want to seem, even to themselves, ambitious. The bind chafes; they feel themselves split apart. They fear accusations—even self-accusations. They dislike thinking themselves ambitious; ambition implies to them an unappealing middle-classness, which is unpleasant for them to contemplate. They may already have discipline, be instinctive planners, be security-minded, live for the future, thrive on work—all middle-class virtues, these—never mind, deep down, they do not feel these qualities properly expressive of their true qualities, or so they prefer to think. They even, many of them, have grave doubts about their accomplishments. Such success as these have brought they sometimes view as aligning them with the haves, the oppressors, the executioners of the world. This makes them often squirm with guilt; it sometimes drives them into therapy. But, be it noted, it scarcely ever pushes them into living less well.

V. S. Naipaul has the narrator of his novel, *A Bend in the River*, remark about a group of well-set-up people listening to a recording of Joan Baez: "You couldn't listen to sweet songs about injustice unless you expected justice and received it much of the time. You couldn't sing songs about the end of the world unless . . . you felt that the world was going on and you were safe in it." So frequently it is with people who worry about their success, who are concerned about being thought too ambitious —such worry and concern are among the luxuries afforded those who have nearly everything else. The fear of coping with success, it might be said, is the mental equivalent of listening to a Joan Baez song; it makes one feel a little better about one's situation without actually doing anything about it.

Menacing greed, spiritual vulgarity, untrammeled corruption have never been in short supply in the world, but these cannot be made the exclusive property of ambition. Ambition, the fuel of achievement, has chiefly to do with the desire to mold one's own destiny, to get the best out of oneself. Having ambition is no guarantee of good character or bad. Ambition repels when it is in too great a disproportion to ability; or when it is unrestrained, or heedless of contending claims. Ambition is sad when it is out of all proportion to gifts: when a man or woman tormented by the need to rule an empire hasn't the competence to run a good shoe store. "This disparity between aspiration and equipment," H. L. Mencken noted, "runs through the whole of American life; material prosperity and popular education have made it a sort of national disease." But neither can the blame for this be laid to ambition. If people are to feel comfort in deserved success, if they are to retain the energy that ambition can give—and, as Dreiser writes in *Sister Carrie,* "there is nothing so inspiring in life as the sight of a legitimate ambition, no matter how incipient"—then a clearer view is needed about what ambition is and what it entails.

Curiosity Shop □ The "hippoisie"—that is what they called themselves. A nice phrase, comical but accurate, too. It denotes people who in the middle and late 1960s were in college or graduate school and connected with protest movements of one kind or another but who are now, in their thirties, more interested in the traditional bourgeois comforts of furniture and food, wine and prints—and thus in many of the things that, a decade or so earlier, they contemned.

At table a great fuss was made over the pasta dish; the wine generated much talk about similar vintages, other vineyards. The fish was not all one had hoped for, but the salad, crisp and delicately dressed, marked a distinct comeback, or so everyone agreed. Coffee, fruit, cheese, and extravagant pastries were served in the living room—"Yes, these older apartments are laid out so much better than the new"—along with a rousing good attack on elitism, sexism, and what were felt to be other establishmentarian ploys against the downtrodden and the better elements in the society, such as those of us gathered around this coffee table. What an extraordinary country the United States is, a place where one can have one's cake and eat it, too, and with a Rémy Martin on the side, please.

What does ambition entail? In his book *On Happiness,* the French philosopher Alain remarked that "Everyone has what he wants." Alain thought that ambition was in large part a matter of taste, and it is not altogether clear whether it was to his, but he did have a serious respect for it. "Society," he wrote, "gives nothing to the man who asks for nothing, I mean, firmly and persistently; and that is not a bad thing, for education and aptitude are not the only things that count." Alain thought that in such matters realism was of the greatest necessity. "The point," he wrote, "is that if you take it upon yourself to tell unpleasant truths to a man who is in a position to open doors for you, do not say that you wanted to pass through them; you dreamed that you were passing through them, as we sometimes dream that we are a bird."

Alain was absolutely in earnest when he wrote that "everyone has what he wants." He is in interesting company, for Goethe, in the epigraph to his autobiography, cites the proverb that runs, "Whatever we desire when we are young we have in abundance when we are old." What Alain felt was that—apart from the odd accident, the arbitrary infliction of disease—each of us determines his own destiny. "Many people complain about not having this or that; but the reason is that they did not really want it." Alain felt that the world did not, in the matter of ambition, offer much in the way of equilibrium. "People who have made their fortune have done so by striving to dominate something. But the man who would like a nice little business where he could be happy in a nice friendly atmosphere, where he could indulge his preferences and fancies, where he could be easygoing and even generous—such a man evaporates, like rain on a hot pavement."

Alain was no booster, no Dale Carnegie got up in pellucid

French prose; he was, among other things, the teacher of Simone Weil and the winner, in 1951, of the first Grand Prix National de Littérature. But this highly cerebral and learned man believed that, above all, one must be truthful with oneself about one's own motives, especially if one is to survive in the world. "It takes rigor, and it takes courage," he held, to will one's way to what one wants; and, in a crucial distinction, Alain added, "to hope is not to will." Will is of the utmost importance for Alain. "The colonel who retires on a farm in the country would have liked to have become a general; but if I could examine his life, I would find some little thing that he neglected to do, that he did not want to do. I could prove to him that he did not want to become a general."

In mentioning his hypothetical colonel—and this is all that is said about him—Alain did not mean that he could find some secret or psychically hidden motive for the colonel's inability to rise in rank. What he meant is that the colonel, assuming he had the ability to rise to general, had not the will to do so. A more perfect obedience, a muting of his critical sense, greater attention to the social side of military life, any of an ample assortment of lapses of this kind could have cost our colonel his promotion. He may have lost it through a deliberate and quite moral decision to speak his mind about a policy with which he disagreed. He may have chosen not to leave an alcoholic wife; or he may have chosen to leave a quite respectable wife for a younger woman. But be it moral or tactical or personal, there was, Alain implies, something the colonel did not do because he would not, he could not, do it.

So it seems to be with other careers. Wish to be a great poet? Assuming one has the ability, it may nonetheless mean having to give up the pleasures of family life. Wish to become a millionaire? It may mean having to cease thinking about spending money and concentrate completely on earning it. Wish to live in an atmosphere of unstinting cultivation and refinement? It may mean falling out of touch with contemporary life, or shutting oneself off from caring about the world's injustices, or even doing work of a repulsive kind that will bring in enough money to make such a life possible. Alain's larger point is that, assuming we stand ready to pay the price, we all get what we want. The rub is, of course, the price. Why not be a great poet with a happy family? Why not a great poet with a happy family who, through recognition of his wondrous gifts, becomes a wealthy man? Why not a great poet, etc., etc., who is also a fine athlete and an operatic-class baritone? Glory, greatness, riches, love—who doesn't want them all? But acquiring the one often precludes acquiring one or more of the others. This is mere wanting, hoping, fantasizing. For one thing, talents are not so lavishly distributed. The acquisition of one sort of ability often makes that of another unlikely, if not impossible; imaginative sympathy, a strength in an artist or historian, can cripple a man of action. Even the extravagantly gifted often find themselves weighted down by countervailing forces: indolence, a violent temper, a quickness to grow bored. To take the gifts one does have, to concentrate one's strength upon their development, to disallow distractions—none of these is an easy task.

What among other things makes them difficult is that so often those things that people do best interest them least. On this point Henri Frédéric Amiel, the nineteenth-century diarist, wrote: "Everyone sets his heart on what he aspires to, and aspires instinctively to what he lacks. This is an unconscious protest against the incompleteness of every nature." Yet even if one does wish to develop such gifts as he has, obstacles everywhere arise, in the form of personal temperament, moral scruples, insufficient firmness of will. But there is another, really quite staggering problem, and this is that most people do not truly know what they want from life. "I wish," a Long Island housewife in a recent novel says, "to die thin." To few among us is such clarity of purpose given.

When a person asks himself what he wants out of life, he is asking a question that cuts to his soul. To answer it with candor and precision and realism about one's own limitations requires self-knowledge of the highest kind. Napoleon may have known what he wanted out of life, Gandhi most certainly knew, but at those lower reaches where most people abide, knowledge about what one wants, truly wants, becomes more complicated. Knowledge about the extent of a person's ambition is not knowledge of a theoretical kind. It comes only from experience. A set of bleeding ulcers may tell a man he has gone as far as he can, and not to push things further. A decision that one cannot bring oneself to make even though it favors one's own career, may, similarly, tell a man that he has come to the end of the line. Yet things can work as readily the other way round. A person can discover that he hasn't the strength to back up the things he truly believes in. Or he can learn that nothing gives quite the same pleasure as mastery over his work, or that he thrives under pressure, or thrills at the prospect of competition. Ambition can be almost systematically encouraged or discouraged, but it is only out in the world where it can be tested and its true strength revealed.

Curiosity Shop □ He taught writing to the young at a university, and they seemed to like writing, or at least the notion of being a writer. It was one of those few jobs that the young, or some among them, nowadays thought to be honorable. Many admired what they took to be the freedom and independence of the work; some thought it was glamorous; for all it was, somehow, an okay thing to do. Over the years he discovered an enormous range of ability among these students: a few were inept, some were pedestrian, but a surprisingly large number were extraordinarily good. He, the teacher, never openly encouraged them beyond telling them that this or that discrete composition was solid or winning or witty. He felt it would be wrong to say to any one of these students, "You really have it, kid; if you work at it, devote yourself to it, you one day could be a considerable writer, the real thing." But he didn't want the responsibility for this kind of encouragement, especially since writing was one of those jobs that, if you failed at it, made nothing else seem quite worth doing in life. Besides, he felt that no more encouragement than he gave was required. Those of his students who would become writers would do so because they passionately wanted to or needed to. By this standard, of the hundreds of students who had passed through his classes, he thought only two had anything like a chance to end up writing for a living. Both came of working-class families. One was a tall, taciturn young man, a brooder, who had a very complicated relationship with his father. The other was a little fellow who had more desire than talent, but possibly desire enough, the teacher thought, to make up for the talent he lacked; and this boy would, he felt, one day be writing for the movies or create a not very good television series. The first boy needed it, the second wanted it, but the more the teacher thought about this distinction between needing and wanting the blurrier it became, until in the end they seemed quite the same thing.

Does human nature change? This is one of the great and continuing questions—great because if the answer to it were known so much else about the human condition would be knowable, and continuing because the answer to it cannot, ever, be known with certainty. But conditions do change, and changed conditions do change views, and changed views result in changed behavior. "If human nature does alter," E. M. Forster wrote, "it will be because individuals manage to look at themselves in a new way."

A new way in which many people have begun to look at themselves has to do with work. More specifically, a distinction, fairly recent, can now be made between those who live for work and those who work to live. For the former, work is central to their lives; their work defines them not only to the world but, more important, to themselves; life and work for them are nearly coterminous, and to them not to be able to work would be a crushing deprivation. For the latter, work is at best an unavoidable necessity; life is most intensely, most gloriously vivid not on but outside the job; work is more or less an intrusion upon life, dampening, irritating, alienating. One cannot know with any certainty whether a greater number of people live for work or work to live. But among the young—people still under, say, thirty-five—it seems as if greater and greater numbers fall into the latter category. Whatever work might be offered them, they would, frankly, rather be on the slopes in Aspen or eating crêpes in San Francisco.

The world has never known a short supply of stupid and

odious jobs; nor of cruel work: stoking furnaces, going down into mines, fourteen-hour days in sweatshops. Much of this has been eliminated; much has ameliorated. But though the worst work has fallen to the lot of the working classes, the most strident complaints about work have come from the educated classes. Work, the argument runs, has deteriorated to the point of choking the spirit. "Most work," as one writer on the subject puts it, "is unrewarding, unfulfilling, meaningless . . . one would not perform it if one could get out of it . . . insofar as one is absorbed too deeply in it, it destroys the body and soul."

Some who hold these views believe that the problem with work set in with the advent of industrial capitalism; others who hold them argue that work, dreary and dreadful though it currently is, can be made more creative and enticing; others still imagine utopian schemes in which necessarily unpleasant work is shared on a rotating basis, thus allowing everyone to be able to develop to his or her highest potential. Yet, when all this is set aside, doesn't the proposition obtrude that much of the world's work is not pleasant, some of it is furiously boring, and has always been so—though perhaps much more in the past than now—and probably always shall be so? Although as recently as a generation ago people did take pride and put craft in less than glamorous jobs (butchering, say, or auto mechanics), the reasons for working well even at jobs performed under harsh conditions seemed more compelling then than now. Some of these reasons were : survival, one's own mobility, one's children's future, self-respect.

There also seemed less room to turn around in; one chose a job and stuck with it. A family lived in one city, one neighborhood even, for generations. The options, as people nowadays say, were fewer. On this point, the late Lionel Trilling remarked:

I think that we must take into account the kind and amount of gratuitousness that has come into contemporary life for all sorts of reasons. That is, our choices are freer now than they ought to be. The control of our lives by necessity is less than it formerly was. We are put under a diminishing pressure of what we can call duty, we are put under a diminishing pressure of what we call necessity. Not that these things have gone from us, but the confrontation of danger, the confrontation of death, the confrontation of suffering, this we do not have to make as frequently as people formerly did. We're pretty sure we're going to be fed, we're pretty sure that we will not die at one of those early ages that people used to die at.

None of which is to say that many men and women do not find pleasure in their work, and intrinsic pleasure in the work itself, not alone in its extrinsic rewards. People do, and doubtless will continue to. Many leave more lucrative jobs for work they hope will prove more satisfying. But these people are more often than not in search of fulfillment—that is, of contentment. Contentment and ambition are often very different things. However hard or even degrading certain jobs were thought to be, years ago it was precisely ambition that was to pull one up; and if a person was not ambitious for himself, he was ambitious for his children. ("I am the daughter of a dining-car waiter," Secretary of Health and Welfare Patricia Harris once told a Senate committee, her rise marking a tribute to her father fully as much as to herself.) Now, though, one can attack the character of work itself. Ambition at least left open the possibility of individual effort, of climbing up and out, which is precisely what so many people did. But to attack work itself is to perceive reality very differently indeed. "If men define situations as real," wrote W. I. Thomas, "they are real in their consequences."

Much evidence already exists of people acting on the assumption that work is drudgery and worse by dropping out. In the late 1960s and early 1970s there was the commune movement, now all but dead. Over the same period there were, on the part of the young, many instances of deliberate downward mobility, in which the sons and daughters of the upper-middle classes took up careers as artisans and craftsmen, as if in protest of the ideal of perpetual upward mobility. More recently, it is said that something like 40 percent of the unemployed in the United States choose not to work. These people live off one kind of hustle or another: food stamps, unemployment payments, welfare programs. How many among them are well schooled is not known, but the percentage may not be insignificant. Their complaint is grounded in psychology. They do not find work, as they say, "meaningful." They have, as a result, laid themselves off. These are people who have taken seriously all the talk about the "rat race," the "overstructuring" of work, vapidities about the "system," and other clichés. The consequences are sad waste, chiefly of their own lives.

Yet perhaps nothing is better calculated to drive people to drop out than the current advocates of the rewards of work, the success merchandisers of the day. Chesterton once said that people who write books about success cannot even succeed at writing books, but that does not mean that their books, however ill made, are not often very profitable. The most recent batch of such books preach an unapologetic selfishness that is rather a new element in the history of this degraded literature. Take, for example, the work of Michael Korda, author of *Power! How to Get It, How to Use It*, and *Success! How Every Man and Woman Can Achieve It*. Mr. Korda is no tub-thumping fundamentalist, no Rotarian enthusiast, no snake-oil salesman, but a New York book editor, English born, Oxford educated, a spokesman for the rights of women (he is also the author of a book entitled *Male Chauvinism! How It Works!*). Korda's books— and particularly his book *Success!*—are especially interesting in representing the view not of the yokel but of what passes for the sophisticate: the man with bespoke clothes, elaborate one-upmanship tactics, the connoisseur of contemporary status symbols.

What Michael Korda is saying is that success is much to be preferred over failure, that the pleasures success brings are not to be sniggered at, that striving for success is a superior game —"the ultimate turn-on," he calls it. *Success!* is a how-to book written for people who have not succeeded, and probably are not likely to. Its author has succeeded in the publishing business, rather more substantially with his how-to books, but that does not mean that he, Michael Korda, is cynical or even disingenuous. The successful men he describes he seems truly to admire; they almost look out from the upper stories of Manhattan skyscrapers, their well-shod feet on desks of good wood; or are being trundled about in the warm dark of limousines (while others, the rabble, await buses in the rain); or taking savory yet unfattening meals in the most expensive restaurants. Korda seems genuinely dazzled by this world.

But what sort of world is it, this world of the successful that Michael Korda bids his readers to? It is, to begin with, a world of scathing insecurity, in which everyone assumes that the other fellow is trying to do him in—and everyone is probably correct. People manipulate each other and all situations; the great thing is to keep everybody else off balance. The greatest enemies are those in your own company. Work itself seems secondary, even tertiary, to wielding, and at the same time keeping an eye out for, the long knives. The biggest fool in the world, Korda describes, is he who merely does his work supremely well, without attending to appearances.

Appearances, in Korda's world, are nearly everything. He provides diagrams on how to sit at a meeting, how a suit coat ought to fit over the back and shoulders, how to use glasses and cigarettes for rhetorical flourish. ("If you don't smoke and don't wear glasses, my suggestion would be to buy a pair of glasses and have clear lenses put into them.") Telephones, their kind and number and color, are a limitlessly useful weapon in the struggle for success: "The more people you yourself can put and keep on hold, the more successful you will seem. You can't have too many buttons." This last remark almost but not quite applies as well to the sleeve cuffs of a suit, which ought, for someone intent on succeeding, to have at least three, possibly four buttons: "Ideally, the sleeve buttons should be real—i.e., you should be able to button and unbutton them—but to get this small, correct touch, you have to go to a tailor." A successful woman carries a handbag or a briefcase, but never both at once. For men, "short sleeves are out." And for both: "It pays to be thin."

But beneath the concern with appearances that take up the better part of Michael Korda's book is a world absolutely hellish. Any values or point of view one might have is so much excess luggage, the first things to be jettisoned in a crisis: "If you *don't* want to change jobs, but feel your success values are unsuited to the place you work, start changing them—fast." One needs, in this world, to develop expensive tastes and "the impulse towards hedonism needs to be cultivated as well"—both as goads to succeeding. And rightly so, if Korda is correct, for what else is there but costly toys and fleshly pleasures? Everyone around you is certain to be duplicitous: those above are out to suppress you, those below to cut you down. Even a wife or husband—envious of your success, or fearful of your rise—can be an enemy working against you. "The true test of success is the degree to which one can isolate oneself from others." A line of demarcation is everywhere to be drawn "between ordinary people and those who are successful."

Despite his own fascination with it, Michael Korda makes success seem a nightmare. Fraudulence lurks everywhere. No one is to be trusted. One's own values count for nothing; one's true point of view is best suppressed. Paranoia, in such a world, is the better part of valor—if valor itself has any place at all. And Michael Korda, recall, is a devotee of success, an advocate of ambition. Read with care, his book would be sufficient to make a Maoist out of a 4-H kid.

Curiosity Shop □ Insanity is not good for the complexion or for the figure. So it must be concluded, watching the trickle of men and women who live in the halfway house in the neighborhood, from the luminous stupor of their pallid faces and the bagginess of their bodies. Halfway is of course one of those euphemisms of our day; more than half mad is what these broken people are, drugged to passivity, shambling and shuffling down this otherwise quite unexceptional middle-class American street. The women all wear white cotton socks and an odd unmatched assortment of second- and third-hand clothes; the men tend to run thinner than the women, their very skin hanging upon some of them like ill-fitting garments. The ages of the men and of the women cannot in most cases be reckoned within twenty years. But they are beyond ambition, beyond caring; vanity of every kind has collapsed in them. They have met with more than life's ordinary little vengeances. They have been judged harmless, and yet their presence wandering up and down this street always brings one up, causing a flutter of horror in the heart. There is no way of knowing what has caused the dimming of these minds: what mistreatments, accidents, shocks, or terrors caused them to find life so insupportable that they had to turn away from it. But they are a sharp reminder, too, of the tight string we all walk. To see the bewilderment in their eyes is to know that there are greater burdens than those imposed by life's daily struggles.

The attacks on ambition are many and come from various angles; its public defenders are few and unimpressive, where they are not extremely unattractive. As a result, the support for ambition as a healthy impulse, a quality to be admired and inculcated in the young, is probably lower than it has ever been in the United States. This does not mean that ambition is at an end, that people no longer feel its stirrings and promptings, but only that, no longer openly honored, it is less often openly professed. Consequences follow from this, of course, some of which are that ambition is driven underground, or made sly, or perverse. It can also be forced into vulgarity, as witness the blatant pratings of its contemporary promoters. Such, then, is the way things stand: on the left angry critics, on the right obtuse supporters, and in the middle, as usual, the majority of earnest people trying to get on in life.

Many people are naturally distrustful of ambition, feeling that it represents something intractable in human nature. Thus John Dean entitled his book about his involvement in the Watergate affair during the Nixon administration *Blind Ambition,* as if ambition were to blame for his ignoble actions, and not the constellation of qualities that make up his rather shabby character. Ambition, it must once again be underscored, is morally a two-sided street. Place next to John Dean, Andrew Carnegie, who, among other philanthropic acts, bought the library of Lord Acton, at a time when Acton was in financial distress, and assigned its custodianship to Acton, who never was told who his benefactor was. Need much more be said on the subject than that, great and important though ambition is, there are some things that one must not sacrifice to it?

But going at things the other way, sacrificing ambition so as to guard against its potential excesses, is to go at things wrongly. To discourage ambition is to discourage dreams of grandeur and greatness. All men and women are born, live, suffer, and die; what distinguishes us one from another is our dreams, whether they be dreams about worldly or unworldly things, and what we do to make them come about. "To fulfill the dreams of one's youth," says Father Vaillant, in Willa Cather's *Death Comes for the Archbishop,* "this is the best that can happen to a man."

The quality of an age's ambitions distinguishes it from other ages. An age's ambitions, similarly, mark the quality of its human energy. Sometimes great causes will let loose this energy —the founding of new religions, great new movements in the arts, wars and revolutions; sometimes inventions and radical technological advances will spring this energy forward—steam power, air travel, space exploration; sometimes there is a concentration of great men—as in Periclean Athens, in Renaissance Italy, in the France of Louis XIV; and sometimes all these forces come together—as the Industrial Revolution, the quest for empire, and an efflorescence of statesmen, artists, and intellectuals did in Victorian England. Yet our own age, whose chief accomplishments are likely to be considered by history as scientific and technological, appears otherwise strangely enervated, oddly shorn of human energy. "Moderation," says La Rochefoucauld, "is languor and idleness of the soul, ambition is its activity and energy." But neither, it must be added, is ours an age noted for moderation.

The current age is beginning to seem an age of social insecurity, whose leading belief is in the inability of individuals to change the drift of things. A dash of Marxism, a touch of Freudianism, a vague groaning about something called the System, a distrust of action, a denigration of success—such appear to constitute the chief strands of social thought of the day. None of this allows much leeway for the use of intelligence, courage, and resolution on the part of individuals. It is almost as if we subscribed to a form of social determinism that has no name and whose causes and effects we haven't quite managed to formulate, but to which we feel ourselves helplessly hostage.

The discouragement of ambition is partly—even greatly—responsible for this feeling of helplessness. It may seem an exaggeration to say that ambition is the linchpin of society, holding many of its disparate elements together, but it is not an exaggeration by much. Remove ambition and the essential elements of society seem to fly apart. Ambition, as opposed to mere fantasizing about desires, implies work and discipline to achieve goals, personal and social, of a kind society cannot survive without. Ambition is intimately connected with family, for men and women not only work partly for their families; husbands and wives are often ambitious for each other, but harbor some of their most ardent ambitions for their children; yet to have a family nowadays—with birth control readily available, and inflation a good economic argument against having children—is nearly an expression of ambition in itself. Finally, though ambition was once the domain chiefly of monarchs and aristocrats, it has, in more recent times, increasingly become the domain of the middle classes. Ambition and futurity—a sense of building for tomorrow—are inextricable. Working, saving, planning, these, the daily aspects of ambition, have always been the distinguishing marks of a rising middle class. The attack against ambition is not incidentally an attack on the middle class and what it stands for. Like it or not, the middle class has done much of society's work in America; and it, the middle class, has from the beginning run on ambition.

Of longer standing is the argument against ambition holding that, in the long view, it is finally worthless. Recall Dr. Johnson's "The Vanity of Human Wishes," with its view that all but the most serious religious faith is vanity. Dr. Johnson is of course correct—again in the long view. But George Santayana's riposte, in a poem of his young manhood, seems closer to the mark for most of mankind, who must, after all, take the short view and live in the world as we find it:

> *That all is vanity is undeniable,*
> *But joy is no less joy for being vain*
> *And evils to which everything is liable*

Are evils of which nothing should complain.
The facts are fixed, our mood alone is pliable
And call it dew or drizzle, rain is rain,
And by the proof that life is an inanity
We cannot change the fortunes of humanity.

It is not difficult to imagine a world shorn of ambition. It would probably be a kinder world: without demands, without abrasions, without disappointments. People would have time for reflection. Such work as they did would not be for themselves but for the collectivity. Competition would never enter in. Flutes and oboes would play. Conflict would be eliminated, tension become a thing of the past. The stress of creation would be at an end. Art would no longer be troubling, but purely celebratory in its functions. Flowers and vegetables would be grown. Children, necessary to the preservation of the species, would be raised in common. The family would become superfluous as a social unit, with all its former power for bringing about neurosis drained away. Longevity would be increased, for fewer people would die of heart attack or stroke caused by tumultuous endeavor. Anxiety would be extinct. Time would stretch on and on, with ambition long departed from the human heart.

Ah, how unrelievedly boring life would be!

An Unknown Soldier

He left home at seventeen, not angry, not feeling unloved, but eager to be on his own and out in the world. Never good at bookish things, he did not bother to finish high school. Not that he was dumb, or even slow; it was that he had the itch, the urge to prove himself that no classroom could satisfy. He had grown up in a hard neighborhood, tough kids all about, many of whom would put in time in jail. No playgrounds there but streets and alleys whose chief forms of recreation included crap games and petty theft and fistfights. What the neighborhood taught was street smarts—these you either learned or went under—and it was street smarts and $150 saved from boyhood jobs that were all he took along on his venture out into the world.

What does a boy of seventeen do, in the early 1920s, when he arrives in a strange city with no trade, no education, no known talent? He takes a flunky job. He seeks experience. Good experience, a sage once said, is another name for a bad job. He soon had lots of good experience—that is to say, bad jobs. He worked in restaurants, he worked filling orders at mail-order firms, he worked as a messenger boy. All these were dead-end jobs, and he knew it. But then one day he found a job selling yard goods in the bargain basement of a downtown department store. He had found his vocation: selling. He was not a bad talker; he was agreeable to begin with, and could make himself more so without seeming to be heavy-handed about it. Persuading someone to buy something—most of his customers in the bargain basement were working-class women who made their own clothes—easing their doubt, erasing their hesitation, gave him, each time he did it, a small but real thrill.

Selling was a job with true prospects, especially for a kid with no well-developed interests, no schooling, nothing really but a strong if still unfocused drive to get on in the world. He had, let it be said, good instincts. Working in the bargain basement with the other young men, he noted one co-worker who was very keen about keeping the stock in order, spending goodly portions of the day tidily folding away the long bolts of cloth, filing them in their proper places. Such neatness is all very well, he thought, but this guy is neglecting his sales—and it's for selling that we've been hired. He was right. When after the Christmas rush it came time to lay people off, this tidyer of the stock, having written fewer orders than the other salesmen, was fired. First things first was the lesson to be learned from this.

He soon learned, too, that if he were ever to make any kind of serious money as a salesman he would have to get from behind the counter and out on the road. It was an age for salesmen; a first-class salesman was a personage, a figure. With a good line and a solid territory, a salesman could earn more than most doctors then did, more than all but a few lawyers; and there was no education required, only a sharp wit and good sense. In those days salesmen took on young men, paid their expenses and a pittance of a salary, and taught them the art of selling; they "broke 'em in," in the phrase of that day. In exchange the young men lugged the salesman's sample cases, wrote up the orders, saw to train tickets, picked up dry cleaning and laundry, went for coffee. The job was a combination of student, porter, gofer, clerk, and valet. He was able to get such a job with a man in his early fifties of erect carriage, a man of bearing and high principle, whose territory was the western United States. Off they went, traveling by train, the older man, who looked upon selling as a profession, teaching the younger man by precept and example. He showed him when to be patient in dealing with customers, how to set the groundwork for future sales, when to press to close a deal, when to hold back. He corrected his dress, once told him to dump a Stetson he had bought in Wyoming, chastised him for bumbling while handling his samples during a call on an important customer, yelled at him for writing up orders sloppily. Sometimes the criticism came in such torrents that the young man, feeling himself worthless, nearly cried himself to sleep; not generally religious, he asked God's help. Indelicate the older man may have been, but he taught the younger man how it was done; he taught him a craft. He stayed with the older man three years—he would later name a son after him—and then went out on his own.

A good salesman could sell anything: handkerchiefs, real estate, watches, shoe trees, fine linen. But the great thing was to get a good line and to be given a good territory to sell it in. At first he got neither. But he took what he could get, worked hard and steadily at it. Selling, his head was abuzz with his former tutor's maxims; where these didn't apply, his own good instincts came to the rescue. He was beginning to make a name for himself when the Depression arrived. Having come from a poor family, not yet having acquired enough to lose, he was himself not hard hit by the Depression. It slowed his progress, to be sure, and it also left a slightly pessimistic cast to his mind. The floor could give way, nothing was guaranteed in life. This didn't mean a man ought to be tame—in the middle of the Depression he himself married and began a family—but only that, somewhere in your calculations, you had to allow for catastrophe. The Depression taught others abandonment—a sense of what the hell, nothing's safe in the world—but the lesson he learned from it was a qualified caution. He was, he knew, alone in the world; if he stumbled and fell, no one would be there to pick him up.

Throughout the Depression he was never without work. He went from job to job, trading line for better line. He became very good at what he did. He developed a reputation for solidity, for being a man whose word, once given, could be counted on. As a big-city boy himself, nothing appalled him more than being lied to or conned. In later years—by then a maxim-giver himself—he would say: "It's a hard world. No one expects anyone to be an angel. But that doesn't give anybody a right to be a son of a bitch either." He was without neurosis; status held no serious interest for him; his vanities were few, and none got in the way of his work. He attended to business. First things first: he was a salesman, in business, and business for a salesman meant writing orders, which he did, abundantly. After one particularly good month, he was called into the office of his current boss, a hard man, noted for being ungenerous and unhumorous, who said to him, "Kid, this desk I'm sitting behind, it's not for sale. I tell you this because you seem to have sold everything else in the joint."

Not long after World War II, along with a partner, he went into business for himself. The plan was that the partner was to be the inside man; he, as a salesman, would be the outside man. Their offices were far from grand, their profits less than great. Going into business meant a substantial drop in his income—he had begun earning handsome commissions—at least for the present. Still, there was a special feeling about it. He used to arrive at the place between 7:00 and 7:30 A.M., sit behind his second-hand desk, walk through the dusty storerooms checking stock before starting out on his calls on customers. As his and his partner's talents were very different, so were their tastes. The partner bought six or eight pairs of shoes at a shot, wore no shirts without monograms, went in for flashy cars. He could not care less about such things.

At one point, at his partner's insistence, they rented Cadillacs. He drove his half-ashamedly, quickly clapping it into the garage when he arrived home at night. But in making his calls on customers, especially on new customers, he noted that they were greatly impressed with the fact that he drove so costly a car. They assumed that, having such a car, he must be a man in the know, and hence someone worth listening to. This did not, he felt, speak well for the intelligence of most people, but there it was. The point for him—and he was always looking for the point to experience—was to take the measure of men and yet not grow cynical.

In time he bought out his partner, and had the business to himself. He ran it inside and outside. His way of running a business was to lavish care on small details, insofar as possible to prevent waste, to buy carefully, to go for the dough and forget the show. He could not delegate responsibility very well, chiefly because he loved all the small responsibilities of the business too much to relinquish them to others. Although its profits increased year by year, the business did not grow in the contemporary sense: he didn't occupy larger quarters, he didn't open branches in New York, Houston, L.A. He didn't mind running a small operation; he preferred things to be of a size that he could control, stamped with his own personality. Besides, he was, slowly, becoming a rich man.

The money mattered; it always would to someone who had been born poor and had been nearly cut down because of the Depression. Money was a useful and accurate way of keeping score; in business, it told a man where he stood. But as he grew older, as his children came of age and went out on their own, money meant increasingly less to him. He liked being in his own place of business; he liked the action; he liked work. Years after he needed to, he still arrived early and continued to come down on Saturdays. He was never happier than when he had heavy mail, customers in the place, fresh merchandise on its way up on the service elevator. At such moments he felt most alive.

One of the greatest benefits of owning his own business was that no one could forcibly retire him, which, in his case, was important. Over the years he had acquired none of the habits of leisure. He read *The Wall Street Journal, The New York Times* on Sundays, watched the news on television, went to one movie roughly every two years. He hadn't the patience for reading books, but he was nonetheless thoughtful. Driving to and from his place he considered what Nature intended in its creations, both glories and disasters. Often he felt he saw distinct patterns, was on the verge of grasping designs; but when he attempted to formulate what, fleetingly, he had glimpsed, it disappeared. Pondering the greater scheme of things never tired him; it was perhaps the closest he came to having a hobby.

What was his own place in the greater scheme of things? Did he ever stop to ask? He was, assuredly, no saint, a man of normal and altogether human appetites. He had not broken another man or stepped on anyone's neck to get where he was. He had, true, contributed no new ideas, changed nothing significantly in the world around him, would leave little after him. He raised a family; he gave to charity. What he bought and sold the world could have easily survived without. He paid taxes; he contributed to the traffic and growth of the economy. He had principles; he was businesslike—and businesslike, for him, was a compliment, which he used to mean dependable and orderly and sensible. He was serious, a man not to be fooled with. There was nothing trivial about him. He had worked his life long, and it had given him character; he had realized his dreams, and it had given him pleasure. He was a man who never complained; if he doubted, he kept his doubts to himself. Ambition served him well. How many others are there like him? More, perhaps, than one might guess.

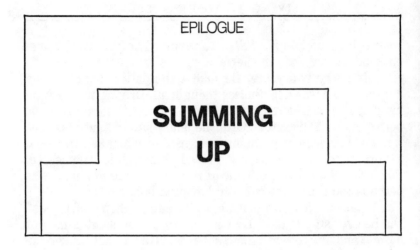

SUMMING UP

Much has happened to deprive ambition of its former unequivocal allure. The family, for example, has come to seem less solid than it once was. Money, formerly a traditional goal of a certain kind of ambition, has been heavily taxed and devalued, both spiritually and materially. Failure, once a snake to avoid at all costs, has lost much of its bite. And over the past two hundred years the spokesmen for ambition, among them Thomas Jefferson and Benjamin Franklin and Ralph Waldo Emerson, have been replaced by less and less impressive figures.

Through the biographical portraits in this book I have attempted to illustrate the range of kinds of ambition and the variety of its representative figures: from Benjamin Franklin, who was never without worthy goals to place his ambition at the service of, to Joseph P. Kennedy, whose ambition seems never to have traveled beyond the promotion of himself and his family; from Henry Adams, whose natural advantages seem to have helped to sink him, to Edith Wharton, whose natural advantages allowed her to succeed. Looking rather closer than I had hitherto done at men such as John D. Rockefeller, Sr. and the first Henry Ford, I found each man's ambition had less to do with money and power than one normally might have thought; and I found both men more impressive, for all their flaws, than the conventional picture makes them out to be. As Justice Holmes once wrote, in a letter to his friend Lewis Einstein, the diplomatist and historian: "But I don't quite sympathize with your scorn of Rockefeller. I don't enjoy that kind of society, but I believe him (typically, I don't know much about him personally) to be a great man, and I think we should do justice to those who do big things however little we want to dine with them." Thinking about ambition has caused me to disregard the notion that our final judgment about the men and women of history hangs on the question of whether we should like to dine with them. For this usually comes down to our asking if they share our views on politics, art, social questions, and so on down the line.

Although people will always argue about the ends to which ambition is put, the real question posed by ambition is whether or not each of us has a true hand in shaping his own destiny. People who believe that our control over our own destinies is slight, if not nonexistent, will not think very well of ambition: it may even seem rather comical to them. For such people forces, not individual will, are what count; history, not biography, is decisive. One would be foolish not to grant historical forces their due; nor should the importance of accident be overlooked. But give forces too much due, allow too much importance to accident, and the significance of our actions becomes nil. "No," Alexander Solzhenitsyn wrote, "we must not hide behind fate's petticoats; the most important decisions in our lives, when all is said, we make for ourselves." To the extent that one believes that each of us is largely responsible for his own fate, to that extent will one believe in the importance of ambition, which, in one of its aspects, is the expression of the desire to shape one's own fate.

Ideas have consequences, bad ideas fully as much consequence as good ones. Some people hold that we are, essentially, what we keep hidden about ourselves, our fears and secrets. Other people hold that, whatever our personal secrets and fears, we are what we do. There is often a conflict among men and women of good heart between those who believe that it is what one achieves that matters and those who believe that what one is and how one lives matter more.

Some of us are Hamlets in our outlook, some Don Quixotes. In many the two types are combined in unending battle. But at the moment, among the best educated, Hamlet's view seems to predominate. Oddly—and ironically—the loss of confidence in ambition comes at a time when the gates of opportunity have never been thrown so wide open. Until fairly recently, for example, women were discouraged from harboring large ambitions, and only truly exceptional women had a chance to make their mark. The same can be said for minority groups. Ambition has never seemed a possibility for so many. Equality of opportunity has grown greater and greater. Yet ambition has not kept pace.

There is a strong view that holds that success is a myth, and ambition therefore a sham. Does this mean that success does not really exist? That achievement is at bottom empty? That the efforts of men and women are of no significance alongside the force of movements and events? Now not all success, obviously, is worth esteeming, nor all ambition worth cultivating. Which are and which are not is something one soon enough learns on one's own. But even the most cynical secretly admit that success exists; that achievement counts for a great deal; and that the true myth is that the actions of men and women are useless. To believe otherwise is to take on a point of view that is likely to be deranging. It is, in its implications, to remove all motive for competence, interest in attainment, and regard for posterity.

We do not choose to be born. We do not choose our parents. We do not choose our historical epoch, or the country of our birth, or the immediate circumstances of our upbringing. We do not, most of us, choose to die; nor do we choose the time or conditions of our death. But within all this realm of choicelessness, we do choose how we shall live: courageously or in cowardice, honorably or dishonorably, with purpose or in drift. We decide what is important and what is trivial in life. We decide that what makes us significant is either what we do or what we refuse to do. But no matter how indifferent the universe may be to our choices and decisions, these choices and decisions are ours to make. We decide. We choose. And as we decide and choose, so are our lives formed. In the end, forming our own destiny is what ambition is about.

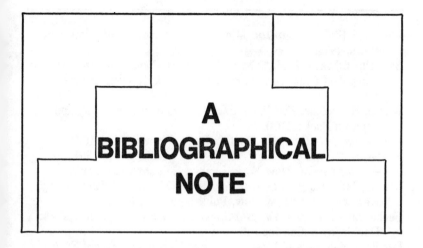

A BIBLIOGRAPHICAL NOTE

This is a book built in large part upon other books, and hence, like all such books, quite fairly open to charges of piracy. Some of the books I have read in preparation for the composition of this book have been helpful to me for the ideas in them; others have supplied valuable factual information; and still others have been useful to argue with. I have plundered freely from history and literature; but my depredations upon biography for the biographical portraits in this book have been especially heavy. Ambition is one of those ample subjects to which, once one begins to think about it, nearly everything one is reading or has ever read seems to have pertinent application. I am not certain that I can recall all the books I have made use of in the making of this book. But below I have listed the major books to which I feel a debt.

Adams, Henry. *Democracy: An American Novel.* New York: H. Holt and Co., 1908.
———. *The Education of Henry Adams: An Autobiography.* Boston and New York: Houghton Mifflin Co., 1918.
Alain. *See* Chartier, Émile.
Amory, Cleveland. *Who Killed Society?* New York: Harper & Row, Publishers, Inc., 1960.
Auchincloss, Louis. *Edith Wharton.* Minneapolis: University of Minnesota Press, 1961.
———. *The Partners.* Boston: Houghton Mifflin Co., 1974.

———. *A Writer's Capital.* Minneapolis: University of Minnesota Press, 1974.

Baltzell, Edward Digby. *The Protestant Establishment: Aristocracy and Caste in America.* New York: Random House, Inc., 1964.

Balzac, Honoré de. *The Black Sheep.* Harmondsworth, England: Penguin Books, 1970.

———. *Eugénie Grandet.* Boston: Little, Brown & Co., 1927.

———. *Lost Illusions.* New York: Avil Publishing Co., 1901.

———. *Old Goriot.* New York: Limited Editions Club, 1948.

Barzini, Luigi Giorgio. *O America: When You and I Were Young.* New York: Harper & Row, Publishers, Inc., 1977.

Beebe, Lucius Morris. *The Big Spenders.* Garden City, New York: Doubleday & Co., Inc., 1966.

Bendix, Reinhard, and Lipset, Seymour Martin, eds. *Class, Status, and Power: A Reader in Social Stratification.* Glencoe, Illinois: Free Press, 1953.

Berg, A. Scott. *Max Perkins: Editor of Genius.* New York: E. P. Dutton & Co., Inc., 1978.

Beyle, Marie Henri (Stendhal). *The Red and the Black: A Chronical of 1830.* New York: E. P. Dutton & Co., Inc., 1922.

Birmingham, Stephen. *The Late John Marquand: A Biography.* Philadelphia: J. B. Lippincott Co., 1972.

———. *Real Lace: America's Irish Rich.* New York: Harper & Row, Publishers, Inc., 1973.

———. *The Right People: A Portrait of the American Social Establishment.* Boston: Little, Brown & Co., 1968.

Boorstin, Daniel Joseph. *The Americans: The National Experience.* New York: Random House, Inc., 1965.

Borneman, Ernest, ed. *The Psychoanalysis of Money.* New York: Urizen Books, Inc., 1976.

Brooks, Van Wyck. *The Ordeal of Mark Twain.* New York: E. P. Dutton & Co., Inc., 1933.

Carnegie, Dale. *How To Win Friends and Influence People.* New York: Simon & Schuster, Inc., 1952.

Cawelti, John G. *Apostles of the Self-Made Man.* Chicago: University of Chicago Press, 1965.

Chartier, Emile (Alain). *On Happiness.* New York: Frederick Ungar Publishing Co., 1973.

Collier, Peter, and Horowitz, David. *The Rockfellers: An American Dynasty.* New York: Holt, Rinehart & Winston, 1976.

Curtis, Charlotte. *The Rich and Other Atrocities.* New York: Harper & Row, Publishers, Inc., 1976.

Davis, John Hagy. *The Guggenheims: An American Epic.* New York: William Morrow & Co., Inc., 1978.

Davis, Kenneth Sydney. *Politics of Honor: A Biography of Adlai E. Stevenson.* New York: G. P. Putnam's Sons, 1967.

Doyle, Edward P., ed. *As We Knew Adlai: The Stevenson Story by Twenty-Two Friends.* New York: Harper & Row, Publishers, Inc., 1966.

Dreiser, Theodore. *An American Tragedy.* Cleveland: World Publishing Co., 1948.

———. *The Financier: A Novel.* New York and London: Harper & Brothers, 1912.

———. *Sister Carrie.* Cleveland: World Publishing Co., 1927.

———. *The Stoic.* Garden City, New York: Doubleday & Co., Inc., 1947.

———. *The Titan.* Cleveland: World Publishing Co., 1959.

Duke, Marc. *The Du Ponts: Portrait of a Dynasty.* New York: Saturday Review Press, 1976.

Farr, Finis. *O'Hara: A Biography.* Boston: Little, Brown & Co., 1973.

Faulkner, William. *The Hamlet.* New York: Random House, Inc., 1940.

———. *The Mansion.* New York: Random House, Inc., 1959.

———. *The Town.* New York: Random House, Inc., 1957.

Fitzgerald, F. Scott. *The Crack-Up.* New York: New Directions, 1945.

———. *The Great Gatsby.* New York: Charles Scribner's Sons, 1925.

———. *Letters.* Edited by Andrew Turnbull. New York: Charles Scribner's Sons, 1963.

Franklin, Benjamin. *The Autobiography of Benjamin Franklin.* Boston and New York: Houghton Mifflin Co., 1906.

Galbraith, John Kenneth. *Money: Whence It Came, Where It Went.* Boston: Houghton Mifflin Co., 1975.

Gissing, George Robert. *New Grub Street.* Baltimore: Penguin Books, 1968.

Harrington, Michael. *Fragments of the Century.* New York: Saturday Review Press, 1973.

Hill, Napoleon. *Think and Grow Rich.* New York: Hawthorn Books, Inc., 1966.

Hoyt, Edwin Palmer. *The Guggenheims and the American Dream.* New York: Funk & Wagnalls, Inc., 1967.

Johnson, Walter. *How We Drafted Adlai Stevenson.* New York: Alfred A. Knopf, Inc., 1955.

Kaplan, Justin. *Mr. Clemens and Mark Twain: A Biography.* New York: Simon & Schuster, Inc., 1966.

Korda, Michael. *Power! How To Get It, How To Use It.* New York: Random House, Inc., 1975.

————. *Success!* New York: Random House, Inc., 1977.

Lawrence, D. H. *Studies in Classic American Literature.* New York: Penguin Books, 1976.

Leggett, John. *Ross & Tom: Two American Tragedies.* New York: Simon & Schuster, Inc., 1974.

Lewis, David Lanier. *The Public Image of Henry Ford: An American Folk Hero and His Company.* Detroit: Wayne State University Press, 1976.

Lewis, R. W. B. *Edith Wharton: A Biography.* New York: Harper & Row, Publishers, Inc., 1975.

Lorimer, George Horace. *Letters from a Self-Made Merchant to His Son.* New York: Outerbridge & Dienstfrey, 1970.

Lundberg, Ferdinand. *The Rockefeller Syndrome.* Secaucus, New Jersey: Lyle Stuart, Inc., 1975.

Lynn, Kenneth Schuyler. *The Dream of Success: A Study of the Modern American Imagination.* Boston: Little, Brown & Co., 1955.

Marquand, John Phillips. *H. M. Pulham, Esquire.* Boston: Little, Brown & Co., 1941.

————. *The Late George Apley: A Novel in the Form of a Memoir.* Boston: Little, Brown, & Co., 1938.

Martin, John Bartlow. *Adlai Stevenson and the World: The Life of Adlai E. Stevenson.* Garden City, New York: Doubleday & Co., Inc., 1976.

Maurois, André. *Prometheus: The Life of Balzac.* New York: Harper & Row, Publishers, Inc., 1966.

Mizener, Arthur. *The Far Side of Paradise: A Biography of F. Scott Fitzgerald.* Boston: Houghton Mifflin Co., 1965.

Mosley, Leonard. *Blood Relations: The Rise and Fall of the Du Ponts of Delaware.* New York: Atheneum Publishers, 1980.

Muller, Herbert Joseph. *Adlai Stevenson: A Study in Values.* New York: Harper & Row, Publishers, Inc., 1967.

Nevins, Allan. *Ford.* New York: Charles Scribner's Sons, 1954.
——. *John D. Rockefeller: The Heroic Age of American Enterprise.* New York: Charles Scribner's Sons, 1940.
Nisbet, Robert A. *Tradition and Revolt: Historical and Sociological Essays.* New York: Random House, Inc., 1968.
Podhoretz, Norman. *Making It.* New York: Random House, Inc., 1967.
Proust, Marcel. *Pleasures and Days and Other Writings.* New York: Doubleday Anchor Books, 1957.
Rischin, Moses, ed. *The American Gospel of Success: Individualism and Beyond.* Chicago: Quadrangle Books, 1965.
Rosen, Bernard Carl; Crockett, Harry J., Jr.; and Nunn, Clyde Z., eds. *Achievement in American Society.* Cambridge, Massachusetts: Schenkman Publishing Co., Inc., 1969.
Samuels, Ernest. *Henry Adams: The Major Phase.* Cambridge, Massachusetts: Belknap Press of Harvard University Press, 1964.
——. *Henry Adams: The Middle Years.* Cambridge, Massachusetts: Belknap Press of Harvard University Press, 1958.
——. *The Young Henry Adams.* Cambridge, Massachusetts: Harvard University Press, 1948.
Schlesinger, Arthur Meier, Jr. *Robert Kennedy and His Times.* Boston: Houghton Mifflin Co., 1978.
Schumpeter, Joseph Alois. *Capitalism, Socialism, and Democracy.* New York: Harper & Row, Publishers, Inc., 1950.
——. *Imperialism and Social Classes.* Fairfield, New Jersey: Augustus M. Kelley, Publishers, 1951.
Simmel, Georg. *The Philosophy of Money.* London and Boston: Routledge & Kegan Paul, 1978.
Stein, Gertrude. *Everybody's Autobiography.* New York: Random House, Inc., 1937.
Stendhal. *See* Beyle, Marie Henri.
Stevens, Holly Bright. *Souvenirs and Prophecies: The Young Wallace Stevens.* New York: Alfred A. Knopf, 1977.
Stevens, Wallace. *Letters.* Edited by Holly Stevens. New York: Alfred A. Knopf, 1966.
Swanberg, W. A. *Luce and His Empire.* New York: Charles Scribner's Sons, 1972.
Thorndike, Joseph J. *The Very Rich: A History of Wealth.* New York: American Heritage Publishing Co., Inc., 1976.

Tocqueville, Alexis de. *Democracy in America.* New York: Alfred
   A. Knopf, 1945.
Van Doren, Carl Clinton. *Benjamin Franklin.* New York: The
   ʼViking Press, 1968.
Veblen, Thorstein. *The Theory of the Leisure Class.* New York: The
   Viking Press, 1967.
Wecter, Dixon. *The Saga of American Society: A Record of Social
   Aspiration 1607–1937.* New York: Charles Scribner's Sons,
   1937.
Whalen, Richard J. *The Founding Father: The Story of Joseph P.
   Kennedy.* New York: The New American Library, Inc., 1964.
Wharton, Edith. *The Age of Innocence.* New York: Charles
   Scribner's Sons, 1968.
———. *A Backward Glance.* New York: Charles Scribner's Sons,
   1964.
———. *The House of Mirth.* New York: Charles Scribner's Sons,
   1951.
Wiseman, Thomas. *The Money Motive: A Study of an Obsession.*
   London: Hutchinson Publishing Group, Ltd., 1974.

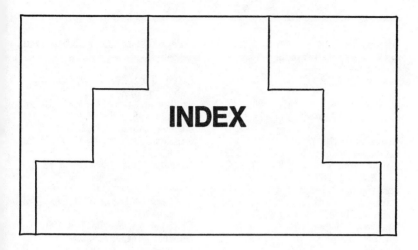

INDEX